I0866441

The Forager's Treasury

The Forager's Treasury

The essential guide to finding and using wild plants in Aotearoa

JOHANNA KNOX

ALLEN&UNWIN
SYDNEY • MELBOURNE • AUCKLAND • LONDON

Contents

Preface

> **Ka ora te whenua, ka ora te tangata.**

I wrote the first edition of this book during 2012, and from the moment it went to print, I started making a list of things I'd love to change. Nine years later the list was quite long, and when Jenny Hellen from Allen & Unwin asked if I'd like to revise the book for a second edition, I had already half-written it in my head.

Obvious changes include identification photos and the longed-for index. I've updated some plant details, changed recipes and corrected a few errors. I've taken some sections out so that other ideas can be included, and I've fixed the way I've expressed some things to better reflect my current world view. Admittedly, that process has made me feel like a bit of a fake, hiding and overwriting the past, but I remind myself that the first edition still exists. I still like it and I hope that, with all its differences, it remains a resource in its own right.

Since I wrote the first edition, the world feels — for many of us — like it's changed a lot. Certainly we're further along a trajectory we've been fearing.

But some things remain the same: whether your environment is urban, suburban or rural, foraging connects you to the land, the air, the waters and the life all around you. Day by day, month by month and year by year, you watch the changes and cycles. You become increasingly aware of the connections between every little thing. And the more you get to know them, the more you see and hear how the Earth calls on us to do better, to try to put things right — however hard and uncomfortable that might be. Even if the Earth is in pain, she's determined and she's hopeful. And, because we're a part of her, so should we be.

Kia hora te marino,
Kia whakapapa pounamu te moana,
kia tere te kārohirohi mua i tōu huarahi,
āianei, ā ake tonu atu.

Introduction

> **The deeper you go into your whakapapa, the easier it is to connect with all things.**
> — Ruby Solly, in conversation with Kahu Kutia in *The Pantograph Punch*, June 2020

Aotearoa New Zealand is a land of foragers. According to my mum, my own foraging life began at the age of about three when I unexpectedly squatted in the middle of my grandmother's garden and ate a pansy. I recall adoring pansies with their little monster faces, so perhaps I was thinking, 'I'll eat you up, I love you so.' Then again, I might simply have been exhibiting the instincts to pick and test that fire in so many children's minds.

I grew up visiting my grandparents and aunt at Ōtaki Beach on weekends and holidays. We gathered pipi, and took home empty shells, driftwood, sea glass, pussy willows and toetoe. I was aware of our whakapapa to the whenua there — our ties to Ngāti Raukawa ki te Tonga, as well as to Ngāti Kahu ki Tauranga further north — but I didn't know back then what that could or should mean for me. Then my grandfather died and my grandmother moved to Auckland.

We lived in Maungaraki, a raw, new bush-clad subdivision in the western hills of Te Awa Kairangi/the Hutt valley. Our section offered plenty of flora to explore, both native and introduced. My father, Fred Knox, worked hard to create a garden and orchard there. My mother, Mary Knox, was a busy environmental activist, continually dragging my sister Andrea and me to protests, fundraising stalls and meetings. A Pākehā back-to-nature movement was in full swing, and I was entranced by some of its

manifestations — particularly the herbal medicine and natural-body-care revivals.

As a child, I embarked on my own projects. I made creams, washes, poultices and face packs. I enlisted my younger sister Andrea to lie still each morning while I plastered her face with bananas, oatmeal and bits of random garden plants. I stripped apples from my father's tree and dug a small pit in the ground so I could bury them, hoping to surprise and delight my family by bringing out this fresh supply in the depths of winter. (They were definitely surprised.)

I also remember making a birthday present for my friend Vanessa by infusing water with rosemary and decanting it into an old perfume bottle. When Vanessa upended the bottle onto her wrist, out plopped a shocking lump of blue mould that quivered on her skin until she shrieked and hurled it off.

Despite early failures, I continued this kind of dabbling throughout my teenage years. Then, in my early twenties, something changed. For the first time I started to earn my own money. Buying things suddenly seemed more fun than scrounging them and materialism ruled.

Within a few years, another wave of change broke over me. My first child, my son Marlon, was born and I was washed into a twilight world of human body fluids, disintegrating sleep patterns and single-minded dedication to this small new cause. The dull band of pain across my head became a part of me, and my inability to remember what I had done a day, or even an hour, before grew legendary. Just when I thought this period might never end, it did.

I resurfaced. Lo and behold, I had a new little friend who liked to pick me small bunches of forget-me-nots from garden borders and eat nasturtium leaves at the park. He reminded me of how I used to be, and I started gathering and experimenting again.

Eventually, my long, stumbling journey to reconnect with my Ngāti Tukorehe, Ngāti Raukawa ki te Tonga and Tauranga Moana iwi whakapapa would lead me to spend a year studying for a rongoā diploma at Te Wānanga o Raukawa, learning from Rita Tupe, Maudy Tupe and Mate Tihema. And, just like that, I was an absolute beginner again, wide-eyed and hungry to understand.

More recently, my daughter Nova and I have been learning to harvest harakeke correctly as we embark on learning raranga together.

I think we're all foragers at heart. From birth, the drive kicks in. We snuffle around, smelling, feeling and able to see only as far as we need, to find food in our tiny caregiver-sized domains. Months pass, then years, but we still employ all our senses in the hunt for health and sustenance. We might be lucky enough to grow up with foraging traditions. Or perhaps we follow our noses towards delicious-smelling takeaways or surreptitiously feel avocados at the supermarket.

Gathering speaks to many needs at once: to escape, to explore, to discover, to collect, to heal, and to provide for ourselves and our loved ones. Most of all, though, I believe it speaks to our need to connect to the world around us.

Each of us forages differently. We have our own gathering routines, favourite plants, and methods of harvest and use. We also have our own ways of ordering our ideas and experiences. And, wherever in the world our ancestors are from, we carry with us a specific legacy of foraging tradition and knowledge — whether we know many parts of it already or we are trying to recover it. Gathering lore is a changing, evolving body of knowledge and every person has their pieces to add. I've enjoyed jigsawing together what pieces I can to make this book, and I'm grateful to the many people who've generously shared their experiences and expertise with me.

I'd like to think this is a book you can dip into and out of at whatever points catch your interest, or to use to follow your own trails. It's by no means exhaustive. Nonetheless, it provides a host of accessible ideas and approaches that I hope you will explore, alter, add to and make your own in ways that I can't even imagine.

A brief history of foraging in Aotearoa

Tūpuna Māori were explorers, sailors, scientists, horticulturalists, farmers, builders, weavers, artists, hunters, fisherpeople and healers. And, of course, they were gatherers. In Aotearoa they created societies based on hapū relationships, and they developed kawa and tikanga to live by. Their lives, laws and mātauranga were indivisible from the land and the surrounding waters.

The British Crown's invasion began stealthily. It was marked by the arrival of Captain Cook, bearing instructions to look for land that Britain could take. European whalers, sealers and missionaries came next, and some hapū developed productive relationships with them. At this point, Europeans were dependent on Māori goodwill to survive.

Māori showed Europeans local plants that could be utilised for food and medicine. Europeans introduced Māori to useful foreign species, such as kohukohu (chickweed). The new plants often escaped and naturalised.

In 1840, many rangatira signed Te Tiriti o Waitangi. It enshrined the sovereignty of Māori hapū over their lands and taonga, while giving the British Crown permission to set up a governorship here to manage *its own* people.

The British had different ideas. Nonsensical as it is to think that powerful chiefs and their people simply decided to hand over sovereignty to some foreigners — that is exactly how the British chose to interpret things. With the treaty signed, the British wilfully misunderstood or disregarded land agreements. They brought in troops, wiped out communities, and passed legislation to give themselves permission to take even more land. By 1937, they'd taken almost everything.

The society that Britain brought here was rapidly industrialising. This coal- and oil-fuelled juggernaut rolled across the country, shifting earth, extracting resources, pouring concrete and excreting pollution. New plants and animals also invaded — and continue to do so. (When we forage in urban environments today, these are the plants we mostly gather.)

Throughout this crisis, sometimes tenuously and against all odds, Māori were keeping their mātauranga around gathering practices alive. Pākehā, meanwhile, were inclined towards peaks and troughs of foraging. The peaks often coincided with tough economic times, such as during the wars and the Great Depression.

In the 1970s, oil shocks rocked the global economy, and many people in the Western world were realising that industrialisation was hurting life on Earth. A widespread new interest in environmentalism and thrift arose, as did another peak in foraging activity, both here and overseas. You can see some of the books this era produced in the Resources section.

Indigenous rights struggles were gathering power globally, and Māori were fighting on many fronts for their whenua, mātauranga and taonga. From this period emerged the groundbreaking Waitangi Tribunal claim Wai 262. It sought recognition of the indivisible relationships between Māori and their whenua, as well as a righting of the enormous breaches of Te Tiriti o Waitangi that were taking place as government and industry exploited native species and mātauranga Māori. The claim was lodged in 1991. It was another twenty years before the resulting report, *Ko Aotearoa Tēnei*, was published. This beautiful, information-rich document is, perhaps inevitably, also disappointing. However, the determined work by the original claimants continues to inform and influence in powerful ways.

The affluence of the 1980s saw Western enthusiasm for foraging wane — until the early 2000s. Then came a renewed backlash against industrialisation's effects on personal and planetary health. Foraging blogs sprang up across the internet, and new foraging books rolled off the presses.

But who will stop the juggernaut? Today, commercial-industrial destruction continues unabated, and, alongside that, interest in foraging has powered up another level. Collecting from farms, cities and suburbs brings us face to face with the stories of our lands. For many of us, that impels us to think harder about what we can do to set things right, to help pull ourselves out of trouble. Some people are already stretched, doing all they can; others, and I am one of them, know we've got room, somehow, to do more.

The work needed feels massive. Perhaps turning to our ancestors — wherever they are from — is more important than ever. One way or another, most of us are here in Aotearoa because we or our ancestors planned hard, took great risks and met immense challenges in order to make change. We too carry this power inside us to turn things around.

Why forage?

There are many compelling reasons to gather from the wild: for health, for economy and for connection.

To keep healthy

The cultivated foods we buy in shops today have been bred for the commercial market, which values size, sweetness, colour, storability and uniformity. Nutritional value isn't always high on the list of priorities, and consequently many modern cultivars have a lower nutritional value than their ancestors. Wild foods are often more densely packed with nutrients, and a wild-food diet can offer greater species variety.

To save money

In both the short and long term, foraging can save dollars. Relatively few people in this country will live entirely off what they gather, even for a short time, but if you have a pantry stocked with cheap staples you can combine them with many fresh, richly nutritious wild ingredients to make a wide range of dishes.

While I was writing the first edition of this book, money was tight for my family. But I had stores of rice, pasta, flour, sugar and beans. By spending money on only a few extra essentials and foraging for the rest, I killed two birds with one stone: I tested the recipes in this book and helped to keep my family well fed.

To explore *terroir*

Every plant is a storehouse of valuable phytochemicals — natural chemicals made by plants. Each plant or group of plants specialises in certain chemicals and holds them variously in its roots, sap, bark, leaves, flowers and seeds. Some chemicals appear throughout a plant and others only in one part of it.

The same chemicals can pop up in diverse parts of the plant kingdom. For example, anethol gives liquorice, fennel and star anise their aroma, even though they're from quite different plant families.

Chemicals give plants their individual colours, flavours, fragrances, and nutritional and medicinal values. But the exact mix and relative strength of a chemical in any given plant can be affected by many things, including genetics, soil, moisture, altitude, surrounding light levels and temperature, as well as patterns of change in all those things. So, a plant's exact location in space and time affects what it will yield.

All this is what winemakers call *terroir*. More recently, producers of artisan foods have adopted the term. Kairongoā and herbal-medicine practitioners, natural perfumers and fibre-crafters have also long understood these principles.

As a forager, you're in a unique position to discover the effects of *terroir* on the plants that grow in your patch. A quick stroll can reveal, for example, that the lavender flowers growing outside a local cafe have a strength and softness to their fragrance that is quite different to those in the plants growing beside a neighbour's gate, which may have a quieter scent with a sour note.

Learning about the interactions of place and plant is a fascinating, never-ending journey. Even if you reach the geographical edges of your roaming space, you will never reach the edges of time, as plants grow and change each day, each season and each year.

To provoke thought

As human populations sweep around the globe, they deliberately take with them collections of plants useful to them or loved by them, and they also carry stowaways. Just as some human cultures invade others, the same is true of some plant communities.

In any new location, some plants are well behaved, staying where you put them and posing little or no threat to their neighbours. Others storm a landscape, overrunning other plants in their path. While foraging, you see the effects of this process.

Human history and plant history are deeply entwined, and thinking about one sheds light on the other. You cannot really know, for example, why this dandelion grows on this grassy bank in this suburban park, unless you also know that 200 years ago the bank was full of rich, dark, damp native ngahere, loud with birds and threaded with the tracks of gatherers. You cannot know why this dandelion grows right here, waiting for you to pick it, unless you know what happened between then and now to clear the bush, remove the people who held mana whenua, and seed the new plants.

If we love the land we forage on, we need to be determinedly curious about its past, to be fearless in facing what we might find out, and to be prepared to think about how to make things right and then act on those thoughts. Who took care of this land before? Who takes care of it now? Who doesn't? Who should take care of it in future? What does 'take care of' mean?

To restore ties to the Earth

I reckon we all know, deep inside, that a reciprocal relationship with the planet isn't just about creating pristine reserves. It's about getting in there and entangling ourselves with the land and the life around us in a relationship of give and take. When we go too far one way or the other, we lose what it is to be a part of the Earth.

Modern industrialised society does this odd thing where it exploits large tracts of land, taking but not giving, and then sets aside a few reserves, decreeing that there shall be no taking from there. In contrast, traditional foraging involves both give and take with all the lands you traverse, and it gives you a genuine relationship with those lands.

> *When I think about the space between myself and the stream I live on, I realize that the hardest work to be done in tending to that relationship is realizing that we were never, and are never, separate. Not even concrete, I realize, can block me, block us, from the knowing that we have a responsibility to nurture our relationships with place, starting with the ground beneath our feet, no matter how far below, or through how many layers of concrete, that ground may be.*
>
> — EMALANI CASE, *HE WAHĪ PA'AKAI: A PACKAGE OF SALT*, <HEWAHIPAAKAI.WORDPRESS.COM>, FEBRUARY 2020

Ready to forage

I've been taught that the most important thing to take into nature is respect: respect for the land, the seas, the sky and all the life they nurture. You'll also want love, curiosity and wide-open senses. Be ready to slow down, take care and become absorbed.

Above all, carry and offer gratitude.

You may be taking karakia with you, or a prayer or incantation in English or another language. Or perhaps you don't need words and will enter conversation with the life around you in other ways. It's not for me to say how you should do this — just be true to yourself and do it in a way that feels natural to you and right.

Foraging equipment

To make your life as a forager easy, you'll need some basic equipment. Below is a list of useful things to take:

- sharp, sturdy scissors and secateurs for tougher jobs
- a selection of plastic bags for damp stuff
- a selection of paper bags or reusable mesh produce bags for things that should breathe
- good shoes or boots with grip, strength and flexibility — you never know when you might need to walk across sharp rocks or through prickly things, or scramble up a bank
- a friend or family member who is either deeply patient or just as enthusiastic about foraging as you — it's no fun when you want to stop every minute to examine or collect something and your companion wants to keep moving.

If I were more organised, I'd have a foraging bag by the door, ready to pick up whenever the urge to forage strikes. Good outdoors shoes would sit right beside it.

Getting going

Below are some basic tips for harvesting and processing foraged treasures.

- Harvest from places where plants are growing lushly. Bitterness concentrates in slow-growing plants, and the choicest forageables will often be in the fastest-growing patches.
- The youngest, newest leaves and stems on a plant will generally be more tender and delicious than older ones.
- Avoid stunted, damaged or diseased plants.
- Cut greens just above leaf nodes to encourage more growth.
- To remove flowers from their sepals, gently squeeze the sepals and, if necessary, pull or twist a little.
- Some plants are too delicate to be washed. For the ones you do wash, dry them in a salad spinner, or become a human salad spinner by wrapping washed leaves in a clean tea towel, bunching the corners together to seal the leaves, and swinging the towel at arm's length in fast circles.
- Some flowers are full of very tiny black bugs. If you don't want to rinse the flowers, place them onto a white plate or piece of paper and watch the exodus. Transfer the flowers to another plate or paper and more insects will emerge. Keep transferring them back and forth until the exodus is pretty much complete.
- Many leaves and flowers wilt quickly. Unless using them straight away, keep them in the fridge or stand them in water.
- Some foraging is time-consuming and labour-intensive, especially when you're gathering or processing lots of small items such as mallow seedpods or dandelion buds. Treat it as a meditative activity, or turn it into a social occasion with friends and get a production line going.
- When you finish, return your foraged remains to where they came from or as close by as possible. That's unless they're weeds that mustn't spread, in which case dispose of them in a way that prevents this.

Store-cupboard staples

Below is a list of the ingredients I like to keep on hand to complement foraged produce. With these in the cupboard I can cook up most of the recipes in this book.

CARBOHYDRATES

- breadcrumbs
- brown and white sugar
- chickpea (chana or gram) flour
- chocolate — your favourite kind
- high-grade wheat flour — for bread and pasta
- honey
- popping corn
- rice and pasta
- rice flour
- rice-paper sheets
- rolled oats
- standard plain wheat flour — for cakes, biscuits and sauces
- vanilla wine biscuits
- vermicelli (bean threads)

FLAVOURING AND BLENDING AGENTS

- agar
- apple cider vinegar, or a selection of vinegars
- baking powder
- cashew nuts
- citric acid, especially if you don't always have lemons
- coconut aminos (salty, savoury sauce made from fermented coconut palm sap and sea salt)
- gelatine (I prefer sheet gelatine, but powdered will do)
- ground salt — your favourite kind
- ground spices, including cumin, garam masala, paprika and turmeric
- kecap manis (sweet Indonesian soy sauce)
- miso paste
- nuoc mam (fermented fish sauce)
- olive oil

- peppercorns for grinding
- rennet (vegetarian rennet is also available)
- rice bran oil
- sesame seeds
- sherry or other fortified wine
- soda water, tonic water or water kefir
- spirits with a low odour, such as vodka or gin
- tamari or shoyu
- tomato paste
- vanilla essence (see recipe, page 26)
- wine

IN THE FRUIT AND VEGETABLE RACK

- carrots
- garlic
- ginger
- kūmara
- lemons
- onions
- potatoes

FROM THE FRIDGE

- Cheddar cheese
- coconut cream
- condensed milk or dairy-free condensed milk (see recipe, page 258)
- cream or a cream substitute
- eggs
- milk or milk substitute
- mozzarella
- Parmesan
- salted butter or butter substitute
- tofu
- unsalted butter or butter substitute
- yoghurt

HOMEMADE VANILLA ESSENCE

To make about a cup of strong vanilla essence, all you need is around eight dried vanilla bean pods and a cup of vodka. Chop the pods into small pieces and place in a jar or bottle with the vodka. Leave to infuse for a month or so, shaking whenever you remember. You'll end up with a delicious, strong essence.

OF FORAGERS AND FARMERS AND FALSE DICHOTOMIES

Embracing a diet that incorporates a mix of wild and cultivated foods is a time-honoured way of life. Most cultures around the world have lived this way for centuries. Zareen Bharucha and Jules Pretty noted in 'The Roles and Values of Wild Foods in Agricultural Systems', their 2010 *Philosophical Transactions of the Royal Society B* paper, 'Many . . . wild foods are actively managed, suggesting there is a false dichotomy around ideas of the agricultural and the wild.'

Living things in the store cupboard

If you have the time to look after them, it's rewarding to keep some live fermented foods in your store cupboard to go with your foraged foods. You can make endless probiotic creations from them. Three of the most commonly available cultures are described below. Starters for all these cultures are available from suppliers online.

WATER KEFIR

This colony grows as firm, irregularly shaped, jelly-like grains and will ferment almost any sugary liquid. It seems to prefer dark, raw sugars, and thrives with added lemon and ginger. You can also make a range of fermented wild cordials with water kefirs, or ferment a basic kefir and add some infused syrup (see recipe, page 170).

MILK KEFIR

With slower-growing, more globby-looking grains than water kefir, milk kefir is used mainly to ferment dairy products. A spoonful of milk kefir grains in a jar of milk transforms it into a nutritious, yoghurty-tasting drink. In cream, the grains produce an excellent sour-cream substitute. Adding finely chopped foraged herbs and greens to fermented cream makes a delicious dip or sauce.

CASPIAN SEA YOGHURT

Sometimes called viili, matsoun or matsoni, this lesser-known yoghurt is very easy to produce with a culture starter. It's different from the yoghurt we're used to, as it's not solely bacteria-based but instead fermented by a symbiotic colony of bacteria and yeast. With its yeasty tang, it can be an acquired taste. However, it's much easier to make than other yoghurts, as no heating or temperature control is needed. It ferments and thickens in an almost foolproof way at room temperature. The warmer the room, the faster it ferments.

Useful kitchen equipment

- baking paper
- blender
- bowls
- heavy-bottomed frying pan
- heavy-bottomed pot
- lidded casserole dish
- measuring cups
- measuring spoons
- mortar and pestle
- muslin for filtering and covering
- oven tray
- pie dish
- rolling pin
- scissors
- sharp knife
- sieve
- storage jars
- tinfoil
- whisk

Foraging rules and regulations

Before beginning your foraging journey, familiarise yourself with the relevant guidelines and legislation. Most importantly, don't take anything from national parks or marine reserves unless you have a permit to do so. And, secondly, don't go onto private property, including farmland, without the owner's permission.

At the local level, there's a tangle of city, district and regional authority rules surrounding public spaces, including local parks and reserves. If you're unsure, check with your local council to find out where you can forage and what plant material you can and can't collect. For example, if a restoration project is under way, you may not be able to touch native plants, but you could be doing everyone a favour if you remove introduced weeds.

While the lack of clear national guidelines may sometimes feel frustrating, it seems important that these kinds of rules and processes are developed to suit the individual locations and communities to which they apply. Generally, collecting a bit of seaweed from a beach — as long as it's not a marine reserve — and removing a few weeds or picking flowers, leaves or fruit from an untended local park or the edges of local bush should be fine. The edges of railway lines can also be good places to forage, but be sure to stay a safe distance from the tracks.

As for private property, any plant part enticingly poking through or hanging over a fence into your property or into public property is legally owned by the person who owns the soil in which the plant is growing. This means that, strictly speaking, you need to ask permission to take any material from such a plant. On the other hand, nipping off a few errant leaves or flowers is probably not going to bother anyone. However, use discretion and common sense at all times and remember that people are usually happy to give permission if you ask — especially if you offer them some preserved gatherings as a thank you.

Pollution

You also need to be careful to forage away from areas of pollution, especially if you're going to be consuming your haul. If you're going to be using the plants for dyeing or some other craftwork, this concern isn't quite so important.

In general, avoid areas subject to farm run-off, or busy roadsides where exhaust fumes and rubber from tyres may coat the plants. Avoid areas that have been sprayed with herbicides or pesticides, or, if you're unsure where these are, ring up your local council to check. They should be able to tell you what areas are being sprayed, and what sprays are being used and when, or they may put you in touch with the contractor who does the spraying. Occasionally it won't be possible to find out.

If you're going to be gathering from waterways or coasts, it's worth making sure you know the area isn't polluted. The patch of coast near me, for example, is often very polluted, especially after heavy rains, thanks to nearby landfills and a

disastrous sewerage system. Few people know how bad it is unless they live right by the sea, and local authorities have been reluctant to share information on pollution levels with the public.

Identify everything you gather

It's important that you positively identify every plant you gather. There's no room for confusion about this, as plants that look similar may not be the same and one may be poisonous. It's good to get to know the poisonous plants you may come across in your area (see 'Common poisonous plants in Aotearoa', page 31). It can be hard to identify a plant from a single image or description, so it's important to have several different images and resources to cross-reference.

Many plants are easiest to identify by their flowers, so you may want to keep an eye on a plant you're unsure of until it blooms. Searching images online is useful, although beware that among the grab bag of internet resources some plants will be incorrectly labelled — you need to know that your sources are reliable. A list of recommended sources is given on page 343.

Listen to your body

It's always important to introduce new foods to your diet gradually. If you find some new foraged foods that you love, go easy on them at first, giving your body time to adjust. Sudden changes in diet, whether in quantity or content, can stress your system. Try things tentatively, introducing one new thing at a time and listening to your body to check whether it's telling you it doesn't like something.

ALLERGY ALERT

There's another reason to go carefully when trying unknowns: there's always the small risk of a food allergy. While some food allergies result in only mild symptoms, a few cause anaphylaxis, where there may be intense swelling, closure of the airways and a sudden drop in blood pressure. Anaphylaxis is life-threatening and needs medical attention straight away.

If you already know you have an allergy, avoid foraged plants that are similar. For example, if you react to potatoes, tomatoes or aubergines, avoid the nightshade family. If you have a tree-nut allergy, you may need to avoid chestnuts. And, although foraging for edible insects, snails and grubs is out of the scope of this book, I'll just say that if you have a seafood allergy, then it's not advisable to eat land invertebrates either.

If you have multiple food allergies, it may well be that foraging is just too risky. However, you will have done your research and you know your body. Remember, too, that an allergy can always strike out of the blue. If after eating a new food you find yourself with stomach cramps, difficulty breathing or some worrying swelling, or if you're feeling faint, seek medical attention straight away.

OXALATES WARNING

Oxalates are organic compounds produced by many plants, both wild and cultivated. Some of these — including rhubarb, wood sorrel, kōkihi (New Zealand spinach and bower spinach) — contain particularly high levels of the compound.

Oxalates bind with calcium, so consuming an oxalate-rich food along with one rich in calcium will neutralise some of the calcium, making it less accessible to the body. Certain foods, such as wild chenopodiums, have a high calcium-to-oxalates ratio. This means that, despite their high oxalate levels, the calcium will generally be absorbed by your body as if the plants had low oxalate levels. Other plants, including docks, contain little calcium, so their oxalates are highly available.

There are other factors to consider, too. Different people metabolise oxalates differently, so there is plenty of variation between individuals in how much oxalic acid we can comfortably consume. Some oxalates can also be broken down by cooking, or leached out of a food by boiling.

The general consensus seems to be that oxalates are fine for most people in moderate amounts. However, if you have gout, kidney trouble, rheumatoid arthritis or some other condition that makes oxalates dangerous for you, then you should avoid foods that contain them. If you are worried, check with your doctor.

Common poisonous plants in Aotearoa

Aotearoa has many poisonous plants, both native and introduced. The following list is by no means comprehensive, but it includes some of the most common poisonous species. For a fuller list, including plants that cause only mild reactions, see the Royal New Zealand Institute of Horticulture's poisonous plants web page or the section on toxic plants in Andrew Crowe's *A Field Guide to the Native Edible Plants of New Zealand* (both listed in the 'Resources' section).

BUTTERCUPS

Buttercups (*Ranunculus* species) contain the toxin ranunculin. Many species grow all around Aotearoa — often in fields and overgrown grass. Most are easily recognised by their five-petalled yellow flowers with a bright, buttery shine. Those that are not in flower can still be recognised by their distinctive leaf form. Some people find that they initially mistake the leaves for those of dove's-foot crane's-bill. This may be the urban forager's biggest concern. Check carefully until you know you can tell the difference.

HEMLOCK

Hemlock (*Conium maculatum*) grows abundantly throughout Aotearoa. It contains the neurotoxin coniine, and it doesn't take much of this stuff to kill a person. Along with parsley, celery, fennel, carrot and coriander, hemlock belongs to the Apiaceae family (see page 48). Fears abound that foragers will mistake it for one of its more edible wild relatives, all of which are herbaceous and have lacy leaves, hollow stems and tiny flowers in umbrella-like clusters.

Hemlock is considered to look most like wild carrot, which has similar leaves and white flowers, but the form of hemlock flowers is generally more like those of parsley and wild celery (although these are yellow). Wild carrot, unlike hemlock, has hairy stems. Mature hemlock has smooth stems, which can be further distinguished from those of its relatives by purple spots or streaks. Note, however, that these spots may be absent or hard to discern on very young plants.

JERUSALEM CHERRY

The ornamental Jerusalem cherry (*Solanum pseudocapsicum*) is a member of the nightshade family that has become naturalised here and grows across Aotearoa. Its attractive orange berries are very poisonous.

OLEANDER

Oleander (*Nerium oleander*), an evergreen shrub or tree, is widely grown as a garden ornamental and naturalised all around Aotearoa. All parts of the plant

CLOCKWISE FROM TOP LEFT Buttercup; mature hemlock stalk; oleander; yew; tutu; ongaonga; hemlock.

are very toxic. Since at least the 1950s, a story involving either a party of Boy Scouts or a family roasting sausages on sticks of oleander, with fatal results, has circulated. Although it's an urban legend, it's a cautionary tale worth heeding.

ONGAONGA

The endemic ongaonga or tree nettle (*Urtica ferox*) is the Terminator of nettles, sometimes growing over 2 metres (6 feet) high. A serious brush with it could be the end of you or at least make you very sick. Look out for it in scrubland and around forest margins throughout the country.

Ongaonga deserves respect. Like other native nettles, it is an important part of the ecosystem, providing vital food and habitat for the endemic kahukura or red admiral butterfly.

TUTU

Several native species in the genus *Coriaria* are commonly known as tutu. These straggling trees or shrubs generally grow in bush and scrub all around Aotearoa, and have drooping clusters of flowers and berries. All parts, except the petals, contain the highly toxic substance tutin.

COMMON YEW

The common yew tree (*Taxus baccata*) is an introduced conifer that now grows up and down the country. Almost all parts of it are poisonous, including the seed of the appetising-looking red berry-like aril.

The treasures

Some of the most easily forageable plants in Aotearoa are native, but most are introduced species. Where possible, I've given the Māori name, the common English name and the botanical name, in that order, for all the plants described in this section — although note that in some cases there may be no Māori or English name that I've been able to find.

There are many ways to categorise plants, but I've grouped them here by taxonomic family, as it often feels useful to compare and contrast different members of the same family. Within each family, plant species are listed according to a broad set of principles: genuses are grouped together, native plants are listed before introduced plants, and common Māori names are given before common English names. Botanical names appear in italics. Within these bounds, the plants are listed in alphabetical order by common name.

TAXONOMY IN A NUTSHELL

Botanists divide the plant kingdom into orders, the orders into families, the families into genera, and the genera into species. Many species are further divided into smaller groups called subspecies and varieties.

A plant's botanical name is generally made up of two words: the genus, which has a capital letter, followed by the species, which begins with a lower-case letter. The name is italicised. For example, garden parsley is *Petroselinum crispum* (*Petroselinum* is the genus name and *crispum* the species name). A subspecies or variety name may follow, also in italics and lower case.

Sometimes a genus name has passed into everyday, informal English — for example, we talk about begonias (genus *Begonia*), pelargoniums (genus *Pelargonium*) and brassicas (genus *Brassica*). In these cases of common usage, the name doesn't need to be italicised or capitalised.

Cultivars are plants that humans have selected, in cultivation or from the wild, for desirable characteristics, then maintained through continued propagation. The word 'cultivar' is usually thought to come from the words 'cultivated' and 'variety'.

Adoxaceae
Moschatel family

In Aotearoa, Adoxaceae plants that grow wild include species of *Viburnum* (a genus that is rarely on the forager's radar) and *Sambucus* (a genus that sets the radar on high alert). Some *Viburnum* species have moderately edible berries or specialised medicinal uses, but others are toxic. *Sambucus* species, commonly called elder or elderberry, have many uses. Of these species, elder is the most sought-after.

The Adoxaceae family is closely related to the Caprifoliaceae or honeysuckle family, and until recently was considered part of it.

Elder

ELDER
Sambucus nigra

SPOTTING IT

While many elderberry plants grow as shrubs, some eventually end up as trees. With their seeds spread widely by birds, they grow throughout the country. However, they prefer cooler temperatures, and so you'll find them mostly in the South Island and southern half of the North Island. They're deciduous and grow in unmanicured parks, old gardens, on farms and along country roads.

The jagged-edged leaves of elder are distinctive and grow darker as the season progresses, but the flowers are their showiest feature. From afar, the flowering bushes look as if they're covered in bright white saucers. Once the flowers finish, they give way to clusters of berries that start green and gradually turn a deep, dark reddish purple — almost black.

You can catch the flowers from October to January, but any individual tree will flower for only a few weeks. Ten years ago I would have said they usually start flowering in mid-November, but where I live they've been flowering earlier and earlier. (The first few years I wondered; now I'm sure.)

Beware that some related ornamental species look very like *Sambucus nigra* but aren't very edible. A telltale sign is their long flowering period — the flowers go on and on for months. While they look beautiful, they make disgusting cordial.

CLOCKWISE FROM TOP Harvesting elder; elderflowers in bloom; making elderflower cordial.

USING IT

Only the flowers and berries of elder should be eaten. All the green bits are mildly toxic, and some people find the raw berries indigestible even when ripe.

Elderflower syrup and cordial is expensive to buy in shops, so it's satisfying to make your own at home for little more than the cost of the sugar. The flowers — either fresh or dried — can also be infused as a tisane and they're stunning as the star of a flower fritter (see recipe, page 249). For the very best flavour, choose open flowers that still have a sprinkling of yellow pollen, and use them as soon as possible after you've gathered them, because the flavours start to change rapidly. You can keep them for up to 48 hours, so long as they are cool and hydrated, but the fresher the better.

There's something surprisingly moreish about sweet, creamy things flavoured with elderflower. Infuse milk and cream with elderflowers to make panna cotta, try elderflower syrup over vanilla ice cream, or use the syrup as a flavouring for milkshakes or ice-cream sodas.

You can also use the berries to make syrup, jam and jelly, or add them to fruit pies. For some, they're an acquired taste. My children, for example, could always taste a single elderberry in a litre of smoothie and would reject said smoothie instantly.

Both the flowers and the berries have cooling properties, making elder drinks great on a hot day. I try to save some loose berries and elderflower syrup in the freezer throughout summer for those sweltering days that can crop up as late as March.

If you can save some syrup or berries even longer, they can be beneficial during flu season. Syrups, tisanes and other infusions made from elder flowers and berries are used in many cultures for treating colds, coughs, fevers and inflamed sinuses. They have both anti-inflammatory and antioxidant properties, they promote sweating, and they also work as an expectorant. In addition, they contain antiviral compounds, and recent research strongly suggests they're effective against symptoms of some colds and flu.

Elderflowers have also traditionally been used in natural and handmade skin toners.

Aizoaceae

Ice plant or fig marigold family

Members of this family grow around the world on beaches and in deserts, and include many succulents. Only a few Aizoaceae species grow wild in Aotearoa, but most of those that do are edible, including ice plants and kōkihi, or New Zealand spinach.

Ice plants

HOROKAKA, NGARANGARA, RUERUEKE | NEW ZEALAND ICE PLANT
Disphyma australe

FIG MARIGOLD, SEA FIG
Carpobrotus chilensis

SOUR FIG
Carpobrotus edulis

SPOTTING THEM

Ice plants sprawl in mats across beaches around the country. The fig marigold is a large yellow ice plant with thick, finger-like leaves that are three-sided in cross-section. It's an invasive pest from South Africa that overruns native plants and changes the structure of sand dunes. The purple-flowered sour fig has also become naturalised here.

Our native ice plant, horokaka, needs to be cherished. It has smaller pink flowers and its leaves are smoothly curved like tapering tubes, rather than three-sided. Horokaka fruits open in the rain, while *Carpobrotus* fruits don't.

Carpobrotus species prefer to grow in sand, while horokaka is more likely to be found on stony beaches. There is some overlap, though, and sour fig plants can overrun native horokaka and even hybridise with them. You may be able to recognise the hybrid offspring — they're not quite as big as sour fig and their flowers are pink, orange, yellow or creamy white. They don't produce seeds like their parents, but they can propagate from pieces of stem.

Sour fig and its hybrids are on the National Pest Plant Accord, so, when you can, it's good to do your bit and pull up a few by the roots and dispose of them. Just be sure you're not pulling up horokaka.

CLOCKWISE FROM TOP LEFT Horokaka (New Zealand ice plant); horokaka in flower; kōkihi (bower spinach).

USING THEM

Succulent ice plant leaves are harshly tannic and only barely edible raw, but they can be sliced and pickled. The plants flower all year, but most prolifically from around October to February. When a flower dies back, the plant produces a fruit that, when ripe and yellowish, can be peeled or squeezed to reveal an edible, interestingly sweet mucilage. In South Africa ice plant fruits are a valued jam and syrup ingredient.

Pākehā haven't used ice plants much, but Māori uses are known and foragers sometimes pick them as a wild treat. Greg Bennett from the Coastal Restoration Trust of New Zealand says, 'When the flower dies off, pick the receptacle, and carefully squeeze it. A pinkish liquid will ooze out. This is very sweet and delicious.'

The astringent and antiseptic properties of ice plant juice have been appreciated around the world. Pound the leaves up to release the juice and use it neat or in vinegars or tisanes. Applied externally, the juice soothes and protects grazed, irritated or inflamed skin. It can also be gargled or ingested for stomach upsets.

Kōkihi

KŌKIHI | BOWER SPINACH, BEACH SPINACH
Tetragonia implexicoma

KŌKIHI | NEW ZEALAND SPINACH
Tetragonia tetragonoides

SPOTTING THEM

These two closely related species form spreading bushes around the coast, preferring slightly shady places such as the dips between dunes. Bower spinach looks very like New Zealand spinach but has smaller leaves, is more scrambling and is much more widespread.

Kōkihi are native to Aotearoa and other parts of the South Pacific, and were seized on by early European settlers for their commercial possibilities. By the 1920s, New Zealand spinach in particular was being promoted in Burpee seed catalogues in the United States as 'hot weather spinach'. Although it was exported to the United Kingdom, France, other parts of Europe and the United States, the vegetable never caught on hugely, and to this day remains something of a cult overseas, where it is sometimes called tetragon.

USING THEM

Both species of kōkihi can be treated similarly. The leaves are dark and fleshy, and they have a sour, salty taste. The plants produce small red berries that taste like the leaves, except just a little sweeter and juicier.

If you find a lush patch, treasure it. As with many plants, pick the young growing tips — these make the best eating, and picking them encourages the plant to grow more voluminously.

Once picked, kōkihi lasts for days, especially in water or in the fridge. It also holds its shape and volume when cooked. I like to strip the leaves from their stems and use them in the same way I use kale: boiled or steamed, and served either on its own or with butter or sauce; chopped and thrown into soups, sauces and casseroles; or shredded into salads.

The tanginess of kōkihi comes from oxalic acid, so bear in mind the 'Oxalates warning' on page 31.

Amaranthaceae
Amaranth family

This large family includes spinach, beets and quinoa, and takes on diverse forms. For example, huainanga (lamb's quarters) is a nondescript but very nutritious little garden weed, while ureure is a distinctive-looking succulent that loves the coast.

Chenopodiums

HUAINANGA | LAMB'S QUARTERS, FAT HEN
Chenopodium album

NETTLE-LEAVED FAT HEN
Chenopodium murale

SPOTTING THEM

Numerous species in the *Chenopodium* genus grow wild in Aotearoa. Some are hard to find; some have small, barely edible leaves; others smell terrible. But two that you'll find throughout the country that have decent-sized, pleasantly edible leaves are *Chenopodium album* and *C. murale*. Both have a potentially bamboozling array of common names, but *C. album* is most commonly referred to as lamb's quarters, fat hen or goosefoot, and *C. murale* is often called nettle-leaved fat hen.

Lamb's quarters is well known as a wild edible, while nettle-leaved fat-hen is something of an unsung hero. Both are annual plants that form ball-shaped flowers in clusters huddled around the stems. Nettle-leaved fat hen is erect and can grow to about 75 centimetres tall. Lamb's quarters is often erect but can also spread, depending on the conditions.

USING THEM

When chenopodiums are young, cook both the leaves and stalks or eat them raw in salads. As they grow larger and older, the stalks toughen, so eat the leaves only. The flowers and seeds can also be eaten cooked.

Treat both lamb's quarters and nettle-leaved fat hen like their relative spinach: boil, steam or sauté them. They lose volume quickly and need only a minute or two of cooking. Both work well in any of the recipes for wild greens, and like many other sour-tasting greens they can be particularly delicious in a cream sauce.

FROM LEFT Huainanga (lamb's quarters) in closeup; ureure (glasswort, beaded samphire).

Food writer Elizabeth Schneider describes the flavour of lamb's quarters thus: 'Raw, it tastes quite different from cooked, with a suggestion of peanuts, grass, and oddly, fruit. Cooked, the slightly waxy, fleshy, flavorful leaves have an earthy, walnut-like savor, and although green and spinachy, lack that vegetable's iron tang.'

Again like spinach, the chenopodiums generally contain oxalic acid — nettle-leaved fat hen is particularly rich in the compound. For more information, check the 'Oxalates warning' on page 31.

Garden orache

GARDEN ORACHE, MOUNTAIN SPINACH
Atriplex hortensis

SPOTTING IT

Originally introduced by European settlers as a culinary herb, garden orache has spearhead-shaped leaves that can range from green through to red. In fertile soil it can grow to 2.5 metres high. It isn't widely grown these days to eat on its own, but is often found as part of a mesclun mix. Having escaped from cultivation, it now grows wild in many parts of the country, including Canterbury, Otago, Wellington and Hawke's Bay.

USING IT

Garden orache is bitter — so much so that it's best mixed with other milder greens or boiled for just a minute to reduce the bitterness. As with chenopodiums, use whole young plants or older leaves stripped from the central stalk.

Ureure

> **UREURE | GLASSWORT, BEADED SAMPHIRE**
> *Salicornia quinqueflora*

SPOTTING IT

Around the world, 'samphire' and 'glasswort' refer to various species in the *Salicornia* and *Sarcocornia* genera. These herbaceous plants have succulent jointed stems and no leaves. They are salt-tolerant and grow around beaches and salt marshes.

In Aotearoa, ureure grows around the North Island and parts of the South Island. The stems are best eaten in spring and early summer; after that, they become tougher. That said, in Wellington I've found plants in early autumn whose stalks were tender enough to eat.

USING IT

Ureure can be sliced and added to salads for salty crunch. Eaten in quantity it can be almost overpoweringly salty, but this can be reduced by boiling it in a decent amount of water. It's delicious boiled or steamed for 2–5 minutes and served hot with a lemon-butter sauce or simply slathered in unsalted butter, perhaps with a dash of lemon juice or a sprinkling of lemon zest.

Potato is a good friend to ureure. Try adding ureure to a potato frittata, a warm or cold potato salad, or hot, crushed potato.

Ureure also lends itself well to pickling, as well as frying in a tempura batter, and it's great in soups and creamy pasta sauces. Whatever you add it to, remember to taste the dish before seasoning it, as you may find it is salty enough already.

Amaryllidaceae
Amaryllis family

This family includes popular flower genera such as *Agapanthus* and *Amaryllis*, but it's perhaps most beloved for containing the edible *Allium* genus. Alliums include everything oniony, from chives and leeks to garlic and onions. They can be overenthusiastic plants, sprouting up where they're not welcome, but they are good pickings for foragers.

Alliums

NAPLES ONION
Allium neapolitanum

ONION WEED, THREE-CORNERED GARLIC
Allium triquetrum

ROSY GARLIC
Allium roseum

WILD ONION
Allium vineale

SPOTTING THEM

More and more introduced alliums — including garlic and chives in some places — are escaping to become naturalised in Aotearoa. The four listed above have all been growing wild here for many decades.

These bulb plants have grass-like leaves and clusters of flowers at the top of leafless stalks. Rosy garlic has pink flowers and the other three have white flowers. However, their most readily recognisable feature is the oniony or garlicky smell evident when you snap or crush a leaf.

The wild allium that many New Zealanders are particularly familiar with is onion weed. It's a native of Europe, including Britain, and was brought over by settlers as a culinary herb. Today it grows rampantly throughout the country, announcing its presence from a distance with clouds of onion smell.

However, it's the less obvious wild onion that's taken most seriously as a problem plant. It's a pasture pest, and if it grows where cows graze it gives their milk an oniony taste.

THIS PAGE Onion weed in flower.

USING THEM

If you know of a patch of onion weed, dig up the small bulbs from the soil in winter and pickle them. It's best to soak them in water first and rub off the papery skins. You can also steam or sauté the bulbs or chop them into salads.

If young and tender, the grown plants can be sautéed whole or chopped and used just like a spring onion. Chop the stringy, larger, older stems very finely.

Onion weed flowers are a decorative addition to any salad or meal, with an oniony taste that's more delicate than the rest of the plant. They also make excellent tempura (see the tempura recipe, page 229).

Chopped finely, onion weed leaves and flowers can be mixed into butter to make a delicately flavoured garlic-butter substitute. This is delicious spread on French bread and baked like garlic bread or daubed over fish. It's also good in combination with other wild herbs such as wood sorrel (see page 116) or parsley (see page 51).

While onion weed is the allium you'll probably find most often, you may also come across others, which you can use similarly.

Apiaceae

Carrot or parsley family

This is another family that gives us a cornucopia of commonly cultivated species — parsley, carrot, celery, fennel, dill, coriander, parsnip and more. The family used to be called Umbelliferae because its species have umbels of flowers — umbrella-like clusters on short stalks that radiate from a central point.

Apiaceae plants are usually herbs rather than shrubs or vines, and they're often aromatic. Many are edible, but others are highly poisonous and can kill you. The most notorious of these is hemlock (*Conium maculatum*) — make absolutely sure you don't mistake it for a similar-looking relative (see page 32).

Of the commonly foraged members of the Apiaceae family, wild carrot (*Daucus carota*) — often used in Western herbal medicine for bladder, kidney and menstrual problems — is most likely to be confused with hemlock. One of the ways it is distinguished from hemlock is by its noticeably hairy stems.

Ngā herewī | Celeries

TŪTAE KŌAU | NEW ZEALAND CELERY
Apium prostratum

WILD CELERY
Apium graveolens

SPOTTING THEM

Tūtae kōau is native to Aotearoa, Australia and some Pacific islands. It grows around the coast and looks a bit like parsley, but has thicker, more markedly ridged stems and fleshier leaves. It's an immediately rewarding plant.

Wild celery, on the other hand, is an introduced plant that has escaped vegetable gardens. It's the same species of celery that our cultivated varieties come from. The cultivars have been bred to have enormous juicy stalks and people often discard the leaves, even though they're quite edible. However, when *Apium graveolens* cultivars escape to weed-dom, their offspring rapidly reassume the species' original wild form, becoming more leafy and less stalky, much like their sibling parsley. They grow in localised places throughout the country but are not among the easiest of wild plants to find.

FROM LEFT
Taru haunga (fennel) fronds; taru haunga in flower.

USING THEM

Both plants can be used like a robust parsley and are delicious teamed with lemon zest and garlic as a flavouring, or with onions and mushrooms or carrots.

The complex and aromatic flavour of tūtae kōau is particularly entrancing. It's a lot like parsley and a little like celery, but with an indefinable extra quality to it.

Taru haunga | Fennel

TARU HAUNGA | FENNEL
Foeniculum vulgare

SPOTTING IT

Fennel is a perennial that grows prolifically in waste places, along roadsides, in weedy gardens and anywhere else it gets a seed-hold. It can grow up to 2 metres tall. With its crisp, strongly aromatic green stalks, feathery leaves and bright yellow flowers sending out clouds of aniseedy scent, it's hard to miss.

The fennel roots or bulbs you buy in stores are really the fleshy bases of the stalks from Florence fennel, a variety specially bred for this purpose. In the wild, fennel is much stalkier and leafier.

USING IT

Fennel was introduced to this country by European settlers, probably as both a culinary and a medicinal herb. It may have first arrived with European sealers on Codfish Island/Whenua Hou, just off Stewart Island/Rakiura, where local Māori and sealers formed a community. A century later, fennel was reportedly growing rampantly on the island. Taru haunga is its Māori name.

Wild fennel has edible stems, leaves, flowers and seeds, and the pollen is considered a delicacy. Grainy and yellow, it's highly flavourful and can be used any time you'd use the finely chopped leaves, bearing in mind that it has a stronger taste.

Fennel has a natural affinity with dairy in both sweet and savoury dishes. Add the pollen or very finely chopped young fronds to buttery shortbread. You can also add them to white sauce or melted white chocolate (letting small spoonfuls set into fennel chocolate buttons). Milk or cream infused with any part of the plant is ideal for making panna cotta, ice cream or junket.

Use the pollen or very finely chopped fronds in butters, oils, creams, sauces or marinades for chicken, pork, fish or vegetables. If you like, add a little orange zest as well, whether the dish is sweet or savoury. Fennel and orange is a classic combination.

You can roast, grill or barbecue wild fennel stalks with other vegetables to serve hot or to add to a cold roasted vegetable salad. Choose the younger, lighter-coloured, more tender stalks, chop them to appropriate lengths and cook them for about 10 minutes. You may want to strip away the outer layer of a stalk if it's a bit stringy.

Fennel, in all its aniseediness, also makes a fantastic base for a spiced tea. Use it as the sole spice or add whatever other sweet spices you have in your pantry — cloves, cinnamon, ginger, cardamom . . . and vanilla, real or fake. There's a quick, mild way to enjoy it: steep black tea as you normally would, add a few fresh young fronds or flowers of fennel, then add sugar or honey to taste.

If you have more time and want a stronger syrup that you can store, put a handful of fennel (again, fronds or flowers) into a saucepan with a teaspoon or two of sugar or honey and cover with water. Let the brew simmer with the lid on for around 20 minutes, then turn it off. Add two or three teaspoons of black tea and let it steep for another 5 minutes. Strain the syrup into a jar or bottle, then add a few drops of vanilla if you have it. Keep it in the fridge and get it out to make spiced tea whenever you fancy a brew: simply put 2–3 centimetres in the bottom of a cup, then add water or your favourite milk — hot or cold.

The chemical that makes fennel smell aniseedy is anethol. The plant also contains coumarins, the compounds that give drying hay its scent. As fennel pollen dries, the fresh aniseedy fragrance of the anethol gives way to a pervasive coumarinic scent reminiscent of fenugreek, which also contains coumarins. However, when you crush the fennel pollen or taste it, the anethol aroma is still strong.

Partly owing to its anethol content, fennel is considered helpful for digestion. It's most famous as a carminative, meaning it gets rid of gas. Fennel essential oil is used in aromatherapy and perfumery.

HOW TO GATHER FENNEL POLLEN

Fennel pollen can be gathered in summer by shaking the flowers into a plastic or paper bag. The easiest method is to cut off the flowers first, then place them upside down in the bag with the stems sticking out, grip the stems and bag in your fist, and shake. Store the pollen in an airtight bag or container. Keep it in the fridge if you want it to hold its aniseediness for as long as possible. Even then, though, a slow progression to a more coumarinic flavour is inevitable — not that this is a bad thing.

Garden parsley

GARDEN PARSLEY
Petroselinum crispum

SPOTTING IT

Wild garden parsley grows in many parts of the country, often in waste places, around bush edges and near the coast. Occasionally you may find curly-leafed varieties in the wild, but usually flat-leafed parsley is more common. That's because parsley's natural wild form has flat leaves. Curly-leafed parsleys have been bred to that form, and plants that escape cultivation and end up self-seeding soon return to the wild form.

USING IT

Wild parsley can be used just as you'd use cultivated parsley. Every part of the plant is nutritious — the leaves, stems, flowers, seeds and roots. The beauty of finding wild parsley is that there's often a lot of it, so you can feel free to dig it up by the roots. 'Bartowich Long' is a cultivated variety grown specifically for its long roots, but there's no reason why you shouldn't also use the roots of the wild versions for soups, sauces and roasts.

THE SIREN CALL OF PARSLEY

My second pregnancy gave me a new perspective on an ancient tale. Consumed with a craving for raw dark greens, I ate mesclun salad as if it were popcorn and devoured bunches of parsley. Unbeknown to me at the time, my iron levels were, as our midwife said later, in my boots. All I knew was that I had to have those greens.

I thought of the story of Rapunzel and suddenly comprehended how a mother-to-be, staring over a wall at the lush greens in a witch's garden, might feel such a strong bodily need to eat those plants that, in a moment of desperation, she or her panicked husband might say or do almost anything.

In many versions of Rapunzel, including that recorded by the Brothers Grimm, the green is rampion, the name given to edible plants of the *Phyteuma* genus in the Campanulaceae family. However, in an earlier version of the tale from Naples, the plant is parsley and the baby's name is not Rapunzel, but Petrosinella.

Despite the story and my own gorging, pregnant women are not supposed to consume too much parsley or the closely related wild celery, especially not the oil-rich seeds, as they contain known abortifacients. I've occasionally wondered whether the Rapunzel and Petrosinella stories — of hunger for nourishing greens — are coded warnings about the loss and grief that could be caused by eating too much of a particular species.

Asparagaceae
Asparagus family

As well as the vegetable asparagus, this family gives us popular cultivated flowering plants such as hostas and hyacinths, and also agave, from which the sugar alternative agave syrup is derived. In Aotearoa the most celebrated member of the family is tī kōuka, the cabbage tree. Its relationship to asparagus is not surprising once you taste its edible leaf shoots.

Rengarenga or rock lily (*Arthropodium cirratum*), which has edible rhizomes, is also a member of this family. It grows wild throughout the North Island and the top of the South Island. With its vigorous clumps of green leaves and small, attractive white flowers, rengarenga has found favour as a garden ornamental.

Tī trees | Cabbage trees

TĪ KŌUKA | CABBAGE TREE
Cordyline australis

TĪ NGAHERE | FOREST CABBAGE TREE
Cordyline banksii

TĪ RAURIKI | DWARF CABBAGE TREE
Cordyline pumilio

TŌĪ | MOUNTAIN CABBAGE TREE, BROAD-LEAVED CABBAGE TREE
Cordyline indivisa

SPOTTING THEM

Trees in the *Cordyline* genus grow all around the Pacific. Tī kōuka is the most common in Aotearoa. It grows in open places throughout the country, often on farmland or bursting up through areas of native scrub.

USING THEM

In Aotearoa, Sāmoa, Tonga, Hawaiʻi and many other island groups, *Cordyline* trees have a long history as sources of food, medicine and fibre. Across the Pacific, 'ti' or 'ki' appears in local names for the species, indicating that knowledge of these trees dates back to the earliest island voyagers. Māori selectively bred and cultivated tī kōuka and its siblings.

THIS PAGE
Tī kōuka (cabbage trees).

Tougher and more weatherproof than harakeke, tī leaves were used to thatch roofs and were woven into mats, ropes and sandals. The leaves are also highly flammable. They catch fire quickly and make great kindling, even when slightly damp. Dried fallen leaves can be gathered and bunched together for use as fire starters. As a form of rongoā rākau, tī leaves are crushed, pounded or pulped to release the juice, which is soothing and antiseptic for sores and cuts.

To harvest food from tī trees sustainably, reach inside the 'leaf explosions' for the central growing shoot, snap or twist it off, and leave the plant to grow new shoots. Peel back the tough outer leaves of the shoot. Inside you will find delicious paler leaves surrounding a 'heart'. Through trial and error you will be able to tell how far you need to peel back the leaves. It's better to strip away too few leaves to start with. Before cooking a shoot, remove the stem from its middle. Chef Charles Royal (Te Whānau-a-Apanui, Ngāti Raukawa ki te Tonga) recommends harvesting them before the tree starts to seed.

Cooked, these shoots offer up a beguiling mix of sweet and bitter tastes with similarities to artichoke and asparagus, and you can use them in recipes as substitutes for both. Boil them for about 6 minutes or roast them. If you throw them in with roasting vegetables, put them in towards the end, when there's about 10 minutes left to go.

Tī trees produce creamy clouds of flowers in spring and summer. The scent is heady, distinctive and highly indolic (see page 112 for information about indoles). In her stunning book *Hiakai*, chef Monique Fiso discusses the edibility of tī flower buds and stems: eat the stems raw, and try dehydrating the flower buds.

Tī flowers also have potential in perfumery, and you can make beautiful scented infusions at home using the stalks of the flowers. Bear in mind that *Cordyline* flowers don't tend to tincture well, but they do make a divine pomade (a scent-infused fat) if this is the kind of earthy scent you like. For a pomade recipe, see page 306.

Asphodelaceae
Aloe family

Worldwide, *Aloe vera* is perhaps the most widely known species in the Asphodelaceae family, but in Aotearoa the most treasured members are harakeke and wharariki, the New Zealand flaxes. For Māori, harakeke especially has always been a vital source of fibre for baskets, clothing, fishing nets, rope and more. Māori also discovered the medicinal and culinary uses of these plants.

New Zealand flaxes

HARAKEKE | NEW ZEALAND FLAX, SWAMP FLAX
Phormium tenax

WHARARIKI | MOUNTAIN FLAX
Phormium cookianum

SPOTTING THEM

With their enormous fibrous, strap-like leaves and imposing flowering stalks, harakeke and wharariki are easy plants to spot. Wharariki has slightly shorter and softer leaves than harakeke, but the easiest way to tell the two species apart is to check the flowers and seedpods. Harakeke flowers are reddish, while wharariki flowers are greenish. Harakeke seedpods curve upwards like bananas, but wharariki seedpods are slightly twisted and dangle downwards. The two species can hybridise with each other.

USING THEM

The flowers of both harakeke and wharariki are edible. They also produce a lot of nectar and pollen, both of which can be collected and added to dishes. The nectar is a sweetener that contains several sugars and small amounts of vitamins.

Harakeke seeds are highly edible. When white or greenish, they are sweet and meaty; when black and shiny, they can be bitter. The sweet ones are nice on their own, sprinkled on a salad, or ground into a pesto or dip. You'll generally find the sweet seeds early in the season — late spring or early summer. As the weeks go by, the seeds acquire their shiny coats, and it gets harder and harder

THIS PAGE Harakeke (New Zealand flax), including the seedpods in closeup.

to find young sweet ones (although a few harakeke plants seem to hold on to them very late into summer). The seedpods also make a valuable dye, yielding a range of rich browns.

The flaxes are treasured as fibre plants by Māori. Iwi and hapū groups around the country are involved in growing and preserving the most valued heirloom varieties, and the weaving arts are thriving under expert leadership.

PROPAGATING HAREKEKE

If you find one of those precious flax bushes that has tasty seeds, you could try propagating it by separating a fan of leaves from the side of the bush and planting it directly into fertile, well-drained soil. Here is advice from the Manaaki Whenua – Landcare Research website (landcareresearch.co.nz) on how best to do this.

> *Taking fans off the parent bush can be hard work! If possible, choose a time when the soil is moist. We like to use a long-bladed planting or trenching spade, a grubber, or even a crowbar to dig around and get under and behind the fan we are lifting.*
>
> *Divided fans are usually trimmed of outer leaves, leaving the rito (growing shoot) and the two 'parent' leaves on either side (awhi rito or matua). The parent leaves should be cut back if too long, but it is a good idea to have some protection of the rito. If possible, plant the harakeke fans together in groups of three. This will give them a good start.*
>
> *The traditional way to plant harakeke is to 'plant the puku to the sun', so that the bulge on the fan faces halfway between the rising and setting sun. This protects the baby fans, which will emerge at the back of the clump, and gives them shade and moisture.*
>
> *Allow three metres between each clump . . . This spacing will allow good air movement among the plants as they grow, which helps prevent build-up of scale and fungal diseases, and allows easier access for trimming and harvesting.*
>
> *If the soil is poor, apply general fertiliser containing phosphate. Plants will also benefit from regular watering. Keep the area around the base of the plants weeded and trim dead leaves.*

Aspleniaceae
Spleenwort family

This is one of many fern families in Aotearoa. Ferns are plants that don't have flowers, but instead reproduce by spores. A lot of ferns contain carcinogens and it's not advisable to eat them. However, Māori culinary traditions include several species that are safe, including mouku and pikopiko, or common shield fern (*Polystichum neozelandicum*).

Mouku

> **MOUKU | HEN AND CHICKENS FERN, MOTHER SPLEENWORT**
> *Asplenium bulbiferum*

SPOTTING IT

This fern has characteristic little bulbils on the tips of its leaves. These curled babies — the 'chickens' — grow furled, then drop to the ground and grow into new ferns.

Mouku is common in lowland bush, especially near streams. The growing season is through spring and summer, although it varies from region to region.

USING IT

People around the world eat a wide range of 'fiddleheads' or 'fiddlehead greens'. These are the coiled shoots of young ferns that burst up from the ground. Once they've unfurled, they're no longer edible.

Mouku fiddleheads are a delicious vegetable, raw or cooked. Raw, they're crisp, have a mild, ever so slightly tart taste, and are juicily mucilaginous as you chew them. They are mildest near the base and become slightly more bitter as you nibble up to the top of the spiral.

They can be chopped into salads, or boiled for about 2–5 minutes, steamed, stir-fried or baked. You can treat fiddleheads like asparagus.

In his book, chef Charles Royal says to harvest fiddleheads by snapping them off at the weak point near their base, taking only those that are less than 25 centimetres long. To prepare the fiddleheads, remove the small fern-shaped leaves along the main spiralling fiddlehead stalk and discard them. Then wash the

THIS PAGE
Mouku (hen and chickens fern).

main stalk well, rubbing off as many of the little brown spots along it as you can, as these are bitter.

The Japanese sometimes serve cooked fiddleheads at room temperature, with shoyu and sesame seeds sprinkled over the top.

With their curls and twirls and flourishes, fiddleheads are a beautiful food, offering many possibilities for gorgeous presentation.

> *Pikopiko will play tricks on you. Always look back after you have harvested an area, and I guarantee you one or two will be waving at you, smiling! You will be amazed you missed them.*
>
> — CHARLES ROYAL, *COOKING WITH CHARLES ROYAL*, 2010

Asteraceae
Daisy family

The enormous Asteraceae family includes daisies, lettuce, sunflowers, marigolds, thistles, chamomile, artichokes, salsify and chicory, as well as foragers' favourites dandelion and pūhā, or sow thistles.

Most members of this family are herbaceous, but a few grow into shrubs or trees and are known as tree daisies. A well-known native tree daisy is rangiora (*Brachyglottis repanda*), with its large, soft, hairy white-backed leaves. As children, my sister and I loved to use those leaves as notepaper for secret messages.

Asteraceae species have composite flowers. This means the flowers are really clusters of much smaller flowers. For example, the centre of a daisy flower is made up of many tiny disc flowers, and the things that look like petals are, in fact, ray flowers encircling them. In contrast, dandelions have no disc flowers, only ray flowers.

The leaves of plants in this family are often highly edible, but they can also be bitter, like a bolted lettuce. The bitterness comes from the milky sap, known as latex. Nutritional experts often say we need more bitter in the modern diet. It's a taste we're not used to anymore, as our diets have shifted towards sweet and salty tastes, but bitters are vital aids to digestion. Bitter tastes trigger a set of responses in the body that stimulate and enhance the digestive process, and help the body absorb nutrients. For the best effect, some people recommend you should eat something bitter about 15 minutes before the rest of the meal.

You can minimise the bitterness of these plants to reveal their subtle underlying flavours by crushing the leaves and stems under running water as you rinse them, thereby releasing some of the latex. Alternatively, you can boil the leaves to release some of the bitterness.

If you have ulcers or a reflux condition, avoid eating too many bitters, or at least check with a medical professional first.

Dandelions

TOHETAKA | NATIVE DANDELION
Taraxacum magellanicum

TAWAO | INTRODUCED DANDELION
Taraxacum officinale

SPOTTING THEM

Dandelions are notoriously tricky to identify at first, because of the many lookalikes that also grow wild. Collectively, plants with dandelion-like flowers have been nicknamed DYCs — damn yellow composites. Dandelions — both the native and introduced species — are distinguishable from other DYCs by their smooth, usually highly toothed leaves, in combination with hollow, unbranching flower stems. But never fear if you mistake a dandelion for another DYC, because they're all more or less edible.

USING THEM

Māori have long used dandelion (first tohetaka and later tawao) medicinally and as a vegetable. A well-known whakataukī compares someone who sleeps in to the tohetaka, which doesn't open its petals until the sun is well up.

Dandelions are extremely nutritious and often described as a wild superfood. You can eat every part of the plant. They're a diuretic, and in Western herbal medicine the leaves and roots (often taken as a tisane) are used to cleanse the kidneys and liver. Meanwhile, dandelion flowers provide a gentle yellow dye for animal fibres.

Dandelion leaves are best eaten in spring before the flower comes up. They can be cooked quickly — wilted in hot oil or steamed — or eaten raw as a bitter salad green. The leaves are often at their most bitter in autumn and winter. They're still perfectly edible at this time, but you'll probably want to collect lots of them and boil them in a good quantity of water. I've never found I needed to boil them for more than 10 minutes to get rid of the bitterness.

When selecting dandelion leaves, choose the youngest leaves (the central ones in the rosette) and snip them off. If you're collecting lots, try to place them with the cut stems end down in the bag so they don't ooze latex onto one another. Note that latex stains as well as tasting bitter.

The new flowers and flower buds of dandelions are edible throughout the year, but they're most abundant in summer. The newest dandelion flowers are delicious, and any you pick to eat do need to be new, because they soon begin to produce fluff for dandelion 'clocks'. This can be hard to see when you examine a flower, but you can definitely feel it in your mouth.

To use the flowers as a vegetable, boil, steam or sauté them, or dip them in batter and fry them as appealingly small, round fritters. Try tempura or a sweet fritter recipe sprinkled with icing sugar (see page 249). You can also pull the flowers apart and sprinkle the yellow parts into or onto whatever dish you are making.

When it comes to dandelion flower buds, you can harvest them in two ways. If you look at the base of a plant that's flowering or getting ready to, you'll often find one or two new buds right in the centre of its rosette of leaves that are ready to rise up on their stalks. These are the ones to pluck. The plumpest, tastiest buds come from the biggest dandelions, which are often the plants in the longest, lushest grass.

To eat the flower buds, boil them, steam them or sauté them for just a few seconds. You can also pickle them. Alternatively, harvest buds after they've grown a bit larger and begun to sprout up on their stalks. Cut them so that several centimetres of stalk remain, and steam or boil them, stem and all. Serve them like any other cooked green vegetable, with seasoning, butter or a sauce, or cool them quickly in cold water to serve in a salad.

When harvesting buds, be careful not to confuse them with the spent flowers that have closed and are getting ready to turn into dandelion clocks — they're far less appetising!

DANDELION COFFEE

The secret to making dandelion coffee is to oven-roast the roots on a low temperature for a long time. They shrink a lot, so start with a decent-sized bowlful.

Use a trowel to dig up the roots – either whole, or leaving a little in the ground to regrow. Most people say that the colder months are best for digging up and using the roots – that's when they're biggest and sweetest. However, legendary US forager Euell Gibbons wrote that he preferred to harvest them in spring.

Give the roots a good wash and scrub and, if they're big, slice them horizontally into thick pieces. Roast them at 100 °C (200 °F) for about 4 hours. Enjoy the smell that fills the kitchen!

They're ready to take out of the oven when the insides are a darker brown than the outsides and they snap easily between your fingers. You may find that you can remove some before others.

Keep the dried roots whole in a jar until you're ready to use them. Pound them with a mortar and pestle or grind them in a spice or coffee grinder, then use the grinds in a plunger, just like ground coffee. The result is a warming, caffeine-free cuppa, a little bit coffee-like, a little bit nutty and a little bit chocolatey, but ultimately with a flavour all its own.

> You can also blend regular coffee with dandelion coffee to make it go further and at the same time reduce your caffeine intake.

Pūhā | Sow thistles

> **PŪHĀ | NEW ZEALAND SOW THISTLE**
> *Sonchus kirkii*

> **PŪHĀ | COMMON SOW THISTLE**
> *Sonchus oleraceus*

> **PŪHĀ | PERENNIAL SOW THISTLE**
> *Sonchus arvensis*

> **PŪHĀ | PRICKLY SOW THISTLE**
> *Sonchus asper*

SPOTTING THEM

Pūhā plants, or sow thistles, are DYCs. They start growing as a rosette of leaves, then send up a strong central stalk with smaller branches coming off it. They tend to grow flowers in small bunches and thrive in moist, fertile places with a little shade.

Even within species, the plants can look quite different from one another, with their form depending on their age and genes, and the growing conditions. In ideal conditions pūhā grows huge and lush — I've met a few plants that were taller than me. However, those that are forced to lead a harder life often have small, sparse leaves with a purplish tinge.

Sonchus kirkii is the only pūhā native to Aotearoa, but the others naturalised here very soon after European settlers introduced them. *Sonchus kirkii* probably grew much more widely before the introduced species took over, but today it's fairly hard to find compared with the other pūhā (either wild or at specialist garden centres).

USING THEM

Sonchus species grow in numerous parts of the world and are regularly consumed in many different cultures. Pūhā are a vital part of Māori cuisine. Every above-ground part, including the buds and flowers, can be eaten raw or cooked in a very similar way to dandelions (see page 63). You can also substitute pūhā for spinach in any recipe. Like spinach, it loses a lot of volume when cooked, so do allow for this.

The young leaves and stalks are quite bitter. As the plant grows older, the stems fill with more bitter, oozing latex, but the leaves often seem to lose some bitterness. If you're using older stalks, bruise or crush them as you rinse them to let the latex wash away before cooking them.

More damn yellow composites (DYCs)

ACRID LETTUCE
Lactuca virosa

PRICKLY LETTUCE
Lactuca serriola

BEAKED HAWKSBEARD
Crepis vesicaria

BEARDED HAWKSBEARD
Crepis barbigera

BRISTLY OX-TONGUE
Helminthotheca echioides

CATSEAR
Hypochaeris radicata

SMOOTH CATSEAR
Hypochaeris glabra

HAWKBIT
Leontodon taraxacoides

SPOTTING THEM

DYCs are all those Asteraceae plants that have yellow dandelion-like flowers. Even common garden lettuce is a DYC. It's interesting how many are named after parts of animal anatomy — even dandelion itself (see page 62), which comes from the French for 'lion's tooth'. All DYCs start as a basal rosette of leaves that sends up stems, and they're all more or less edible.

When writing this book I was determined at the outset to provide a comprehensive guide to almost all the DYCs growing wild in this country, but I soon gave up. The epithet 'damn yellow composite' was not bestowed lightly. Not counting dandelion and pūhā, there are more than 30 DYC species growing wild here — some

CLOCKWISE FROM TOP LEFT Tawao (introduced dandelion); pūhā (New Zealand sow thistle) in bud; bristly ox-tongue; catsear; pot marigold; oxeye daisy; pūhā.

with hairy leaves, some smooth; some branching, some unbranching; some with wavy or toothy leaves, others with smooth-edged leaves; some annuals, some biennials and some perennials.

The eight DYCs I've listed are some of the most widespread in Aotearoa. Others grow more locally. Unless you're a botanist, take DYCs as they come, and use the entries on dandelion and pūhā as inspiration for how to treat them.

USING THEM

When you find a new DYC, experiment with it. Nibble its leaves to see how bitter they are. Decide if you could eat them raw or whether they might be nicer cooked. Experiment with old and young leaves. See if the plants produce flowers or flower buds that you could use. And see if the roots look large enough to roast and use to make a coffee substitute. Catsear and hawkbit can certainly be used this way; see page 64 for the recipe.

As ever, be very sure you have a DYC before experimenting. The best way to be sure is to inspect the plants when they're in flower.

Chamomiles

GERMAN CHAMOMILE
Matricaria recutita

RAYLESS CHAMOMILE, PINEAPPLE WEED
Matricaria discoidea

ROMAN CHAMOMILE
Chamaemelum nobile

SPOTTING THEM

Roman chamomile is a sprawling or creeping perennial plant with a fruity, apple-like scent. It has feathery green leaves and white flowers with raised, cone-shaped centres.

German chamomile looks and smells quite similar to Roman chamomile, but it's an annual that grows upright. In Aotearoa, it's found wild only occasionally in localised patches, although it self-seeds readily in the garden.

Rayless chamomile, an annual in the same genus as German chamomile, grows commonly throughout the country and is easily distinguished. It has feathery leaves and a cone-shaped yellow flower centre; however, the white petals edging the centres are vestigial and barely visible. The plant has a pineapple-like scent. In a lawn it's tiny, trying to cram its entire life cycle into the period between mows. In long grass it grows to a more usable size.

USING THEM

German chamomile is the most popular of the three, but all have some properties in common. Their medicinal uses are numerous, and some people call them 'a pharmacy in a flower'. The flowers are the part most often used medicinally — the yellow centres contain high concentrations of active ingredients.

Chamomile tisane is particularly noted as a mild and gentle sedative, and also a soothing treatment for a stomach upset by anxiety or stress. Note, however, that a few people find this tisane has the opposite effect, making them feel queasy or outright nauseous.

Chamomile flowers and leaves can be eaten either raw or cooked. The flowers can also be used as a flavouring to infuse alcohols, vinegars, oils or syrups, imparting a mix of fruity, green and bitter notes.

Damn white composites (DWCs)

FEVERFEW
Tanacetum parthenium

OXEYE DAISY
Leucanthemum vulgare

STINKING MAYWEED
Anthemis cotula

SPOTTING THEM

Not only do foragers have to contend with DYCs, but they are also confronted by DWCs — damn white composites. These are the numerous plants that have daisy-like flowers with yellow centres and white 'petals'. The chamomiles may be to DWCs what the dandelion is to DYCs. In Aotearoa, there aren't quite as many DWCs as DYCs, but those listed here are three of the most common.

Feverfew is an aromatic perennial that grows as a very small bush. Some flowers are double, while others are single. The leaves and petals tend to be slightly shorter and wider than those of many other similar plants. Oxeye daisy has a relatively flat centre in comparison to the cone-shaped centres of many DWCs,

THIS PAGE
Yarrow leaves and flowers.

and its leaves are not as feathery. Stinking mayweed looks very similar to Roman chamomile (see page 68), but has a strong smell that many people find unpleasant.

There are also a number of wild-growing Asteraceae that have this same daisy-like form but are different colours — often yellow. Examples are the inedible ragwort (*Jacobaea vulgaris*) and dyer's chamomile (*Anthemis tinctoria*) which, you won't be surprised to hear, has long been prized by natural dyers for the beautiful yellows it gives.

USING THEM

DWCs with white 'petals' and yellow centres are generally safe to ingest in moderate amounts, although some people do have allergies to members of the Asteraceae family. The flower buds can be pickled, and the open flowers can be used in salads or as edible garnishes, or for making fritters.

Feverfew has several applications in herbal medicine, most notably as a preventative treatment for migraines.

Pot marigold

POT MARIGOLD
Calendula officinalis

SPOTTING IT

This easy-care plant is widely grown in gardens and sometimes finds its way into the wild. It looks like a cheerful large orange (or pale yellow) daisy.

USING IT

Most marigolds have edible flowers. Generally, the petals are pulled off and sprinkled into salads or across other dishes, or added to infusions or baked goods for colour and extra nutrition. The flowers are also important in herbal medicine, having antimicrobial properties. In addition, they are used in skincare products; an infusion is often recommended as a wash for acne.

Yarrow

YARROW
Achillea millefolium

SPOTTING IT

Yarrow has feathery leaves and tiny, usually white, composite flowers in wide clusters. The flowers can also be pale pink.

USING IT

You can cook and eat yarrow leaves, but the plant is best known for its numerous medicinal uses. As with chamomile, make a calming, sedative tisane to drink by infusing the flowers. Yarrow is particularly well known as a wound treatment, and contains antiseptic and blood-clotting compounds. Some people make a poultice from the leaves and flowers for this; others use only the leaves. You can also make an infusion and use it topically as a compress.

There is increasing pharmaceutical interest in yarrow, and a 2008 review in the journal *Current Pharmaceutical Design* concluded: 'The largest number of data accumulated for antioxidant and anti-inflammatory effects. There are positive results on the analgesic, anti-ulcer, choleretic, hepatoprotective and wound healing activities.'

Boraginaceae
Borage or forget-me-not family

This family is a hairy lot. Almost all of its 2,000 species have hairy leaves, although the forms vary widely from herbs, to shrubs, to trees. Many have blue flowers. Pretty forget-me-not is a well-known family member.

Borage

> **BORAGE**
> *Borago officinalis*

SPOTTING IT

An annual or sometimes biennial plant that can grow up to 60 centimetres tall, borage has hairy stems and hairy leaves with a wrinkly texture. Its distinctive star-shaped flowers will help you identify the plant most reliably. They're usually a shade of blue, although some are white in cultivation.

Borage is found in the wild here and there throughout the country, and in gardens it often self-seeds. Many people like to plant it in their gardens as a companion plant and to attract bees.

USING IT

Borage leaves are crisp to eat and have a distinct cucumber flavour. As with other hirsute plants, if you're eating the leaves raw, disguise their texture in a sandwich or wrap, or by slicing them finely in salads. The leaves also make a delicious cooked green. Whole, cut or torn, they can be boiled for a minute or two just to soften them or they can be very briefly sautéed in oil or butter.

The leaves contain very low levels of toxic pyrrolizidine alkaloids, so some people advise that you enjoy them sparingly. Note, however, that borage doesn't contain the alkaloids in the high quantities found in the related comfreys (see page 74).

Borage flowers, either plain or candied, are a much-loved garnish. Like the leaves, they make a dainty sandwich ingredient. They are also pretty in salads, and you can freeze the flowers in ice cubes for party drinks. UK food writer Frances Bissell makes a striking blue pesto using borage flowers in place of basil.

TOP ROW
Borage in flower.

BOTTOM
Common comfrey.

Comfreys

COMMON COMFREY
Symphytum officinale

ROUGH COMFREY
Symphytum asperum

RUSSIAN COMFREY
Symphytum × uplandicum

SPOTTING THEM

Russian comfrey is a cross between the other two species named here, and grows wild more often around Aotearoa than either of its parents. Comfreys can grow 80–100 centimetres tall. They have large hairy leaves and attractive bell-like flowers in drooping clusters. The flowers of rough comfrey are purplish, while those of common comfrey are creamy white or pale pink — although when they dry they become more purple. Russian comfrey may have pink or purple flowers.

USING THEM

Up until the 1970s, some people liked to eat comfrey leaves by the salad-bowlful, and the leaves and roots were also widely used in herbal medicine. A comfrey tisane was recommended as a general tonic, and poultices, ointments, washes and other preparations were enthusiastically applied to wounds and broken bones. Comfrey contains a number of medicinal compounds, including powerful allantoin, which stimulates healthy tissue growth and helps heal injuries.

Through the 1980s and 1990s, however, concern grew about the toxicity of pyrrolizidine alkaloids, which comfreys contain in quantity. For this reason, many herbalists now recommend avoiding comfrey altogether or keeping its use to a minimum — especially its internal consumption. For the benefits of allantoin, a safer alternative as far as we know is broad-leaved or narrow-leaved plantain (see page 125).

There are, however, less fraught ways to use comfrey. Organic gardeners value it as a mulch and make a liquid fertiliser by fermenting the leaves in water for 3–5 weeks.

Brassicaceae
Cabbage or mustard family

This family of plants has given humans the raw material from which to cultivate many popular vegetables, including broccoli and cauliflower, selectively bred for giant edible flowerheads; kale for firm, delicious leaves; radishes, turnips and horseradish for swollen edible roots; and a number of species for their seeds.

Several species of Brassicaceae grow wild around Aotearoa. Many are cultivated varieties that have escaped from gardens and then, over one or more generations, reverted to their wild form. Almost all Brassicaceae are rich in glucosinolates — compounds that contain sulphur and nitrogen. Sometimes called mustard oils, glucosinolates give the plants their mustard flavour.

Most wild Brassicaceae are edible, but to be on the safe side avoid gathering them from places that are subject to farm run-off or may have been very heavily fertilised. Many Brassicaceae can absorb and retain large quantities of nitrates, which are toxic in very high doses.

Wild mustards

HEDGE MUSTARD
Sisymbrium officinale

ORIENTAL MUSTARD, INDIAN HEDGE MUSTARD, EASTERN ROCKET
Sisymbrium orientale

RADISH
Raphanus sativus

WILD RADISH
Raphanus raphanistrum

PŌHATA | WILD TURNIP
Brassica rapa ssp. sylvestris

TWIGGY TURNIP
Brassica fruticulosa

SPOTTING THEM

You can recognise Brassicaceae most easily when they're in flower. They have distinctive flowers with six stamens and four petals in the shape of a cross (their former family name, Cruciferae, means 'cross-shaped'). The flowers are usually yellow, but they can also be white or pink. The plants grow in all kinds of habitats, but are common on wastelands and roadsides.

It can take a while to recognise the different Brassicaceae species. Once you've identified their flowers, you can keep a close eye on the plants throughout the year and you'll begin to recognise their various stages before they flower. They begin as rosettes close to the ground. The rosettes then send up stalks with leaves that can look quite different to the leaves of the rosette, and often become more bitter.

Wild turnip and twiggy turnip look similar to each other, but twiggy turnip has smaller leaves with slightly more rounded, curvy edges and a smoother feel. Twiggy turnip also has paler flowers and smaller seedpods than wild turnip.

Radish and wild radish are distinguishable from the other species because they have hairy leaves and stems.

USING THEM

All parts of the Brassicaceae species are edible. The leaves and roots are best eaten during the rosette stage (older roots are too stringy), so it's worth getting to know what the plants look like in this form.

The young leaves that have just emerged from the ground in a rosette are bitter and mustardy — good raw or cooked. You need to fry or steam them for only a few seconds as they soon lose their volume — along with a lot of their distinctive mustardiness.

Before they flower, wild mustards form little clusters of edible flower buds that look like mini broccoli heads (although it's really the other way round — broccoli heads are giant flower buds). These are edible, too, and need only the tiniest amount of cooking — from a few seconds to a minute, boiled, steamed or sautéed. They are usually more bitter than the broccoli we're used to, so you may want to add a little salt or sugar during cooking.

The flowers themselves are quite edible and a colourful addition to any dish. After the plants have flowered, they form seedpods that can be collected and dried until they release their hot, edible seeds (see page 78).

CLOCKWISE FROM TOP LEFT Hedge mustard; wild radish; shepherd's purse; twiggy turnip; wild radish flowers.

HARVESTING WILD MUSTARD SEEDS

You can use this method for any of the wild radishes, turnips or mustards listed on page 75. Gather the seedpods and spread them on a plate to dry in the sun. As the pods dry, they split and release their seeds. Collect the seeds and store them in an airtight container.

Use the seeds just like store-bought mustard seeds. To make a basic mustard paste, soak the seeds in vinegar for 1–2 days, topping up with more vinegar if they absorb it all. Then simply pound them to a paste.

Shepherd's purse

SHEPHERD'S PURSE
Capsella bursa-pastoris

SPOTTING IT

Shepherd's purse generally grows as a smaller plant than the wild mustards. Its four-petalled flowers are white and so small that you can only just see they are arranged like a cross. The easiest way to recognise the plant is by the little heart-shaped seedpods it's named for — a ram's testicular sac, sometimes called its 'purse', has a similar shape. It's debatable whether the word 'purse' in the context of a ram's testicles is used simply in the sense of a container for valuables, or whether shepherds really did make purses from ram's testicles — as some sources claim.

USING IT

Shepherd's purse isn't as useful as the wild mustards. Its lush new leaves are good in salads and cooked, and can be treated just like other mustard greens, but its seeds are too small to be of much use.

Ngā kirihi | Cresses

***BARBAREA* SPECIES**
***CARDAMINE* SPECIES**
***LEPIDIUM* SPECIES**
***NASTURTIUM* SPECIES**
***PACHYCLADON* SPECIES**
***RORIPPA* SPECIES**

SPOTTING THEM

A bewildering array of the mustardy, small-leafed greens we call cresses — both native and introduced — grows throughout Aotearoa. They often love damp places — streams, ditches, marshes and boggy paddocks. Many of the native species are now threatened.

It's also harder and harder to find good places to harvest cress as our waterways are increasingly polluted. Not surprisingly, people are very protective of their local patches, often holding the locations close to their chests and always being careful to harvest the cress sustainably. If you don't have a way to harvest naturally growing cress, it's rewarding to grow plants at home.

USING THEM

When using cresses, test the stalks to see how tough or stringy they are, then decide whether you want to leave them whole, finely chop them, or pick them over to remove the coarsest bits. Cresses make marvellous salad ingredients, and with their small leaves they are also pretty garnishes. They're great in soups, sauces and casseroles, but add them at the last minute to ensure they don't lose too much volume or their mustardiness.

Caryophyllaceae
Pink or carnation family

Most Caryophyllaceae are herbaceous, and two genera in the family — *Dianthus* (carnations) and *Gypsophila* — provide floristry staples. Another species, Antarctic pearlwort (*Colobanthus quitensis*), is one of only two flowering plants in Antarctica. As Antarctic air temperatures have risen, the pearlwort has spread to new territory and begun to grow more lushly. Researchers are keeping a close eye on this species to see how it continues to respond to global warming.

Two particularly useful plants of the Caryophyllaceae family — common chickweed and soapwort — grow wild in Aotearoa.

Kohukohu | Common chickweed

> **KOHUKOHU | COMMON CHICKWEED**
> *Stellaria media*

SPOTTING IT

Common chickweed grows wild in gardens and will soon take over a bed of soil you've just cleared. It also pops up in the unmowed areas of parks and reserves, starting life as a mat of tangled stems with small teardrop-shaped leaves. The stems and leaves often become bigger and bushier, and if you cut the plant back it regrows more lushly.

The tiny star-like white flowers look as if they have ten petals, but if you peer closely you can see that they actually have five petals, each split down the middle. Another distinguishing feature that can be difficult to see is the single row of hairs on the stem.

USING IT

Common chickweed contains B vitamins, as well as vitamins C and D. It's also a respectable source of iron, copper, calcium and sodium. It's hard to grab a handful of a plant without also bringing with it bits of other unwanted weeds. The easiest way to harvest it is to find the tips of the plant, pull them upwards and snip off the best-looking bits.

Raw leaves snipped into pieces 2–3 centimetres long make a healthy and

FROM TOP Harvesting kohukohu (chickweed); kohukohu leaves in closeup.

tasty salad ingredient, and remind me of alfalfa sprouts. The plant is valuable in wild salads because it has such a mild taste it balances out other, more intense-tasting wild greens.

You can also cook common chickweed in a stir-fry or add it to a soup, sauce or casserole at the last minute. When cooking it, I like to cut the leaves into shorter pieces, 1–2 centimetres long, to avoid a stringy mouth feel. Common chickweed can also be puréed before being added to a cooked dish.

The species contains saponins — compounds that lather up like soap. This makes it an especially creamy pesto ingredient — and you can throw it into a smoothie for added nutritional value as well as extra frothiness.

The saponins also make chickweed medicinally valuable as a soothing and healing skin treatment. In herbal medicine, chickweed poultices or compresses are used for eczema, insect bites and other itchy skin conditions.

Cerastium chickweeds

MOUSE-EAR CHICKWEED
Cerastium fontanum

STICKY MOUSE-EAR CHICKWEED, ANNUAL MOUSE-EAR CHICKWEED
Cerastium glomeratum

SPOTTING THEM

Mouse-ear and sticky chickweeds look very similar to common chickweed, with small leaves and white flowers that have five split petals, but the leaves are hairy and the plants don't grow as abundantly or lushly.

USING THEM

Although mouse-ear and sticky chickweeds are not as appealing as common chickweed, they're quite edible. Pounded into a pesto or chopped into very short pieces and cooked with other things to disguise the hairy texture, they make a nutritious addition to a dish.

> *Chickweed is an old friend that has sustained me through thick and thin. I pick it and usually eat it on the spot.*
>
> — SANDOR KATZ, *THE REVOLUTION WILL NOT BE MICROWAVED*, 2003

Soapwort

SOAPWORT
Saponaria officinalis

SPOTTING IT

Soapwort does sometimes escape from gardens, but it doesn't seem to travel very far, so patches are localised. It has been spotted growing wild in Tauranga, Picton, Moutere, Christchurch, Darfield, Inangahua and around Alexandra.

The plant has opposite leaves on strong stems and pink flowers in clusters. Single flowers have five petals, but soapwort can also produce double flowers.

USING IT

Soapwort is valued for its leaves and roots, which are full of saponins. To make a gentle fabric cleaner or shampoo, use either the leaves or the grated or finely chopped roots. Add 1 part leaves to 2 parts water, or 1 part roots to 4 parts water in a pot (even so, the roots are much richer in saponins and this will be a stronger soap). Simmer with the lid on for about 20 minutes. Leave to cool, then strain and store the liquid in a jar in the fridge. Your soapwort solution should last at least a week.

Sweet william

SWEET WILLIAM
Dianthus barbatus

SPOTTING IT

If you're lucky, you might come across sweet william in a grassy field or clearing. These plants have spear-shaped green leaves and dense rounded clusters of flowers borne on stalks. The flowers have five petals with serrated edges.

While cultivated sweet williams come in all manner of pinks, whites and reds, the petals are red with a white base when the species reverts to its wild form.

USING IT

The spicy, scented flowers of sweet william are edible. You can use them in salads, as garnishes, or to infuse syrups, cream and other sweet treats.

Fabaceae
Pea or legume family

Fabaceae includes 18,000 species, so there is a huge variety of plant forms within the family. Many of the plants — including peas, beans, chickpeas, soya beans, clover, peanuts, alfalfa, liquorice, gorse and broom, among many others — have been important to humanity. The family is best known for two particular qualities.

The first of these is that as the plants grow they fix atmospheric nitrogen in the soil, increasing its fertility. And second, many species in the family contain isoflavones, a group of plant oestrogens — compounds that mimic the effect of human oestrogens in the human body. There's a bit of paranoia around about the effects of isoflavones, but most research shows that they have some really worthwhile health benefits.

Brooms

MONTPELLIER BROOM
Genista monspessulana

SPANISH BROOM
Spartium junceum

SWEET BROOM
Genista stenopetala

WILD BROOM, COMMON BROOM, SCOTCH BROOM
Cytisus scoparius

MAKING A BROOM WITH BROOM

You can make a simple traditional broom by gathering the branches of a broom plant and bunching them together. Wind cord tightly around the top half or two thirds to bind the branches together into a handle, and leave the bottom part open as the brush end. Use your brush fresh or leave it to dry.

Broom-making has long been a valued art. An array of brooms of different sizes, textures and densities, and for different purposes, can be created from different plants. Brooms for sweeping hot hearths and ovens are sometimes made from aromatic branches, because they release their scent as they brush the hot surface.

TOP ROW
Sweet broom.

BOTTOM ROW
Red clover.

SPOTTING THEM

Numerous plant species around the world are called broom. When I asked local botanist Phil Garnock-Jones to define 'broom', he replied, only half-jokingly, 'Any shrub in the Fabaceae family that you could imagine bundling together the branches of and using as a broom.' Indeed, *scoparius*, the species name for wild broom, means 'one who sweeps'.

Brooms are a group of closely related genera that grow as shrubs, have numerous stems with small leaves, and have small, pretty flowers that are almost always yellow. They include the four species named here.

In Aotearoa, several brooms have escaped from cultivation to become naturalised. Wild broom and, to a slightly lesser extent, Montpellier broom are particularly widespread, and have become despised pests in some regions.

Sweet broom also grows throughout the country but in a more localised way, and is one of the most lusciously scented plants you will ever encounter. It turns on flowers for most of the year, but particularly profusely in summer. When the sun warms its petals, an almost impossibly sweet and fruity scent fills the air. This distinguishes it from similar-looking brooms, which are unscented.

Spanish broom is another species identifiable by its strong scent. It can grow up to 3 metres tall and its mature rounded green twigs have few, if any, leaves.

USING THEM

A 2007 European study in the *Journal of Ethnobiology and Ethnomedicine* found that across Bulgaria, Italy, Macedonia and Romania about 108 plant species from 37 different families were used to make brooms. Of these, eight were from the Fabaceae family.

Aside from their use as brooms, the other common application for broom plants — those that have fragrant flowers — is in perfumery. Spanish broom in particular has a whole industry built around it. An extract made from the flowers of this species is a very subtle and expensive perfumery ingredient known as genêt, the French name for this plant. Genêt has a floral fragrance, mingled with notes of honey, hay and tea. Both Spanish broom and sweet broom are amazing ingredients for handmade perfumes (see page 312).

Clovers

ALSIKE CLOVER
Trifolium hybridum

RED CLOVER
Trifolium pratense

WHITE CLOVER
Trifolium repens

SPOTTING THEM

There are several clovers of the *Trifolium* genus growing wild in Aotearoa, but the three listed here are probably the most common. They're distinctive for their (usually) three-part leaves and orb-like flowers.

USING THEM

City folk sometimes overlook clovers, thinking of them as common lawn flowers and cow food. Children see them as more special — often including the flowers in the small bouquets they like to lovingly gift to family members.

When I was growing up, I would spend ages poking through clover patches trying to find four-leaf clovers, until we discovered a motherlode beside the garage. We then suspected that any number of these mutants could be created with a little exposure to petrol, rubber or exhaust!

Clover petals have sweet nectar at their base, and can be pulled apart and sprinkled into salads or onto biscuits, cakes and desserts as an edible garnish. The leaves are quite edible, too, although most people are underwhelmed by that thought. Where they grow lushly, red-clover flowers have a gorgeous honeyed fragrance, but this doesn't last long after picking and is hard to capture. It's probably best enjoyed on the plant.

Clovers are also highly valued by some for the oestrogenic isoflavones they contain, and are said to help with troublesome symptoms of the menopause. Many over-the-counter treatments contain red-clover extracts, but some people swear by a simple tisane of the flowers, taken daily (it's pleasant and mild in flavour).

Gorse

> **GORSE**
> *Ulex europaeus*

SPOTTING IT

You can hardly miss gorse in this country. Introduced by European settlers as a hedge plant because it was easier and cheaper than building fences, it soon ran wild. This spiky pest does have one redeeming feature — it's a good nursery plant for areas of regenerating native bush. Leave a field of gorse alone for a few decades, and natives will seed and grow in the nitrogen-rich soil under its prickly protection. Eventually, the natives burst through and shade out the gorse. Having served its purpose, the gorse dies.

USING IT

Gorse flowers are edible, although I'd exercise moderation as there are health concerns around consuming flowers from related broom species.

The flowers have a sweet, coconutty smell that fills the air on a warm day. Many foragers have tried unsuccessfully to capture this aroma in wines, cordials and ice creams. All the same, you can use them for their sunny colour as a garnish, thrown into salads, or steeped in liquid to impart a golden hue.

Fagaceae
Beech family

Fagaceae is a family of trees and shrubs that have catkin flowers. Some are deciduous and some evergreen. The most well-known family members, in Europe and North America at least, are the oaks, beeches and chestnuts. Chestnuts — trees in the *Castanea* genus — are great foraging fare.

Chestnuts

JAPANESE CHESTNUT
Castanea crenata

SWEET CHESTNUT
Castanea sativa

SPOTTING THEM

Old chestnut trees, many planted by early European settlers, grow throughout Aotearoa. There are several species of chestnut worldwide, but those found here are usually the Japanese chestnut or sweet chestnut, or a hybrid of the two.

Chestnuts can be recognised by their green fruits, which have porcupine-like spines. The fruits are called burrs. Don't confuse edible chestnuts with horse chestnuts, whose burrs have sparser spikes that look more like cat teeth than porcupine spines. The horse chestnut is poisonous (see 'Allergy alert', page 30).

USING THEM

Let chestnut burrs ripen on the tree. After they fall in autumn and winter, leave them for a few days to open, as the nuts will then be riper and you can extract them more easily. You may need gloves to protect your hands from the spines. Good shoes are useful too, so you can gently roll and press the burrs under your feet, to help release some of the nuts.

Once the nuts are out of the burrs, you need to remove their shiny brown shells. Score the shells with a knife or cut the whole chestnuts in half, then drop them into boiling water — shell and all. Boil them for 5–10 minutes if you're in a hurry, or for up to half an hour for very easy peeling.

Drain the liquid and, when the chestnuts are cool enough to handle, remove the loosened shells, which should now be easy to pull off. You're not finished yet though! The nuts inside the shells have a fuzzy brownish skin, which is unpleasantly tannic and needs to be peeled off. While the cooked nuts are still warm, use a combination of knife and fingers to do this. You could also buy a chestnut peeler.

If the nuts cool before you finish, they become harder to peel. If this happens, just reheat them in water and try again. Once peeled, they can be eaten as is. Another popular way to eat chestnuts is roasting them in their shells for 20 minutes in an open fire or an oven heated to 200°C (400°F). Again, score the shells or cut the chestnuts in half first so they don't explode.

In his book *Food for Free*, Richard Mabey notes that the traditional way to gauge roast-chestnut readiness is to put one unpierced nut in the fire with the rest, make sure everyone is sitting well back, and wait. When the unpierced nut explodes, all the others are ready!

You can eat chestnuts raw, but people seldom do, probably because it's hard to get the skin off when the nut is cold. Whichever way you eat them, they're best consumed as soon as possible after harvesting. They contain a lot of water, so they don't store well fresh. However, you can peel them and air-dry or oven-dry them to keep them longer (see page 194). You can also grind dried chestnuts to make flour.

CHESTNUTS AS A SUPERFOOD

Chestnuts are high in protein and starch but much lower in fat than other nuts. They're the only commonly eaten nuts that are rich in vitamin C. They're also a good source of vitamin B6, potassium, magnesium and iron. What's more, chestnut flour is great in gluten-free baking.

Geraniaceae
Cranesbill family

The large Geraniaceae family includes the genera *Geranium*, *Pelargonium* and *Erodium*. All three were lumped together in the genus *Geranium* until 1789, when the pelargoniums and erodiums were given their own classification. Confusingly, pelargoniums are still often called geraniums.

To add to the confusion, true geraniums are commonly called cranesbills, while pelargoniums are called storksbills, and erodiums are called storksbills or heronsbills. The names are inspired by the long, beak-shaped columns that emerge from the flowers to hold their fruit capsules.

Pelargoniums all have edible leaves and flowers, but the scented pelargoniums, from South Africa, are especially exciting for foragers, offering numerous possibilities for cooking and perfumery. The *Pelargonium* genus features a whole palette of aromatic chemicals, and different aromas and aroma combinations come to the fore in different species, varieties and cultivars.

Dove's-foot cranesbill

DOVE'S-FOOT CRANESBILL
Geranium molle

SPOTTING IT

This modest little weed grows in gardens and parks around the country. Because of its leaves, it's often confused with buttercup. Once it flowers, though, there's no confusing the two. Dove's-foot cranesbill has mauve flowers with five jagged petals — completely different from buttercup's shiny yellow flowers.

USING IT

Dove's-foot cranesbill leaves, although downy, are very edible. With their mild flavour, they can be thrown into any cooked dish, chopped lightly and added to salads or sandwiches, or blended into pastes and smoothies. The pretty flowers are also edible.

TOP ROW
Dove's-foot cranesbill.

BOTTOM ROW
Rose-scented pelargonium.

Scented pelargoniums

LEMON-SCENTED PELARGONIUM, LEMON-SCENTED GERANIUM
Pelargonium crispum

NUTMEG PELARGONIUM, NUTMEG GERANIUM
Pelargonium × fragrans

PEPPERMINT PELARGONIUM, PEPPERMINT GERANIUM
Pelargonium tomentosum

ROSE-SCENTED PELARGONIUMS, ROSE GERANIUMS
Pelargonium × asperum, P. capitatum

SPOTTING THEM

The scented pelargoniums listed here are among those that most commonly grow wild in Aotearoa. You'll also find them, and others with more domestic natures, in cultivated gardens. They persist in old, neglected or abandoned patches and, like lavender and rosemary, often lean into public spaces because people like to grow them along fence lines. *Pelargonium × asperum* is probably the one you'll come across most often. It's thought to be a hybrid of two other rose-scented pelargoniums, *P. graveolens* and *P. radens*.

When you pass a pelargonium that you think might be scented, stop, rub a leaf between your thumb and forefinger, then sniff your finger to see what it's offering you. It's the scented pelargonium secret handshake.

Pelargonium flowers usually have five petals and ten stamens. The two upper petals on the flower are usually larger and brighter than the bottom three, and there is only one line of symmetry through the flower.

Look for wild pelargoniums in coastal places, where they tolerate wind and salt.

USING THEM

The fragrant compounds in scented pelargoniums run plentifully through the leaves, stems and flowers, but are most abundant in the green parts, which practically drip aromatic oils. Pelargonium flavours and aromas are strong and often linger. Some have musky undertones.

The leaves and stems generally have a tough, unpleasant texture for eating, but you can use them to infuse butter, alcohol, vinegar, syrups and oils, or you can use the leaves — fresh or dried — as a herb to flavour both sweet and savoury dishes. Crumble or pound dried leaves to use as a rub, or mix with salts, sugars or dukkahs for dipping or sprinkling. A time-honoured trick is to line cake or cupcake tins with scented pelargonium leaves to impart their flavour during cooking.

The flowers are more mildly aromatic than the rest of the plant and make tender eating. They're great in salads and little sandwiches, pressed into your fresh homemade pasta or used as a garnish on desserts.

If you find a scented pelargonium you love, see if you can take a stem or root cutting. Pelargoniums are a generous, hard-working bunch and they'll try to grow for you from a cutting if they possibly can.

There are numerous species, varieties and cultivars available from nurseries, too, offering an amazing palette of aromas. One of my favourite cultivars is 'Orange Fizz', which has a genuine orange scent and flavour, with just a background hint of rose and less muskiness than many pelargoniums. I love its flavour in combination with jasmine and fennel. Anyone who becomes enamoured with scented pelargoniums will find their own favourites to analyse and experiment with.

THE PELARGONIUM KIDS

If scented pelargoniums were people, they'd be that big, rambunctious family down the road that you always secretly wished you were part of. The loud, outgoing sibling that you have most fun with is rose-scented pelargonium. Lemon-scented pelargonium is her sidekick. Cinnamon pelargonium is the worldly intellectual you could listen to for hours, and mint pelargonium, with its soft, furry leaves, is always cuddly and comforting. There's the quiet, intense one that you like in small doses — that's nutmeg pelargonium — and then there's coconut pelargonium, who's painfully shy but lovely once you get to know him. Apple pelargonium is the sibling who breezes in and out of the house, always doing her own thing.

Iridaceae
Iris family

This family of bulb plants includes the popular garden flowers iris, crocus and gladiolus. It also contains a number of small flowering pasture plants found across Aotearoa, including the *Sisyrinchium* genus, known as blue-eyed grasses, and the *Romulea* genus.

Onion grass

ONION GRASS
Romulea rosea

SPOTTING IT

Onion grass is a small plant, native to South Africa, that grows in fields, along roadsides and in wasteland. Here, it is more common in the North Island. It has flowers with yellow centres and six pink petals, the shade of which varies. Its grass-like leaves can grow up to 10–30 centimetres long.

USING IT

Come spring, the unripe onion grass fruits, which are about 1 centimetre long, grow on the ends of drooping stalks. In South Africa, these are a popular wild-food snack called *knikkertjies*, which children especially enjoy. Filled with sweet little seeds, the fruits are sometimes called puddings or plum puddings. The corms — the plant's swollen underground stems — can be eaten raw or cooked.

Juglandaceae
Walnut family

This family of trees and shrubs contains a number of species valued for their nuts and hard, strong wood. It includes walnuts, pecan (*Carya illinoinensis*) and hickories (*Carya* spp.).

Walnuts

COMMON WALNUT
Juglans regia

JAPANESE WALNUT
Juglans ailantifolia

SPOTTING THEM

Walnut trees grow in many very old gardens, and they self-seed near parent trees and in plantations. The two species named here are the most common in Aotearoa, but there are others. The highly invasive Japanese walnut is on the National Pest Plant Accord, so you may not sell, propagate or distribute it.

USING THEM

In summer, when the outer husks are green, walnuts can be brined and pickled — although you have to catch them before they develop an inner shell. Some people test this while the nuts are still on the tree by making sure they can push a darning needle through the green walnut from the end opposite the stalk.

Later in the year, the hard nuts can be gathered. Wild and self-sown walnut trees tend to produce nuts with thicker shells than those on cultivated trees, and foraging for walnuts is unpredictable. What's inside a shell can vary from a curvaceous, fleshy treat to a bitter, shrivelled disappointment.

However, bad walnuts are not a lost cause. You can make a natural dye from walnut shells that provides a pale, rosy brown colour (see pages 331–332).

Good walnuts — soaked overnight to make them more digestible, drained, dried and then oven-roasted on a very low temperature — make an extra-crisp and delicious treat. You can grind them to make flour, but in my house they always disappear before I get the chance.

FROM LEFT Japanese walnut; young common walnut.

With their high oil content, walnuts can soon turn rancid. To keep them very fresh, don't shell them until you're just about to use them. Many people also recommend keeping them in the fridge or, if you want to store them for several months, in the freezer. This especially applies if you live in a hot climate.

Lamiaceae
Mint family

This much-loved family includes myriad aromatic herbs — mint, catnip, sage, thyme, basil, marjoram, oregano, rosemary, lavender and more. Many have stems that are square in cross-section, and often the flowers have petals that are fused to form two lips.

Dead-nettles

HENBIT
Lamium amplexicaule

RED DEAD-NETTLE
Lamium purpureum

FIELD WOUNDWORT, STAGGERWEED
Stachys arvensis

HEDGE WOUNDWORT, HEDGE NETTLE
Stachys sylvatica

SPOTTING THEM

Dead-nettle is the common name given to plants in the *Lamium* genus, and is sometimes also applied to the woundworts (those in the *Stachys* genus) as they look similar. The dead-nettles probably take their name from the fact that their leaves have a superficial resemblance to nettle leaves, but they're 'dead' because they don't sting.

The four plants listed here all grow throughout Aotearoa, springing up in parks, pastures, wasteland and home gardens. You can recognise them by their square stems, their hairy leaves and their mauve flowers, the latter each with an upper and lower lip. Red dead-nettle can be distinguished by the blush of purple that colours the leaves around its flowering tops.

The woundworts have hairier stems than the two dead-nettles, and distinctive long, thin, pointy sepals around the flowers, often darker in colour or with a dark stripe down the middle. Field woundwort stays small like henbit and red dead-nettle, and these three are easily mistaken for one another. Hedge woundwort looks very like field woundwort, but it grows larger and its flowering stalks shoot up higher.

CLOCKWISE FROM TOP LEFT
Henbit; hedge woundwort; red dead-nettle.

USING THEM

These are among the least aromatic members of the Lamiaceae family. The stems, flowers and leaves of all four species are edible, raw and cooked, and have a fairly mild taste. That said, some people find the scent of the woundworts unpleasant and a bit mousey.

Strip the leaves and flowers from the stems to cook them. They shrink a lot when heated, but as they may feel unpleasantly hairy when you eat them raw, use them in ways that bear this in mind. Throw them onto pizza or into omelettes, chop them finely into salads, pound them into pesto, let them bed down in sandwiches, or cook them in a stir-fry or casserole for just the briefest time.

Plants from the *Stachys* genus are collectively called the woundworts because they contain an astonishing range of wound-healing, anti-inflammatory, antimicrobial and analgesic compounds. They've long been made into poultices or ointments and applied to wounds and inflammations. They also make an astringent tisane for diarrhoea.

Staggerweed is a dangerous plant for grazing stock and contains a nerve toxin that makes the animals lose co-ordination. It gives them 'the staggers', hence the plant's common name.

Lavenders

ENGLISH LAVENDER
Lavandula angustifolia

FRENCH LAVENDER, TOOTHED LAVENDER
Lavandula dentata

SPANISH LAVENDER, FRENCH LAVENDER
Lavandula stoechas

SPOTTING THEM

Everyone recognises lavender, with its purple spike flowers and strong, often medicinal aroma. Lavender doesn't really run wild, generally staying close to home, but it can self-seed. It's often found growing around old homesteads, or planted along suburban fence lines or beside gates and porches.

USING THEM

Lavender has been a staple of cuisine, medicine, cosmetics and perfumery worldwide for centuries, and the *Lavandula* genus includes many species, varieties and cultivars.

English lavender is widely cultivated, and is the most common species used in herbal medicine and perfumery. It's also popular as a garden ornamental. However, in this country French lavender is the species grown most often, especially for ornamental uses. It can be recognised by its delicately tooth-edged leaves, which give rise to its species name, *dentata*.

Any lavender can be used in cuisine — as a herb in savoury dishes (often along with thyme or as a replacement for it), as a flavouring in desserts or as an ingredient in handmade cosmetics. You can use both the flowers and the leaves.

Be sparing with lavender, as its aroma can be overwhelming. If you're unsure, start by using less than you think you need. Even within the same species or variety of lavender you'll find differences in flavour and aroma. The time of year and time of day alter the scent, too. The best thing to do is get to know your local bushes, and then experiment.

CLOCKWISE FROM TOP LEFT English lavender; French lavender; Spanish lavender; French lavender in closeup.

Hīoi

HĪOI | NEW ZEALAND MINT
Mentha cunninghamii

SPOTTING IT

I can't in good conscience advise you to go gathering hīoi like I did in the 2013 edition of this book. Back then, its status was updated from 'not threatened' to 'at risk — declining'. Sadly, I didn't get the memo until after the first edition was published. This beautiful little scrambling plant, with gently aromatic leaves and tiny sweet flowers, needs to live. If you can find it at a garden centre or in a place where it can be sustainably harvested, do cherish it, grow it and/or propagate it to help it survive.

Rosemary

ROSEMARY
Salvia rosmarinus

SPOTTING IT

Like lavender, rosemary rarely grows wild, but it does often inhabit the interstices between domestic and public spaces. Rosemary bushes have highly aromatic needle-shaped leaves and lipped purple-blue flowers. Some cultivars stand tall and imposing, while others are low and sprawling.

USING IT

Rosemary leaves are packed with aroma and best used sparingly in strong dishes that can handle it. Infuse dishes with a sprig, then remove it before serving, or very finely chop the leaves. Rosemary branches can be used as kebab sticks to impart extra flavour to whatever you have on the skewer. The flowers are also aromatic, but more mildly so. I love to use just the flowers when I need a milder flavour or a delicate texture.

Rosemary is a popular ingredient in handmade haircare products. Herbalists have long used it to stimulate hair growth, and a small number of recent medical studies have produced evidence that rosemary extracts may help slow down pattern baldness. Additionally, rosemary oil's antioxidants make it an excellent preservative in fragrant or cosmetic products.

Malvaceae
Mallow family

Mucilage is found in many plants, but it runs particularly thickly through the veins of the Malvaceae family — in their roots, their leaves and their seedpods. This thick slime absorbs and holds water. The Dutch call it *planteslijm* and in German it's *pflanzenschleim*, and it's used in many culinary, medicinal and cosmetic products.

Okra is a member of the Malvaceae family, and has long mucilaginous seedpods that you can use to thicken soups and stews. Meanwhile, the marshmallows in every dairy are pale simulacra of true marshmallow sweets, which were once made from the mucilaginous root of the marshmallow plant (*Althaea officinalis*).

Slime doesn't sound very appetising, but I've found it an addictive food texture.

Herb mallows

COMMON MALLOW, LARGE-FLOWERED MALLOW
Malva sylvestris

DWARF MALLOW
Malva neglecta

SMALL-FLOWERED MALLOW
Malva parviflora

SPOTTING THEM

These herbaceous plants are recognisable by their soft, roundish, slightly hairy leaves, which look as if they want to fold up along the main veins that radiate from their centre. The flowers have five pale cream, pinkish or purplish petals, with darker rays emanating from the centre.

USING THEM

The leaves are mild in taste, with little or no aftertaste. Raw, they're perfectly safe and nutritious to eat, but their hairy texture can be off-putting, so shred them or slip them in between other interestingly textured ingredients.

Herb mallows shine in cooked dishes. They don't work particularly well if they are sautéed or fried unless they are included in a fritter, but they're delicious

FROM LEFT
Small-flowered mallow (not in bloom); tree mallow seedpods and flowers.

EXTRACTING MALLOW MUCILAGE

Mucilage is easy to extract from herb mallow leaves. Renowned UK forager Fergus Drennan uses plant mucilage as a nutritious, fat-free salad dressing, and it can also be used in homemade conditioners and skin treatments (see recipes, pages 278 and 283).

To extract the mucilage, start by gathering several handfuls of mallow leaves. Cut or tear them up and place them in a jar or bowl. Pour enough water over them to cover, and poke them down now and then to keep them as submerged as possible.

Let this stand for an hour or two, and the mucilage will often simply seep out into the water. At other times you may want to encourage it out by giving it a good stir or even a bit of a mash. Some people like to use warm or hot water, or boil the plant material to get the mucilage to flow. I find cold water works fine.

boiled. The mucilage swells, giving the leaves a rich, melting texture in soups, casseroles and sauces.

Mallow flowers also make a beautiful, almost melt-in-the-mouth garnish or addition to any salad. They can also be cooked — although do so for just the briefest time. After the flowers die away, the plants produce little round seedpods that are also edible. These resemble miniature pumpkins, which US forager and author John Kallas calls 'mallow peas'.

Pick mallow peas while they're still green and tender — before they begin to dry out and get stringy. Extract them from their husks, then eat them raw or boil them as a vegetable, served plain or with butter or a sauce. Throw them into stir-fries, soups and casseroles.

Mucilage is soothing, and a tisane of mallow leaves will ease an inflamed throat or digestive tract. In the gut, mucilage absorbs water and binds everything together, as well as bulking it up and pushing it all through. Adding mucilaginous foods such as mallow to the diet can therefore help with both diarrhoea and constipation. Mucilaginous plant extracts are widely used in commercial treatments for digestive troubles.

MUCILAGE MERINGUES AND MARSHMALLOWS

Making marshmallow or meringue with mallow mucilage other than from the root of the marshmallow plant is a challenge that has frustrated many a forager. It's tough to turn the mucilage into a froth that's firm and stable enough to match beaten egg whites.

American forager John Kallas has come up with an ingenious solution that uses fewer eggs rather than no eggs. He makes his mucilage by boiling mallow seedpods in water at the ratio of 1 part seedpods to 3 parts water, by volume.

To make the meringue mix, he beats a single egg white to soft-peak stage, as a starter. He then adds around half a cup of mallow mucilage to the egg white in a slow, thin stream, beating continuously. The single egg white gives the mix enough structure to hold it together. Next, he beats in ¼ teaspoon of cream of tartar to stabilise the mix further. Once all the mallow mucilage is incorporated, Kallas slowly adds around half a cup of caster sugar, still beating.

When the mix is beaten stiff (which takes longer than with egg whites alone), Kallas drops blobs onto a tray. He cooks them for 20 minutes at 165 °C (330 °F) to make meringues, or dehydrates them to make marshmallows.

I've tried his technique, but instead of using mallow seedpods I used mucilage from mallow leaves extracted using the technique on page 103. It certainly works and you make a huge amount of creamy, frothy stuff, with a pale green tint. However, you do have to work fast once it's beaten, because the mixture doesn't hold its structure for as long as a pure egg-white meringue.

Vegans can't eat these treats, but for those who can it's a slightly cheaper option than using more egg whites and you don't end up with as many leftover yolks.

Tree mallows

CRETAN MALLOW
Malva pseudolavatera

TREE MALLOW
Malva arborea

SPOTTING THEM

These two species may be the most common tree mallows in Aotearoa. They can grow up to 2–3 metres tall, and their leaves and flowers have the same attributes as herb mallows. Tree mallow often shoots up on a trunk like a tree, but somehow it still looks like a bush that's trying to be something it's not.

USING THEM

The enormous floppy, fuzzy leaves of tree mallows are known as an emergency toilet-paper substitute, but they have a nasty, squeaky, water-repellent feel, like 1970s velour, so 'emergency' is the operative word.

When it comes to culinary uses, the leaves are not quite as appetising as those of herb mallows. Even boiled, their stringy fuzziness doesn't quite disappear. Nonetheless, chopped fine in a stew or soup, a few are perfectly nice. The flowers and seedpods of tree mallows can be used in the same way as those of herb mallows.

I haven't tried extracting mucilage from Cretan mallow leaves, but my experiments with tree mallow didn't yield nearly as much as with the herb mallows.

FROM LEFT Miner's lettuce; flowers in closeup.

Montiaceae

Miner's lettuce family

Montiaceae contains a number of edible greens that grow wild around the world, including those in the *Claytonia* genus. In Aotearoa, the most famous of these is miner's lettuce, sometimes nicknamed winter purslane.

Miner's lettuce

> **MINER'S LETTUCE**
> *Claytonia perfoliata*

SPOTTING IT

Miner's lettuce grows most abundantly in the South Island, but it's also found in the cooler southern parts of the North Island. It sends up stalks with two juicy leaves at the top that are fused to look like one round leaf, wrapping itself parasol-like about the stalk. Above these leaves appear tiny white flowers. The plant is an annual that grows from the end of winter, through spring and into summer.

USING IT

Miner's lettuce is a delicious, mild, nutrient-dense salad green that's also good cooked. If it doesn't grow wild near you, you could grow it in your garden.

Myrtaceae
Myrtle family

The trees and shrubs in this family are evergreen and usually have distinctive flowers with numerous prominent stamens, often red. The family includes pōhutukawa (*Metrosideros excelsa*), bottlebrushes, feijoa (*Acca sellowiana*) and the medicinal tea trees — Australia's melaleucas and our own native mānuka and kānuka. Eucalyptus trees are also members of the myrtle family.

Tea trees

KĀNUKA
Kunzea ericoides

MĀNUKA
Leptospermum scoparium

SPOTTING THEM

Mānuka is a shrub or tree that can grow to 15 metres but doesn't usually reach this height. It bears lots of small, thin, spiky leaves and small five-petalled flowers that are white or pink.

It's easy to confuse mānuka with its relative kānuka, but kānuka has noticeably softer leaves. It also generally grows larger than mānuka, lives longer and has smaller flowers — white only — that tend to grow in clusters. On mānuka the flowers are spread more evenly over the branches.

There is enormous genetic variation in both wild mānuka and wild kānuka, and they are highly adaptable to different environments. Mānuka's capacity for wildly varying forms has made it a popular cultivated ornamental. Red-flowered, pink-flowered, double-flowered, and prostrate or ground-hugging forms are all cultivated.

USING THEM

Mānuka is the go-to source of woodchips or sawdust for smoking meat, fish, cheese, chocolate and more. You can also try using the dried twigs or seedpods for smoking.

Mānuka leaves make a delicious flavouring for both savoury and sweet

CLOCKWISE FROM TOP LEFT Pink mānuka; harvested mānuka flowers gathering bay leaves and mānuka; white mānuka.

dishes. Use slim branches to infuse the cooking liquid, then remove them as you would rosemary. Alternatively, dry the leaves and powder them to use like any other dried herb.

Kānuka, on the other hand, is rarely used in cuisine. It generally has a more harshly medicinal flavour and aroma than mānuka. However, there's no harm in experimenting with it, and its softer leaves are easier to use fresh than those of mānuka. Try young, new leaves, stripped from their branches and finely chopped, in any recipe where you'd normally use thyme, lavender or mānuka. You can use older branches as you'd use mānuka.

Both mānuka and kānuka contain potent antimicrobial compounds. They've long been used in rongoā Māori, and can be drunk as a pleasant and/or medicinal tisane.

Eucalypts

***EUCALYPTUS* SPECIES**

SPOTTING THEM

With their striking blue-grey leaves — sometimes round, sometimes long and thin — these Australian imports are hard to miss, and on warm days their delicious scent spreads far and wide. You can often see both types of leaf on the same tree — the round ones are the juvenile form. Now and then, you may also spot eucalyptus leaves that are either edged in red or red all over — a clue to the pigments they yield.

USING THEM

Keep a few eucalypt branches, fresh or dried, around the house to use in case of colds, flu and blocked noses (see page 275).

The trees are also among the most exciting dye plants around. Heat the leaves in water to create a range of vivid, colourfast reds, oranges, browns and yellows (see page 331). Often when dyeing with eucalyptus leaves, you'll notice that the colour they produce gradually changes from yellow to orange to reddish as you simmer the leaves. Experimenting with this is worthwhile: you can dye one item pastel yellow, another apricot and a third item fiery orange, all in the same session, just by removing the items from the dye pot at different times.

Oleaceae
Olive family

The olive family includes not only olives, but also jasmine and lilac.

Jasmines

COMMON JASMINE, POET'S JASMINE
Jasminum officinale

PINK JASMINE
Jasminum polyanthum

SPOTTING THEM

True jasmines are any plant in the *Jasminum* genus, several of which grow wild in Aotearoa. Jasmine flowers are often small and white with five or six petals. There are, however, species with yellow, pink and red flowers, and some have more petals. All jasmine flowers have two stamens that emerge from a tubular centre. Common and pink jasmine are the two most fragrant species growing wild here.

Pink jasmine hails from China and has become a popular cultivated plant in the UK, Europe and the US. In the UK, it's well behaved and the Royal Horticultural Society even gave it an Award of Garden Merit. Unfortunately, however, when it was brought to the Antipodes it went off the rails and started propagating all over the place. It grows prolifically throughout this country, most rampantly in warm areas such as Auckland and Nelson. It isn't on the National Pest Plant Accord, but it is listed as a pest plant in some regions.

Pink jasmine has pink flower buds that open into five-petalled white flowers with pink blushes on their underside. They have a heady, musky scent. In warmer parts of the country the flowers turn into purply-black berries that are eaten by birds, thereby dispersing the seeds.

In other parts of Aotearoa it's rare for pink jasmine to form berries. Where I live, I've seen only an occasional surreptitious cluster. However, this plant doesn't need seeds to reproduce. Hydra-like, bits of chopped vine easily grow into new plants, so gardeners should burn prunings rather than dump them.

Common jasmine is much less rampant — it doesn't spread too far from

TOP ROW
Pink jasmine.

BOTTOM
European olive tree coming into flower.

where it's planted, and can often be found in old gardens. It looks very similar to pink jasmine, but the flowers are pure white. Its scent is beautiful, but lighter and fresher than that of pink jasmine.

USING THEM

For centuries, jasmines have been pillars of the perfumery world. Today, the most commonly used jasmine species in perfumery — and aromatherapy — are Spanish jasmine (*Jasminum grandiflorum*) and Arabian jasmine (*J. sambac*). Two others grown and processed commercially are *J. auriculatum* and *J. flexile*, but much more rarely. Presumably, these species have been the easiest to cultivate and process on a large scale in the countries that provide most of the raw materials for perfumery. However, there are many others — including common and pink jasmine — that can be used to make divine fragrant products.

Often jasmines have a love-it-or-hate-it fragrance, partly due to their particularly high levels of indole — a strong-smelling molecular compound that's found in many flowers but also in faeces. While it's probably indole that repels the jasmine-haters, others find this flower's grubby notes seductive. In fact, a bit of dirt and a hint of animal are blended into many of the great perfumes — the trick is getting the balance right. Both common jasmine and pink jasmine can be tinctured or enfleuraged for handmade perfumes.

Jasmines also have intriguing culinary uses. Remove the flowers from their green sepals to throw them into salads or use them as a garnish. Syrups or alcohol infused with jasmine make great dessert flavourings and toppings.

You need to be selective about what you combine jasmine with. If you pair it with anything else that also has a slightly animal quality, the jasmine will heighten this, potentially to an unpleasant level. For example, when using jasmine to scent a milk dish like panna cotta, the jasmine will exacerbate the barnyard taste if your milk is anything but farm fresh. Likewise, pairing jasmines with scented pelargoniums in perfumery or cuisine is risky. Many scented pelargoniums have musky or tomcatty undertones that, on their own, may be acceptable, but when teamed with jasmine end up smelling like your least-favourite public toilet.

Blending jasmine with fresh, bright scents such as citrus, mint and apple works well to cut through the indole. Rose and jasmine are a classic duo in perfumery, and there's no reason not to combine them in desserts, too.

> **STAR JASMINE — A WARNING**
>
> Star jasmine (*Trachelospermum jasminoides*) has become popular in Aotearoa. However, it's not a true jasmine — it's not even in the olive family, but is in fact a member of the Apocynaceae or dogbane family. It isn't edible and may even be toxic. Don't confuse it with the true jasmines or use it in anything to be consumed. As always, make sure you carefully identify any plant you're planning to use.

Olive

> **EUROPEAN OLIVE**
> *Olea europaea*

SPOTTING IT

In recent years the number of wild olive trees in Aotearoa has increased as a result of a boom in our country's olive-oil industry and seeds being spread from the new plantations. Olives are also often planted ornamentally.

These evergreen trees have long, thin grey-green leaves and masses of white flowers in clusters that give way to bunches of olives. Olives are ripe when they reach full size. They generally begin 'green ripe', then change to a pinky colour and then to brown, before turning black. They can be picked at any stage of ripeness, depending on the end use.

USING IT

Raw olives are extremely bitter and need to be cured over a long period before they're edible. The curing method depends on when the olives have been harvested — green olives are cured differently from black olives. Some people like to cure olives using lye, commonly known as caustic soda, which works faster than salt (see page 204) or vinegar. However, while it removes more bitterness, lye possibly removes other more subtle and complex flavour components, too.

If you don't have time to cure olives, consider harvesting the leaves. Olive leaves have attracted attention for their anti-inflammatory, antibacterial and antiviral qualities. You can pick them at any time of year, although bear in mind that a tree needs plenty of leaves left on it to grow good-quality olives.

A tisane of olive leaves is prescribed for all sorts of ailments. Olive leaves and bark also make a wonderful bright yellow dye (see pages 331–332).

Onagraceae

Evening primrose family

This family includes many decorative, edible and medicinal flowering plants, including fuchsias and evening primroses. Most fuchsias hail from South America, but Aotearoa has three beautiful native species.

Fuchsias

> **KŌTUKUTUKU | TREE FUCHSIA**
> *Fuchsia excorticata*

> **CREEPING FUCHSIA**
> *Fuchsia procumbens*

> **SCRAMBLING FUCHSIA**
> *Fuchsia perscandens*

> **INTRODUCED FUCHSIAS**
> *Fuchsia* species

SPOTTING THEM

Fuchsia have distinctive drooping, often colourful flowers with four large sepals, four shorter and wider petals, and long, dangling stamens. Some are evergreen and others are deciduous. Most are shrubs, but the largest fuchsia in the world — endemic to Aotearoa — is kōtukutuku, the tree fuchsia. Also endemic is creeping fuchsia, an unusually tiny, rambling species that grows around coasts and has flowers that stick straight up rather than dangle down. Compared to introduced fuchsias, our natives have very small petals or sometimes none at all.

Here and there you'll find an introduced or cultivated fuchsia growing wild, but more often than not they'll stay growing respectably in ornamental gardens, where few people realise they make good food.

USING THEM

All fuchsia berries and flowers are edible but, just as they look different, they offer a wide range of flavours and textures. Some are more appetising than others.

THIS PAGE Introduced fuchsia.

Te reo Māori contains a dazzling array of words to describe different plants and different plant parts at different stages. Kōtukutuku berries are kōnini, and are especially good to eat. Unbeknown to many, the plump berries of the introduced specimens in suburban gardens can also be pretty delicious. The only way to know if you've found a good one is to try it — you might get a mouthful of bitterness or a sweet surprise. Ripe, squishy fuchsia berries can be made into jams, jellies, pies and wine, often in combination with other fruits.

As for the flowers, the sepals are generally fleshier and milder, while the petals and other parts are more bitter. Raw, whole or chopped, the flowers add dazzling colour to salads. Smaller flowers and unpopped buds can be dipped in batter and made into tempura or fritters.

Oxalidaceae
Wood sorrel family

Oxalidaceae species typically have divided leaves that spread and open in the light, then fold and close in the dark. Most members are in the *Oxalis* genus.

Oxalis plants are very sour as they're rich in oxalic acid. The vegetable we call yam in this country is the root of *Oxalis tuberosa*. Native to the Andes, it's usually called oca in other parts of the world or, sometimes, New Zealand yam. It was introduced to these shores in the mid-nineteenth century and has become more popular here than in many other Western countries.

Wood sorrels

TŪTAE KĀHU | WHITE OXALIS, SNOWDROP WOOD SORREL
Oxalis magellanica

BERMUDA BUTTERCUP
Oxalis pes-caprae

HORNED OXALIS, CREEPING WOOD SORREL
Oxalis corniculata

LILAC OXALIS, CRIMSON WOOD SORREL
Oxalis incarnata

SPOTTING THEM

The larger *Oxalis* species are troublesome weeds in Aotearoa. However, the smaller ones are often known as edible wood sorrels. They frequently grow around borders and up against rises and mounds, and look like three-leaved clovers except each leaf is heart-shaped. Like many other members of the wood sorrel family, *Oxalis* species have leaves that open and close depending on light levels. The flowers have five petals.

Tūtae kāhu, with white flowers, is native, non-invasive and currently not threatened. Pink-flowering lilac oxalis and yellow-flowering Bermuda buttercup were both introduced from South Africa. Horned oxalis also has yellow flowers, but its country of origin is uncertain.

THIS PAGE
Lilac oxalis.

USING THEM

The leaves, stalks and flowers of wood sorrels are all edible. They contain oxalates and have a bright, sour flavour that some people describe as lemony. Wood sorrels are tasty on their own, but they also mix well with other foraged herbs.

You can use wood sorrels raw and cooked in both sweet and savoury dishes. They retain their delicious sourness when cooked. The leaves and flowers are nice tossed in a green salad, and the flowers make a good edible garnish. Wood sorrels go well with root vegetables, fish and chicken, and their sourness works well with cream. Try chopping up a large handful of leaves, stalks and flowers and adding it to a potato salad with a creamy dressing.

For a simple but delicious wood sorrel gratin, alternate layers of chopped wood sorrel with pre-boiled, sliced potato and kūmara. Pour over enough cream to cover, and bake or grill at 180°C (350°F) until everything starts to brown.

For desserts, try adding wood sorrel to an apple, peach or pear pie. The resulting flavour is a little like rhubarb, which also contains a lot of oxalic acid.

Pinaceae
Pine family

The trees in the pine family, Pinaceae, have distinctive leaves called needles, and instead of flowers they have cones (which, confusingly, are actually modified leaves). Each tree has both male and female cones. The female cones produce seeds between their scales, and the male cones, which are normally smaller and shorter-lived, make pollen.

Pine

PINE TREES
Pinus species

SPOTTING THEM

Pine trees are common throughout this country. You can distinguish them from spruces and firs by examining their needles, which come in clusters of two to five, joined at the base. The cones are strong and woody. It can be tricky to tell the difference between different species of pine, but the number of needles in each cluster provides a clue. The most common, radiata or Monterey pine (*Pinus radiata*), has three needles in each cluster. It's resinous and strongly aromatic, making it great to use as a culinary herb. Scots pine (*P. sylvestris*) and lodgepole pine (*P. contorta*) both have two needles per cluster, while strobus pine (*P. strobus*) has five.

Fir

FIR TREES
Abies species

SPOTTING THEM

Unlike pines, which carry their needles in bunches, firs have needles that sprout singly from their branches. The needles are two-sided and flat.

CLOCKWISE FROM TOP LEFT Harvesting pine near my home; gathering pine tips; young pine in the wild; pine needles and cones.

Spruce

SPRUCE TREES
Picea species

SPOTTING THEM

Like firs, spruce needles emerge singly from the branches. However, the spruce needles themselves have four sides instead of two. To feel the difference, try rolling a needle between your thumb and forefinger. If it rolls, it's a spruce; if it's too flat to roll, it's a fir. You can use the alliterative mnemonic 'Fir is flat and spruce is square.'

USING PINES, SPRUCES AND FIRS

In the northern hemisphere, Pinaceae species have a long history of both culinary and medicinal use, notably in Japan and Scandinavia, and by Native Americans in North America.

The trees all grow outwards from the tips of their branches, so the oldest needles are those closest to the trunk. The choicest parts of the trees are the 'tips', which are harvested in spring when they first appear. They are the very new, bright, lush needles produced each year at the ends of the branches. Look for tips that are tender enough to chop finely, and add them to salads, cooking and baking. You can also add them to pesto or finely chop them into mayonnaise and other dips and dressings for extra flavour.

Older needles are coarser and have the advantage of being available all year round. Use them to infuse a soup, casserole, roast sauce or syrup, then remove them before serving. They also make a refreshing tisane (see page 166).

Different species of pine, spruce and fir provide an astonishing range of flavours. Many have citrus notes, some smelling and tasting like lime, while jammy, berry notes come through with others. If you're looking for inspiration, use them anywhere you can imagine a citrus flavour working well. Alternatively, combine them with citrus for a complex mix of complementary flavours.

In natural perfumery, essential oils and absolutes from pines, firs and spruces are used to give fruity, fresh and foresty notes (see page 303).

Piperaceae
Pepper family

In the Western world the most significant member of the pepper family is the flowering vine black pepper (*Piper nigrum*), the dried fruit of which is what we call a black peppercorn. Recently, other gourmet peppercorns have reached our local markets. These include fruits from Balinese long pepper (*P. retrofractum*) and Javanese cubeb, sometimes called comet's tail pepper (*P. cubeba*).

In Mexico, the leaves of hoja santa (*Piper auritum*) are a culinary herb, and people in South East Asia use *P. sarmentosum* in salads and traditional medicine. The sedative drink kava, enjoyed throughout the Pacific, is extracted from the roots and stems of the kava plant (*P. methysticum*).

In Aotearoa, we have two native species of pepper tree, both commonly known as kawakawa.

Kawakawa | Pepper trees

KAWAKAWA | NEW ZEALAND PEPPER TREE
Piper excelsum

THREE KINGS KAWAKAWA
Piper melchior

SPOTTING THEM

Kawakawa are small trees or shrubs with heart-shaped, dark green leaves that are often full of holes made by very hungry kawakawa looper moth caterpillars (*Cleora scriptaria*). They can grow to 4 metres tall, although are often much smaller. They have jointed brownish branches, and the trees are either male or female.

Male trees produce long, thin flowering spikes that start green and darken with age. Female trees produce shorter, plumper green spikes that ripen to orange fruit called tākawa. People quite often mistake the male spikes for the fruit, but the differences are clear if you observe the plant over time.

Piper excelsum grows widely throughout Aotearoa around parks and bush margins, as well as in gardens, and likes to be close to the coast. *Piper melchior* is endemic to Manawatāwhi/Three Kings Islands, but it's also grown on the mainland

THIS PAGE
Kawakawa (New Zealand pepper tree).

here and there as an ornamental. It has larger leaves with few, if any, holes. Its fruits are also larger and more bland-tasting.

Kawakawa are susceptible to fungal leaf-curl disease. Don't harvest from trees whose leaves are drying and rolling up.

USING THEM

Piper excelsum leaves and bark are used extensively in rongoā rākau. This kawakawa species has particularly strong anaesthetic properties, which you can test for yourself by chewing a leaf and feeling the resulting tingly numbness inside your mouth. It also has anti-inflammatory and antimicrobial properties. This combination of attributes makes it useful as a gargle for toothaches and sore throats, and it's soothing to the skin when applied as a poultice, oil or ointment. Kawakawa is known as an all-round tonic for cardiovascular health, and, like other members of the *Piper* genus around the world, it has a long history of use for digestive problems.

It's generally believed that leaves with looper-moth holes are the most effective. Recent research indicates that when a caterpillar munches on a leaf, it triggers the plant to produce more active compounds in that area.

Because of the analgesic nature of kawakawa, don't go overboard when using the plants in cuisine — that is, use them as a herb, not a leafy green. In Mediterranean-inspired dishes, kawakawa leaves take on faintly basil-like tones. For inspiration, you could also look at using the leaves as you would hoja santa in Mexican recipes, or *Piper sarmentosum* in Thai and Vietnamese recipes.

Chef Charles Royal is a pioneer in the modern culinary use of kawakawa, and has shown how they can be used in many dishes, both sweet and savoury. One of his simplest recipes is fried kawakawa leaves. A single leaf fried in oil until it bubbles and turns translucent, and then drained on a paper towel, can be used whole or crushed as a delicate, crisp, flavoursome garnish. With their oiliness and strong herbal taste, these kawakawa wafers taste to me like delicious herbed sausages, and I instantly want to team them with a comforting vegetable mash.

Royal has also brought the use of kawakawa as a dessert ingredient into the public eye, flavouring meringues, shortbreads, custards and creams with a leaf infusion. The leaves impart a complex palate containing both ginger and vanilla notes. You can create an even more intense flavour or aroma by making an alcohol infusion using dried peppercorns from kawakawa fruit (see page 124).

Fruits from female kawakawa trees — tākawa — have sweet flesh with a slight passionfruit flavour, and are full of peppery little seeds. They have tiny white spears through their hearts that you pull out before eating. Make a sauce from the fruits to use sparingly, add them to a fruit salad, or dip a few in chocolate. Supposedly you shouldn't eat too many at once or it'll upset your digestion, but some people disregard this advice without ill effect.

Often tākawa will ripen off the bush, especially if they're starting to blush orange already. They'll complete their ripening sitting in a warm or sunny place, usually within 1 to 4 days.

TĀKAWA PEPPERCORNS

Peppercorns are simply the dried unripe fruit of plants in the *Piper* genus. Tākawa (fruits from female kawakawa) somewhat resemble the fruits of the Balinese long pepper in both appearance and aroma.

To make tākawa peppercorns, gather unripe, green tākawa, leaving plenty on the tree to ripen. You can sun-dry or oven-dry your picked fruits.

If you sun-dry your tākawa, put them in as hot, dry and sunny a place as possible. If the temperature is too cool or the air is humid, the drying will take too long and the fruit will begin to degrade before the process is complete. It should take only a few days. Note that some fruit will probably ripen rather than dry. It can be hard to predict which way any given fruit will go when it's green, but to get the best strike rate, pick the least ripe fruits you can find.

If you oven-dry the tākawa, you won't have the same problem. Spread them in a single layer on an oven tray and bake in a preheated oven at 60 °C (140 °F) until they become brown and brittle. They should snap easily. Keep an eye on them to make sure they don't burn. If there is any hint that they might, turn the temperature down immediately. It's a good idea to experiment with two or three in your oven before doing a whole batch. Once the fruit are dry, remove them from the oven and let them cool.

Store your dried tākawa in an airtight container. To retain their freshness, leave them whole and then pound or grind them just before use.

Plantaginaceae
Plantain family

This family includes hebes — a prolific genus native to Aotearoa — and antirrhinums, also known as snapdragons. In addition, it includes *Plantago*, a genus of herbaceous plants commonly called plantains (not to be confused with the cooking bananas that are also called plantains). There are around twenty recorded species of *Plantago* in Aotearoa, about nine of which are native. Many are endemic; some are rare and specific to certain regions, so are best left alone. A few are widespread, including the greeny-bronze kaupārerarera or papa plantain (*P. spathulata*).

Common introduced plantains

BROAD-LEAVED PLANTAIN
Plantago major

BUCK'S-HORN PLANTAIN
Plantago coronopus

NARROW-LEAVED PLANTAIN, ENGLISH PLANTAIN
Plantago lanceolata

SPOTTING THEM

Broad-leaved, buck's-horn and narrow-leaved plantain can be found throughout Aotearoa. Like all *Plantago* species, their leaves emerge from a central base point and have distinctive parallel veins running up them. The plants send up stalks with clusters of tiny flowers on a cone or spike.

Broad-leaved plantain has wide, almost round leaves, while narrow-leaved plantain has longer, narrower leaves. Both are found growing as weeds in open places. Buck's-horn plantain leaves are the narrowest of all, and rather than having straight edges like the other two, they are lobed — that is, they have deeply indented edges. This species tends to grow around estuaries, lakes, lagoons and coastal areas.

USING THEM

Plantago leaves are edible (especially buck's-horn plantain) and are widely used in herbal medicine. Choose the youngest, most tender leaves for eating, and chop them finely if they're fibrous.

CLOCKWISE FROM LEFT Broad-leaved plantain; buck's-horn plantain; narrow-leaved plantain.

Broad-leaved and narrow-leaved plantain have wound-healing properties. Both contain blood-clotting agents and, like comfrey, significant amounts of allantoin, a compound that promotes cell regeneration.

Synthetic allantoin is widely produced and often added to skincare products to soothe itching, heal and smooth, as well as moisturise. You can use plantain in your own handmade natural skin products. As allantoin is water-soluble, I like to use plantain in any of the body-care product recipes on pages 278–285 that have a glycerine, water or mucilage base. Use the plantain leaves fresh. Juice them, or break them up and soak them in glycerine, alcohol or hot water, before adding the resulting liquid to the recipe. Be creative!

Psyllium, a commercially available mucilaginous dietary fibre often included in high-fibre breakfast cereals, is extracted from the seeds of certain *Plantago* species. Use your own plantains at home in the same way, boiling the seeds to extract mucilage, or grinding them and adding them to breads to enjoy their beneficial effect on your digestion.

Poaceae
Grass family

The Poaceae family includes rice, wheat, rye, oats, corn and more, making it one of the most important food families for people worldwide.

The transition of humans from a race of hunter-gatherers to one of agriculturalists, and the subsequent global population expansion from particular regions of the world, has been directly linked to the organised cultivation of grass grains. We developed a close relationship with the grasses several thousand years ago, and this relationship has become somewhat symbiotic, leading some commentators to ask whether people domesticated grasses, or grasses domesticated people.

Bamboo

ARROW BAMBOO
Pseudosasa japonica

BLACK BAMBOO
Phyllostachys nigra

FOUNTAIN BAMBOO
Himalayacalamus falconeri

HEDGE BAMBOO
Bambusa glaucescens

MADAKE
Phyllostachys bambusoides

OLDHAM'S BAMBOO
Bambusa oldhamii

SQUARE-STEMMED BAMBOO
Chimonobambusa quadrangularis

WALKING STICK BAMBOO
Phyllostachys aurea

SPOTTING THEM

The plants we refer to as bamboo are generally from the Bambuseae tribe, a division within the grass family that contains more than 70 genera. Within those genera are nearly 1,500 species.

Bamboo grows from underground rhizomes that send up shoots, which grow into single, straight, hollow stalks with nodes. The stalks become harder and woodier as they age, and are known for their fast growth. In the right conditions, some bamboo species grow up to a metre every 24 hours.

Many bamboo species flower only once every few decades, and some even at intervals of more than a century. When they do, it's as if a genetic timer goes off, and all individual plants from the same seed source — no matter how old they are or where they are — flower within a few years of one another. These mass bamboo flowerings can cause chaos. As soon as the plants flower and seed, they die, so local industries based around a particular species can be devastated. The sudden bounty of seed can also fuel a rodent plague.

Increasingly, certain introduced species of bamboo are becoming naturalised in Aotearoa. The eight bamboos listed are among the most common growing wild here.

USING THEM

Bamboos are valuable for furniture-making, crafts and garden stakes. In recent years there's also been a lot of research into, and discussion about, bamboo's abilities to rapidly sequester carbon.

Virtually all bamboo species have edible shoots, and they're an important and nutritious ingredient in many Asian cuisines. Shoots range in taste from sweet to bitter, and many require extensive boiling to make them safe. This is because bamboo species contain varying amounts of a cyanogenic glycoside called taxiphyllin. Cyanogenic glycosides are chemicals that, when eaten, release the poison hydrogen cyanide. Cassava and the pits of stone fruits also contain cyanogenic glycosides, and different types of these chemicals require different processing methods to break them down.

Luckily, bamboo's taxiphyllin is one of the few that can be reliably broken down by boiling. A small number of bamboo species contain little or no taxiphyllin and can be eaten raw; others take only 10 minutes or so of boiling. However, some contain so much taxiphyllin that they need to be boiled for up to 2 hours to remove all but a trace of the glycoside.

PREPARING BAMBOO SHOOTS FOR COOKING

As yet, I haven't harvested wild bamboo shoots, but each of the species named here is listed as edible in at least one source, with the exception of arrow bamboo, whose shoots apparently are too small to yield enough meat to be worth processing.

General instructions for turning bamboo shoots into an ingredient you can use in cuisine are not too complicated. However, they don't keep well raw, so harvest them as close as possible to cooking time. Select bamboo that is less than 30 centimetres tall. Use a shovel to lever the shoot up out of the ground.

Cut the shoot in half lengthwise and peel off the outer layers to expose the white meat. If you know what species of bamboo you are working with, you may be able to find details for recommended boiling times. If you are unsure, start by boiling the halved shoots for at least 2 hours to be on the safe side, then proceed to use them tentatively.

GATHER YOUR OWN GARDEN STAKES

My friend Madz BatachEl of Manawatu Urban Foraging harvests her garden stakes from the roadside. Here are her tips.

> *The best garden stakes are from a good wild patch that doesn't get cut back too often. I collect thinner bamboo with a pair of loppers or secateurs. If you can find a source of fatter, stronger bamboo you'll need a good pruning saw to get through it. It's usually really long too (often 4–6 metres at least), so a plan for how to get it home is a good idea.*
>
> *Some people are concerned that if you put bamboo in your garden while it's still green, it could take root. I, personally, have not had this happen to me. However, I have heard that the stakes will be stronger and last longer if you do take the time to cut and dry them out well before using them.*

Oats

OAT
Avena sativa

RED OAT
Avena byzantina

SAND OAT
Avena strigosa

SLENDER OAT
Avena barbata

WILD OAT
Avena fatua

WINTER WILD OAT
Avena sterilis

SPOTTING THEM

Oats are grasses with distinctive small clusters of dangling flowers. Cultivated oat is the species most often grown commercially here and around the world to produce oats, and gardeners also use it as a cover crop. All the species listed here grow wild around the country, and some — particularly wild oat — have become troublesome weeds.

USING THEM

All oats are edible. However, without an industrial machine it's near impossible to hull your own harvested oats for eating at home as cereal or porridge. Once the oats are ready for harvest, their hulls are just too hard. But there are other ways you can use these plants.

Milky oats — the green, unripe seeds — are highly valued in herbal medicine to relax and rejuvenate. They're often prescribed if you're feeling stressed, over-stretched, fatigued or burnt out.

To harvest milky oats, catch oat grasses when the dangling flowers are fresh and green. Pinch a seed inside a flower between your fingers to test it. If it exudes a milky juice, it's at the right stage. If it doesn't, try several seeds on different plants before you despair, as they can ripen at different stages. Harvest the whole flowers, and do it straight away as the milky stage lasts only a short time.

You can make a tisane from the fresh flowers, but because the season for

FROM LEFT
Oat; purslane.

milky oats is short and drying them removes some beneficial components, most herbalists favour tincturing them in alcohol instead as a way to preserve them. One way to do this is by filling a jar with the flowers, pouring vodka over to cover, sealing it and leaving it to sit in a dark, cool place for a week or more to infuse. Shake it every now and then, and, when the infusion is ready, decant the liquid into a bottle and seal.

Dosage recommendations vary, but half a teaspoon three times a day would not be unthinkable. Milky oats are considered very safe, so your main concern is how much alcohol you want to consume.

The dried stems of grasses are called straw and have many uses. Oat straw is valued for its nutritional and medicinal qualities. It contains minerals, including calcium, silicon and potassium, as well as plenty of vitamins. You can buy bags of oat straw in health food shops, but it's more satisfying to harvest your own. Gather the stems of oats while still green, then make a healthy infused vinegar from the stems (see page 175) or dry them to save for making tisanes (see page 166).

Portulacaceae
Purslane family

The Portulacaceae family contains only one genus — *Portulaca*, the purslanes.

Purslane

> **PURSLANE**
> *Portulaca oleracea*

SPOTTING IT

Purslane grows as a weed throughout the North Island and in many parts of the South Island. It's an annual that emerges from the ground in summer and dies back in winter. It spreads across the ground, sending out long reddish stems with almost oblong, succulent green leaves. It has small yellow flowers.

USING IT

You can eat the leaves, the smaller stems and the flowers, although some recipes call for only the leaves. All parts have a sour, salty taste, indicating the species' oxalate content (check the information about oxalates on page 31).

Purslane is unusual in the world of commonly eaten greens in that it's a succulent. Its fat, juicy leaves have evolved to store moisture and nutrients over long periods of time so, like other succulents, it's full of mucilage. You can break up the leaves and extract mucilage using the same method as for mallow leaves (see page 103).

Many cultures across Asia, Europe and the Middle East use purslane in their cuisine. It can be eaten raw, and complements cucumber especially nicely. It's also a fantastic addition to many cooked dishes. Fry it quickly to retain its satisfying volume and firmness, or cook it for longer to give it a melting quality.

Purslane is rich in vitamins, minerals and antioxidants. For a leafy green, it also contains unusually high quantities of omega-3 fatty acids, including alpha-linolenic acid (ALA). This is considered a particularly important omega-3 in the human diet as the body can't synthesise it. The other known omega-3 fatty acids can be synthesised to some extent from ALA, which is also found in high quantities in linseed and the seeds of plants such as kiwifruit (*Actinidia deliciosa*).

Rosaceae
Rose family

Rosaceae includes numerous sweet, aromatic fruits and flowers that are enjoyed by many cultures around the world. The *Rosa* genus contains all the roses. The *Malus* genus includes the domesticated apple and its cultivars. *Prunus* claims peaches, plums, nectarines, apricots, cherries and almonds. *Pyrus* boasts the common pear. Quince is the sole member of the *Cydonia* genus. Meanwhile, *Rubus* includes blackberries, raspberries and strawberries. The family produces a fascinatingly connected complex of aromas — there are apple blossoms that smell like roses, and roses that smell like berries.

Certain fruit trees in this family, such as apple and cherry, self-seed relatively often and do grow wild. Others, like pear and quince, rarely self-seed but can appear to be growing wild when you come across the remains of a settlement.

Botanists divide some large plant families into tribes. In the taxonomic hierarchy, tribe falls between family and genus. One tribe in the Rosaceae family that's especially important to humans is the apple tribe, Maleae, which contains plants that produce cored fruits, technically called pomes.

Maleae tribe

COMMON PEAR
Pyrus communis

CRAB APPLE
Malus species

DOMESTICATED APPLE
Malus × domestica

LOQUAT
Eriobotrya japonica

QUINCE
Cydonia oblonga

SPOTTING THEM

These trees all grow in public and wild areas, often in and around old gardens and settlements. They have distinctive white, cream or pink flowers with five petals and a profusion of little stamens in the centre. Often the flowers are delicately fragrant.

Wild apple trees in particular can be found growing beside roads and railway tracks, often a fair way from settlements. Researchers are intrigued by the way this shows how readily they grow from a core chucked out of a window by a traveller whizzing by. Apples also demonstrate a lot of genetic variation and don't breed true from seed — they'll always be a surprise.

Botanist Phil Garnock-Jones told me, 'These throwaways are more likely to be bitter and small or to have other undesirable properties, but occasionally there might be one worth propagating. Many commercial varieties were simply discovered among such variable progeny of seed-grown apples.'

USING THEM

You can store hauls of any of these fruits in syrup (see page 172). Rather than using the fruits simply to infuse the liquid, you can peel, halve and core them, then briefly boil them in the liquid, before sealing them in jars, liquid and all, to preserve them.

Quinces and crab apples are the only fruits listed here that can't happily be eaten raw by most people — they're usually hard and sour, and crab apples are also full of seeds. However, both are rich in pectin and make fantastic jams and jellies. They're also wonderful for chopping and using raw to infuse spirits, wines and liqueurs.

Apples are full of pectin, too — especially when they're hard and unripe. Making apple jelly is an excellent way to use a windfall of unripe fruit.

Before fruiting, the scented blossoms of all these Maleae trees can be used to infuse a softly aromatic syrup or vodka. Some varieties are much more scented than others.

Prunus genus

CHERRY PLUM
Prunus cerasifera

JAPANESE HILL CHERRY
Prunus serrulata

PLUM
Prunus × domestica

RUM CHERRY
Prunus serotina

BELLFLOWER CHERRY
Prunus campanulata

SPOTTING THEM

Plums are easily recognised by their fruit. Cherries are sometimes harder to spot, but they have small red or dark fruits and distinctive leaves with serrated edges.

Plum trees are not invasive, but the closely related introduced wild cherries are a massive and increasing problem in Aotearoa, spreading readily as birds disperse their seeds. In many areas they are displacing native trees and shrubs. Rum cherry is on the National Pest Plant Accord, while Bellflower cherry is listed as a pest plant in some areas. To halt this spread, we need to stop planting flowering cherries as ornamentals.

USING THEM

Plums are delicious cooked or raw, but they develop a much richer taste when cooked. They're also wonderfully user-friendly as they never need peeling before cooking. Plums are delicious chopped up in crumbles (see recipe, page 262), as well as in fruit honeys (see recipe, page 185). They can be preserved in sugar syrup or vinegar, and they happen to be my favourite fruit for making liqueur (see recipe, page 188).

Small fresh plums can be stuffed to make a moreish snack. Halve them and remove the stones. Cut up some soft cheese like feta or ricotta and mix it gently with just a little honey and/or balsamic syrup. Heap it into the cavities in the plum halves, and sprinkle with nuts, pine nuts and/or a favourite herb — foraged options include fennel and kawakawa.

Some of the berries on wild escaped flowering cherries are pleasant enough to eat, but don't do anything to encourage them.

Rosa genus

FRENCH ROSE
Rosa gallica

MULTIFLORA ROSE
Rosa multiflora

RAMBLER ROSES
Rosa wichuraiana hybrids and *Rosa sempervirens* hybrids

SWEET BRIAR
Rosa rubiginosa

SPOTTING THEM

The roses listed here are the ones you find growing wild most often in Aotearoa, but there are others. Roses are perennial, usually deciduous shrubs, and often have prickles. Single roses have five pink or white petals and numerous stamens, like giant apple blossoms. Double roses may sport many petals. Sweet briar is distinguished by the strong apple fragrance of its leaves, but it's listed as a pest plant in some regions of the country.

USING THEM

Fragrant rose petals are hugely useful as aromatic flavourings in cuisine. However, even unscented or barely scented rose petals are quite edible, and when chopped or shredded can be treated almost like a green.

After flowering, roses produce their fruits — rosehips. Treasured culinary ingredients in many cultures, these are noted for being rich in vitamin C. They're taken as a nutritional tisane or, more commonly, a decoction (like a tisane, but prepared by boiling). They contain high levels of pectin and are ideal for syrups and jellies.

Rosehips are pesky to process as they have hairs around the seed that some people find irritating. Boiling the hips whole gets around this problem, but many people still like to cut them in half and remove the seeds and hairs before cooking the fruits. You may also want to top and tail them.

Rosehips are also often preserved by drying, either whole or cut in half. They can then be used for tisanes, syrups, vinegars and other infusions.

CLOCKWISE FROM TOP
Bellflower cherry; blackberry flowers; blackberry leaves.

Rubus genus

TĀTARĀMOA | BUSH LAWYER
Rubus australis, R. cissoides, R. schmidelioides

BLACKBERRY
Rubus fruticosus

CREEPING LAWYER
Rubus parvus

RASPBERRY
Rubus idaeus

SPOTTING THEM

Blackberries and raspberries, both introduced plants, grow out in the open and have aggregate fruit — their berries are formed from lots of little 'fruitlets'.

Raspberries are a good find in the wild, but are not nearly as common as blackberries. If you're planning on harvesting a big blackberry patch, take planks of wood and throw them down over the patch so you can walk into the bushes.

Blackberries are sweetest when very dark and soft. The native tātarāmoa prefers to grow in the bush, and has small pink or yellow edible blackberry-like fruits.

USING THEM

There are many ways to use these berries — they're even great as a pizza topping, combined with your favourite nuts and some chunks of good cheese.

Some blackberries you pick are full of worms. After harvesting, I soak the fruit in cold water for about an hour — the worms simply float out. Many people like to dissolve a little salt in the water first for added effectiveness.

Blackberry leaves can also be harvested and used to make a delicious tea that settles upset stomachs. Take the very new leaves that are paler in colour — if they're still a little curled up, that's fine. The gently fragrant flowers of members of this genus are all edible, too.

Rubiaceae
Coffee or madder family

Rubiaceae is a vast and diverse family. Coffee is made from the fermented and roasted beans of *Coffea* species. Madder, made from the roots of *Rubia* species, is an important source of pigment for textiles, and quinine, extracted from the bark of South American trees in the *Cinchona* genus, is an antimalarial medicine. Meanwhile, members of the *Gardenia* genus are popular ornamentals — with perfumes in their flowers that are frustratingly difficult to extract.

In Aotearoa, an important genus in the family is *Coprosma*. Worldwide, the genus contains more than 100 species of trees and shrubs, and Aotearoa is home to roughly half of them. The first coprosma ever collected and named was the Aotearoa native hūpiro or stinkwood (*Coprosma foetidissima*), which gives off a rotten smell when wounded. Thus, the botanists who described the genus decided to call it *Coprosma*, which is from Greek and means 'dung smell'.

Coprosma genus

KANONO, MANONO, RAURĒKAU | LARGE-LEAVED COPROSMA
Coprosma autumnalis

KARAMŪ
Coprosma robusta

MINGIMINGI
Coprosma propinqua

SHINING KARAMŪ
Coprosma lucida

TAUPATA | NEW ZEALAND LAUREL, LOOKING GLASS PLANT
Coprosma repens

SPOTTING THEM

The *Coprosma* genus is generally divided into large-leafed and small-leafed species. Listed here are some of the most commonly found coprosmas in Aotearoa, but there are many others, including hybrids. Some, like sand coprosma (*C. acerosa*), are becoming endangered and should be left alone if you find them.

During summer and autumn, female coprosmas put forth vivid bunches of small, shiny, juicy berries, each with two seeds. The berries range from purple, red and orange to translucent white, depending on the species, and their flavours can be anything from insipid to sweet and complex. Australia and other places around the Pacific have their own native coprosmas, and the edible berries are generally well known to the Indigenous people in these areas.

You'll find coprosmas in gardens, on bushy margins and in forested reserves. One way to help identify a coprosma is to look at its leaves. On the underside of each leaf you'll see little pits where the main veins join the midrib.

Taupata is perhaps our most instantly recognisable coprosma, thanks to its strong, super-glossy, almost varnished-looking leaves. Clearly, it's well adapted to withstand salt-laden coastal winds, but it also grows a fair way inland.

USING THEM

Coprosma berries often have a high ratio of seed to flesh, so while it's fun to pick them off the tree and nibble on them, the most practical use is in cooking. You can boil them up with a little water and some sugar to taste, then push the mixture through a sieve to make a sauce for sweet or savoury purposes. If you find the sauce slightly bitter, consider adding lemon or lime juice to help neutralise it. Add a little at a time and taste after each addition, until you're happy with it.

You'll need quite a few handfuls of berries to make cooking with them worthwhile. The easiest method I've found for collecting them is to hold a bag or other container under a branch, and strip off clusters of berries in a sweeping motion. Then I remove any shrivelled berries or bits of debris that have fallen into the container. I like the flavour of taupata berries best, but karamū and kanono berries are enjoyable too.

In her book *Hiakai*, chef Monique Fiso details using the leaves and bark of kanono as a flavouring for stocks, syrups and sauces.

COPROSMA COFFEE

In the late 1870s, settler J. C. Crawford was hopeful about the possibility of developing a coffee-substitute industry in this country, based on roasting seeds from the native karamū and taupata. Despite his efforts, it never took off. Since then, foragers like Andrew Crowe and Sheila Natusch have tried making coffee from coprosma seeds, but have been underwhelmed by the results.

CLOCKWISE FROM TOP LEFT Taupata (New Zealand laurel) leaves; taupata with unripe berries; cleavers; harvested cleavers.

Cleavers

CLEAVERS
Galium aparine

SPOTTING IT

Cleavers is a scrambling annual, with long, thin leaves that grow in whorls on thick stems. The hooked hairs on its leaves stick to your clothes like Velcro.

USING IT

The raw leaves taste mild and slightly salty, and some are faintly bitter. The texture is unpleasant, though — who wants to eat Velcro? To soften the leaves for eating, blanch them before using. Alternatively, chop them very finely and add to cooked dishes to disguise the texture. Cleavers leaves are also great for juicing and adding to sweet drinks. To harvest them, use scissors to snip off the smallest, choicest-looking lengths.

Cleavers is nutritious, and in herbal medicine it is considered to be an excellent cleanser of the lymphatic system. It's used as a general tonic, as well as for specific complaints such as swollen glands anywhere in the body (see page 277). In natural skincare, cleavers is considered useful for treating dry, itchy skin, and a juice or tisane made from the leaves and stems can be used as a wash.

Rutaceae
Citrus or rue family

This family contains many plants with fragrant flowers, including the divinely scented *Boronia* genus, prized as a raw material in the perfumery world. The most famous aromatic genus in the family is, of course, *Citrus*, which has a bewildering number of species, crosses and cultivars. It's debatable whether any citrus varieties are truly naturalised in Aotearoa. However, the first plants were brought here by European missionaries in the early nineteenth century and many now grow in old gardens and around abandoned settlements.

Citrus genus

GRAPEFRUIT
Citrus × paradisi

LEMON
Citrus limon

MEYER LEMON
Citrus × meyeri

SWEET ORANGE
Citrus sinensis

TANGELO
Citrus × tangelo

SPOTTING THEM

You can't mistake citrus trees, with their strongly fragrant leaves and twigs, scented creamy flowers, and bright pock-skinned fruits that, when peeled, reveal juicy, translucent segments. They are treasured wherever they grow for their many applications in cuisine, healthcare and perfumery.

Each citrus has its own distinctive aroma that suffuses its leaves, flowers and fruits. If you come across a tree that isn't in fruit and you aren't sure which one it is, try crushing a leaf or sniffing a flower. You may find you can identify it purely on smell alone: grapefruit leaves and flowers smell grapefruity, orange leaves and flowers smell orangey, and so on.

USING THEM

When you eat citrus fruits raw, try also to include some of the white pith. Recent studies show this has high nutritional value, with lots of antioxidants, vitamin C and fibre.

While the fruits are the most obvious culinary treasure, the flowers are also deliciously aromatic. You can use the petals to infuse syrups, oils and vinegars, and they are marvellous ingredients for home perfumery, particularly in enfleurage (see 'Pomades', page 306). Use them straight away, as they can start to exhibit off-notes fairly soon after being picked. If you are infusing a liquid with citrus flowers, do so for only a few hours — or less.

Even citrus leaves have exciting culinary possibilities. For example, you can put them into a baking-paper or cooking-foil parcel to bake fish, letting them impart their flavour in a subtle way.

Home distillers of essential oils love citrus, as the peels yield enough oil to make small-scale distillation worthwhile. Most other plants are only worth distilling for oil on a large scale.

CITRUS-LEAF CHOCOLATES

This is a fun activity to do with children. The resulting 'chocolate leaves' can be used to garnish desserts, and they're delicious as small treats in their own right.

Gather leaves from any citrus tree — young, healthy, well-formed leaves are best. Wash and dry them, then spread them on a plate, with their undersides facing upwards.

Melt chocolate of your choice — white, milk or dark — in a heatproof bowl over a saucepan of simmering water. Stir gently to help it melt faster and more evenly.

When all the chocolate has melted, use a knife or paintbrush to spread it thickly on the undersides of the citrus leaves. There must be no leaf showing through.

Put the plate of chocolate-painted leaves in the fridge for half an hour or more to set, then remove the plate from the fridge and *carefully* peel away the real leaves from the chocolate to reveal beautifully veined chocolate leaves. They will have taken on a delicate citrus flavour as well — especially if you used very young, fresh citrus leaves.

VARIATION

For a stronger citrus flavour, grate a little citrus zest and stir it quickly but gently through the chocolate before you paint it onto the green leaves.

MAKING THE MOST OF CITRUS FRUITS

This is an efficient way to process a haul of citrus fruits to keep over weeks or even months. You'll get three different products – juice, syrup and peel – for different uses. The syrup and peels look pretty in clear glass and, with handmade labels, they make great gifts.

STEP 1: THE JUICE

Cut the fruits in half and squeeze all the juice into a jug. Pour it into ice-cube trays and place in the freezer.

When frozen, transfer the ice cubes into a zip-lock bag and store in the freezer. Whenever you need citrus juice you'll be able to whip out one or more cubes.

STEP 2: THE SYRUP

Pull the pith away from the peels that remain after you have juiced your fruits. Slice the peels into small batons, then blanch these in boiling water for 1 minute. Drain and repeat once or twice, depending on how much bitterness you want to remove from the peel.

In a saucepan, mix equal parts of sugar and water and bring to the boil. Add the blanched citrus peel and simmer for 1 hour.

Drain the liquid and leave it to cool. Before the peels cool, use them for step 3, below. Pour the cooled liquid into bottles for use as a syrup – mix it into drinks or use it as a sauce. It can be stored in the fridge, or you can freeze it for up to a year.

STEP 3: THE PEELS

Sprinkle a layer of any crystallised sugar over a dinner plate. Roll the boiled peels in the sugar while still warm, then lay them out to dry in a single layer on a rack or on a tray lined with baking paper.

Transfer the dried candied peels to a sterilised airtight container. Stored at room temperature, they will keep for up to 3 weeks, or in the fridge they will keep for a few weeks more.

CEVICHE

Fish 'cooked' by marinating in citrus juice is a dish enjoyed in many parts of the world, especially around the Pacific and in South America. The citric acid coagulates the proteins in the fish, just as cooking does, and the flesh turns white. The result is a fresh, cool, delicious and healthy dish. It's one of those exciting base recipes that opens itself up to many creative variations. The word 'ceviche' is derived from Spanish, but the dish has many other names, including *'ota 'ika* in Tonga, *kokoda* in Fiji and *poisson cru* in France.

At its most fundamental, ceviche involves chopping about 500 g (1 lb 2 oz) of fish into cubes, pouring half a cup or so of citrus juice over the top, mixing it around, and then leaving it all to sit covered in the fridge for about 3 hours. In practice, however, herbs and vegetables are also often added to the mix before it goes into the fridge, and this is where much of the regional variation occurs.

Usually, something oniony is added first — finely chopped or grated onion, or chopped spring onion. My unscientific analysis of a selection of recipes from around the world indicates that the second most important addition is something red (often sliced tomato, capsicum or chilli), often followed by something green (often fresh chopped herbs or cucumber). In the Pacific, coconut milk is often added after the fish has turned white. The dish is then finished with salt and, sometimes, pepper to taste.

If you need carbs, ceviche can be served with fingers of toast or tortillas.

VARIATIONS

- Any acidic citrus will do, but lemon and lime juice are traditional — their sourness and extreme acidity work well. Sometimes, orange or grapefruit juice is mixed in with the lemon or lime juice. You can also use other citruses when they're unripe and extra acidic — for example, green mandarins.
- When it comes to the optional extras, ceviche is a great dish for the forager. Onion weed is perfect chopped into ceviche. Other fresh greens and herbs to try include finely chopped chickweed, parsley, wild celery, tūtae kōau, ureure, wood sorrel, borage leaves, pikopiko, beach spinach, dead-nettles, watercress and chenopodiums. Dried and powdered horopito or kawakawa pepper are also delicious additions.

Sapindaceae
Soapberry family

This family of trees and shrubs includes maples, lychees and the *Sapindus* genus, from which soap nuts are obtained — a commercially available alternative to laundry powders. Many members of this family are known for high levels of saponins — soapy compounds that lather up.

Horse chestnut

> **HORSE CHESTNUT**
> *Aesculus hippocastanum*

SPOTTING IT

Horse chestnuts are large trees that produce spectacular clusters of pink and white flowers. These give way to spiky green fruits called burrs, which contain nuts with shiny brown shells. The nuts look a lot like sweet chestnuts, but they're toxic. Still, they have their uses.

USING IT

Horse chestnuts are best known for their use in the game conkers (see page 337). You can also use the nuts as large, smooth beads: paint them or leave them plain.

A fabric soap can be made from horse chestnuts, by chopping up the flesh of the nuts and boiling it in water. The nuts contain large amounts of soapy saponins and also a whitening agent. I haven't had much luck with this, but you can find more detailed instructions online.

Note that, unlike the unrelated edible chestnut (see page 88), horse chestnuts are poisonous. See 'Allergy alert' on page 30 for more information.

Seaweeds

Foraging along the coast, you find a world of diverse, colourful sea vegetables. These are just as nutritious as many of the land-based edibles you can harvest. Indeed, some are more so. They burst with flavour and richly salty and umami tastes. Full of a range of soothing mucilages, seaweeds also offer much to medicine and body care. Two of the mucilages commercially extracted from seaweeds are agar and carrageenan, or Irish moss.

Seaweeds are often classified according to colour — there are brown, green and red seaweeds. Aotearoa's long coastlines host too many species of seaweed to mention here, but all are edible except flattened acid kelp (*Desmarestia ligulata*), named for the sulphuric acid it contains and releases as it dies, discolouring other seaweeds nearby. When alive, it is brown with feather-like fronds, but as it dies it turns what writer Andrew Crowe has described as 'bilious green'.

Brown seaweeds

RIMURAPA | BULL KELP
Durvillaea species

BLADDER KELP
Macrocystis pyrifera

COMMON KELP
Ecklonia radiata

NEPTUNE'S NECKLACE
Hormosira banksii

SPOTTING THEM

Of the brown seaweeds, rimurapa is easy to spot, with its long, thick, almost leathery straps; there are four species around Aotearoa. Other readily identifiable kelps include common kelp and bladder kelp, which has blades emerging from a central stem and gas-filled bladders at the base of each blade.

Another easy species to identify is Neptune's necklace, sometimes called sea grapes, which grows in strings of hollow, textured brownish or olive-coloured beads. In some the beads have a slightly squared-off shape.

FROM LEFT Rimurapa (bull kelp); sea lettuce.

Green seaweeds

SEA LETTUCE
Ulva lactuca

SPOTTING IT

Sea lettuce grows where there is plenty of sunlight. Around Aotearoa, it's easy to recognise, looking a lot like vividly green, thick, soggy lettuce.

Red seaweeds

KARENGO | NORI, LAVER
Porphyra species

SPOTTING IT

Karengo is considered the choicest red seaweed for eating. You'll find it growing on rocks near the high-tide mark, looking like small torn sheets of purplish cellophane.

USING SEAWEEDS

Seaweeds with a pleasant texture, like sea lettuce, can be washed and eaten fresh. Usually, though, it's better to cook or dry them. When their saltiness is overpowering, boiling them in a decent volume of water to reduce that saltiness is a good option. Experiment with boiling times. For example, I think sea lettuce is delicious once it has been boiled for 8–10 minutes, but you may prefer to cook it for more or less time.

You can serve boiled seaweeds hot with butter and/or lemon juice, or a sauce, much like any other vegetable. You can also add cooled cooked seaweed to salads. Experiment with how you cut them before boiling. Thin boiled strings or shreds, almost like vermicelli, work well as a hot side vegetable, or cold as part of a salad.

Let your culinary imagination be sparked by the unique shapes, textures and colours of different seaweeds. Use them instead of lasagne sheets or for an extra layer in a gratin, but be careful because you probably won't need to add much salt. Seaweeds usually have quite enough salt for any dish.

Seaweeds dry well, and their flavours can transform through the process. Follow the methods in the drying section of this book (see pages 194–198), then powder the dried seaweeds and use them as a condiment or keep them in larger pieces for cooking. In hot liquid, they'll expand to their original size.

Make flavoursome seaweed chips by briefly frying or oven-baking small pieces of dried or fresh seaweed until they bubble. The key to making good seaweed chips is removing them at exactly the right time — after they've thoroughly crisped, but before they burn. Kelp chips are especially popular and sometimes sold commercially. When making chips from bull kelp, choose the thinnest, choicest parts of the straps.

You can also use your foraged seaweed to make the Japanese stock dashi (see page 226) or laverbread, a traditional Welsh dish made by boiling well-washed red seaweed to a paste (with or without a bit of extra help from a mincer or blender). The end result can be used in all sorts of ways, including in sauces or mixed with oatmeal and fried.

Very mucilaginous seaweeds can be boiled in milk or cream with added honey or sugar for about half an hour to make a milk jelly. Try 1 part seaweed to 4 parts milk. Back in the day, this was classic 'invalid food'. Remember that using your own gathered sources of mucilage won't offer the same reliable standardised results as store-bought agar or carrageenan.

SUSTAINABLE SEAWEED HARVESTING

Seaweeds generally attach themselves to rocks with a holdfast. Many people say that to harvest seaweed most sustainably you should snip off a few bits, leaving the seaweed plant attached and growing. Another way to harvest seaweed sustainably is by gathering what's been thrown up onto a beach after a storm.

Solanaceae
Nightshade family

This family includes many widely cultivated edible plants, such as potato, tomato, eggplant, tamarillo and cape gooseberries, which self-seed and tend to become weedy. However, it also contains plants that are infamous for their toxicity, including nightshades, Jerusalem cherry (*Solanum pseudocapsicum*) and *Datura* species. Even the edible members have their risks. (For example, it's not a good idea to eat potatoes that have turned green from exposure to light. It's not the green that's the problem — that's just chlorophyll, which is pretty good for you. The trouble is that the presence of chlorophyll indicates that another, more toxic substance has likely been developing in the light as well: solanine.)

Many species in the nightshade family contain powerful alkaloids that are used as medicines and recreational drugs, but in excess these substances can be very poisonous. Deadly nightshade (*Atropa belladonna*) is particularly toxic, although here in Aotearoa it's rare. It grows wild in some parts of Canterbury only. You can recognise it by its five-petalled bell-shaped purple flowers. (As ever, flowers provide a good way to ID a confusing plant.)

The other weedy nightshades around the country have small white flowers. These include black nightshade (*Solanum nigrum*), small-flowered nightshade (*S. nodiflorum*) and velvety nightshade (*S. chenopodioides*).

Poroporo

POROPORO
Solanum aviculare, Solanum laciniatum

SPOTTING THEM

Both species of poroporo grow around the country in scrub and on forest margins, and occasionally they pop up in gardens. Colourful, dangerous-looking characters, poroporo have a lanky trunk; dark, droopy, long-fingered leaves; vivid purple flowers; and dangling fruits that turn from green to yellow to orange. Many foragers have noted that the fruits look like a small orange version of their cousin the tamarillo (*Solanum betaceum*).

CLOCKWISE FROM TOP LEFT Poroporo (note very deeply lobed leaves as an identifier); poroporo flowers in closeup; black nightshade; velvety nightshade.

USING THEM

It's vital to harvest only very ripe poroporo fruits, when the orange skins begin to split. Unripe fruits, along with the rest of these plants — including the leaves and flowers — are toxic. I've experimented with cooking very ripe poroporo fruits with a little sugar, and even though they tasted fine, they still irritated the roof of my mouth. Other people have consumed them with no trouble.

Nightshades

BLACK NIGHTSHADE
Solanum nigrum

VELVETY NIGHTSHADE
Solanum chenopodioides

The one part of these two nightshades that is edible and non-toxic is the ripe, black berry. Make sure it's absolutely ripe, though. I've never been game to taste one myself, no matter how many times I'm told they're safe. Nonetheless, when I lead foraging walks and we come across black nightshade, I always let people know that the ripe berries are edible. Invariably, most people in the group feel nervous, but one person will try a berry or two without hesitation. And every single time they've declared them to be delicious. (And lived to tell other people that they're delicious the next day.)

Deadly nightshade (*Atropa belladonna*) is far less common in Aotearoa than black nightshade, but it is sometimes mistaken for the latter. All parts of deadly nightshade are very poisonous. For this reason, you should avoid collecting black nightshade unless you've really done your research and can identify it with certainty and harvest and process it safely.

Tropaeolaceae
Nasturtium family

There is a single genus is this family — *Tropaeolum*. These plants are native to the Americas, from Mexico southwards, and are especially prevalent in the Andes, where they grow up and down mountainsides.

Only two of the family's many species are widely naturalised in Aotearoa. Chilean flame creeper (*Tropaeolum speciosum*), which is on the National Pest Plant Accord, is a coiling vine that shades out and smothers native plants. The other is nasturtium (*T. majus*), which is usually quite well liked.

This family is in the Brassicales order, which contains many families whose species are noted for their mustard-oil content — including another favourite, the Brassicaceae family (see page 75).

Nasturtium

NASTURTIUM
Tropaeolum majus

SPOTTING IT

Nasturtium is an easily identifiable herbaceous plant. Its distinctive round green leaves have a radiating star pattern of veins on the upperside, and are attached to the stem at the centre of the underside. The trumpet-shaped flowers generally have five petals and most are a vivid orange, although there are also red and yellow varieties.

USING IT

Nasturtium likes celebrations, and is great in a range of snacks and finger foods. Aside from the root, every part of the plant is edible.

The leaves are slightly mucilaginous. One advantage of nasturtium over the leaves of many wild mustard greens from the Brassicaceae family is that it doesn't have the same bitterness mingling with the mustard flavour. You can certainly cook nasturtium leaves, but to preserve their mustardy flavour in its entirety, use them raw.

Nasturtium works well with cheeses. You can finely chop the leaves and/or the flowers into a cream cheese, or lay them flat on crackers or in sandwiches. They also go well with salmon, walnuts, cucumber and chives.

CLOCKWISE FROM TOP LEFT Nasturtium leaves; red-flowered variety; nasturtium growing on a wall; orange-flowered variety.

Pickled nasturtium seedpods have a similar flavour and texture to capers, which come from the caper bush (*Capparis spinosa*), another plant in the mustardy Brassicales order. Sometimes you'll have to rummage through nasturtium leaves and stems to find the seedpods, which grow in groups of three. Choose young, green pods and use one of the pickle recipes on pages 199–203.

PARTY NIBBLES: FILLED NASTURTIUM LEAVES AND FLOWERS

Pick small nasturtium leaves, leaving a long stem on them. Dollop a delicious filling of your choice onto each leaf, then roll it up and secure it by tying the stem around the roll. Separately, arrange some flowers on a plate, and drop filling into their centres. Leave them open for maximum visual appeal.

Urticaceae
Nettle family

This large family contains many species that are used around the world medicinally and for fibre. It includes ramie (*Boehmeria nivea*), whose stalks have been harvested for millennia for their spinnable fibre. There's also a nettle fibre revival going on — just google 'nettles for fibres'.

The best-known family members are those in the *Urtica* genus — the true nettles — which give the whole family its common and scientific names. Used as food, medicine, fibre and dye, they have nourished and inspired since the beginning of recorded history.

England hosts the World Nettle-eating Championships each year, and nettle festivals throughout the United Kingdom and Europe showcase all manner of nettle fare. Perennial nettle and annual nettle are the most commonly mentioned nettles in today's herbal books. Often considered weeds now, they're delicious culinary greens and have a rich, earthy taste with tea notes.

Native nettles

COMMON NAME UNKNOWN
Urtica aspera

PUREORA | SCRUB NETTLE
Urtica incisa

SOUTHERN NETTLE
Urtica australis

SWAMP NETTLE
Urtica perconfusa

Introduced nettles

ANNUAL NETTLE, SMALL NETTLE, DWARF NETTLE
Urtica urens

PERENNIAL NETTLE, COMMON NETTLE
Urtica dioica

THIS PAGE
Perennial/ common nettle.

SPOTTING THEM

Nettles have upright stems and jagged-edged leaves covered in hairs, which are actually glassy little spines, like syringes. They inject histamine and other chemicals into any skin that brushes them. Nettle's flowers cluster close to its stems.

Aotearoa has five native nettles, all of which need to be carefully treasured. Four are edible, and there is also the striking giant ongaonga (*Urtica ferox*; see page 34). Many centuries ago, Kupe — the legendary Polynesian explorer who discovered Aotearoa — sent a formidable squad of thorny shrubs into the landscape to halt pursuers. One of these shrubs was ongaonga.

Nettles — especially the introduced species — like to grow in rich, well-fertilised soil, so look for them in gardens, on farms, around parks and in bush margins.

USING THEM

It's best to gather nettles in spring, before the plants flower. After that, the leaves become more indigestible. Pick the growing tips — just the four to six leaves on the end of each stem. You can also coppice a nettle plant early in spring, chopping it off near the base. Use what you've gathered, and the nettle will regrow. Most people like to wear gloves to harvest and process nettles, although some can use their bare hands.

You can throw nettles into any cooked dish without fear, because cooking them neutralises the sting. Drying also has pretty much the same effect —I say 'pretty much' because I've experienced tongue tingles from dried-nettle tea, although I've been told this shouldn't happen.

Interestingly, nettles also impart delicious flavours to desserts. I have local forager and nettle enthusiast Marianne Vella to thank for introducing me to such sweet applications. The secret to using nettles in desserts is to use vanilla as a complement. This is partly because nettle has a lingering aftertaste, and vanilla's own aftertaste is strong enough to balance this out. A particularly lovely dessert flavour combination is nettle, vanilla and ginger.

You can finely chop nettle leaves into a dessert, or infuse a cream, custard or syrup with them. If you're unsure how much nettle to use in your dessert, err on the side of caution the first time you try it.

Nettle is widely touted for its health benefits. It's rich in iron, magnesium, calcium, chromium, zinc, potassium, phosphorus and silicon, as well as vitamins A, B, C, E and K. It's considered an all-round tonic to boost strength and immunity. A cup of nettle tisane, which can be made using dried or fresh leaves, is a simple way to enjoy these benefits.

One study found that people who suffer painful arthritis in their hands could reduce the symptoms by inflaming the skin on their hands with stinging nettles. This benefit was over and above the effect of replacing one pain with another. Other studies have shown that extracts of stinging nettle (usually *Urtica dioica*) improve lower urinary tract functions.

> *New Zealand's five native [nettle] species tend to hang around on the outskirts of bush and . . . along the side of little-used tracks . . . You have to be brave to consider planting nettles in the garden. But we must.*

Without the nettles our most elegant butterflies will surely disappear. The Admiral Butterflies rely on the nettles for the correct balance of food to feed their rapacious caterpillars as they grow to become a beautiful gold-encrusted chrysalis.

— GEOFF DAVIDSON (FOUNDER OF THE LEGENDARY AND SORELY MISSED ORATIA PLANT NURSERY), *TITIRANGI TATLER*, AUGUST 2010

NETTLES — THE LITERARY WEEDS

In fairy tales around the world, nettles have prominent roles. Shakespeare mentions nettles at least thirteen times, in plays from *Hamlet* to *King Lear*. And this quote, from Part I of *Henry IV*, was one of writer Katherine Mansfield's favourites: 'but I tell you, my lord fool, out of this nettle, danger, we pluck this flower, safety'. Mansfield uses it at the beginning of her short story 'This Flower', written in 1920 after her diagnosis with tuberculosis. The lines also provide the epitaph on her grave.

Meanwhile, in one of my favourite childhood books, *The Piemakers* by Helen Cresswell (first published in 1967), brooding, dreamy Jem is miraculously immune to the eye sting of onions. Her secret? She wears a pendant containing a nettle leaf. Her grandmother gave her the charm because 'a big sting chases away a little sting'.

Winteraceae
Horopito family

This is one of the oldest families of flowering plant on Earth. The trees and shrubs of Winteraceae, which populate the southern hemisphere, are often aromatic. In Australia the leaves and fruits of one family member, mountain pepper (*Tasmannia lanceolata*), have long been used by Aboriginal people as a flavouring and a medicine. Here in Aotearoa, horopito has similar culinary properties.

Horopito

> **LOWLAND HOROPITO**
> *Pseudowintera axillaris*

> **MOUNTAIN HOROPITO**
> *Pseudowintera colorata*

SPOTTING THEM

Mountain horopito is the more prevalent of the two horopito species, and it's also easier to identify. It grows into a shrub or small tree, in and around bush throughout Aotearoa except in the far north. The flowers are small and faintly fragrant, and grow singly, directly from the branches. The ovalish leaves are a pale matt green and often edged with red or covered in red spots, which seem to be a response to injury. You can test this by scratching a small mark into a leaf and then coming back after an hour or so: your mark will have turned red.

Lowland horopito flowers look and smell similar, but grow in small bunches. The leaves are shiny on their upper surface and nearly white underneath, and they don't display the red spotting. The species grows in forests throughout the North Island and in the top half of the South Island.

USING THEM

Mountain horopito is the most frequently used of the two, but lowland horopito is also edible and flavourful. Both species have a heat to them, but mountain horopito is hotter. Try nibbling lightly on a leaf. You may not feel the heat at first — it has a habit of developing gradually. And don't overdo it, as the antidote for chilli burn — milk — doesn't work with horopito!

THIS PAGE Lowland horopito.

Horopito leaves make a hot cooking spice, fresh or dried. They also work well as an infusion for pickles, and in some recipes as a replacement for chilli, but bear in mind that their flavour is different from that of chilli and the heat creates a different sensation.

The leaves are thick and leathery, and they don't soften significantly when cooked, so either dry them and powder them to flavour a dish, or, if using them fresh, keep them whole or tear them into large pieces so they can be lifted out before serving or eating.

Polygodial, the substance that gives horopito plants their heat, is used in industrial foods to enhance mint flavours. Horopito leaves also go well with mint in home cooking — consider adding them to a mint sauce for lamb.

Chef Monique Fiso notes that she especially enjoys the combination of horopito and chocolate. She makes popular chocolate-horopito bonbons.

Occasionally, horopito can knock out some of your taste buds for a while — the more horopito you have, the greater the effect. It can make things you eat or drink afterwards taste odd. I wonder if this is related to research that shows polygodial is an effective deterrent against some bugs that eat your garden plants, as it blocks their sugar receptors?

The polygodial content of horopito has strong antifungal properties, and the plants have long been used in rongoā rākau to treat fungal infections. Medicinally, horopito can also be used in a similar way to chilli. Both are counter-irritants with rubefacient qualities — they dilate blood vessels wherever they're applied and increase blood flow around an area, giving a therapeutic inflammatory response that may help cleanse damaged or toxic tissues. Nettles and mustards also have this effect.

Chef Charles Royal suggests infusing massage oil with horopito by adding the leaves to the oil and heating it gently to help release the active compounds. He also says the leaves work well as an expectorant when added to a steam inhalation.

> *A favourite joke to play on 'newchums' was to offer them*
> *a taste of something 'really delicious' — a horopito leaf.*
> *We soon got the rough edge of their burning tongues.*
>
> — SHEILA NATUSCH, *WILD FARE FOR WILDERNESS FORAGERS*, 1979

Preserving the harvest

As soon as a plant is harvested, its flavours, scents and nutrients have one foot pointed towards the door. So how do you catch and tame these ephemeral qualities?

One of the simplest ways is to use your gathered plants to infuse basic ingredients such as syrup, honey, butter, alcohol, oil or vinegar. Other useful methods include freezing, drying and pickling. In this section of the book you will find a host of simple methods for preserving your wild harvest, along with ideas for using them later. Some infusions and preserves can be enjoyed as they are, but often they're building blocks for other recipes.

There are further recipes in the next chapter, and to find out more about the suggested ingredients for each method you can refer to the previous chapter. This contains details about each plant, along with tips for harvesting and processing.

Recipe key for dietary requirements

DF — dairy-free, or dairy-free versions are possible
GF — gluten-free, or gluten-free versions are possible
V — vegan, or vegan versions are possible

Important notes about hygiene and storage

Many moulds and bacteria are friends to us, enabling us to make fermented foods and drinks. A few, however, are not. Storing food for any length of time can give these unwanted interlopers a chance to reproduce to dangerous levels.

The time-honoured storage methods in this part of the book have been developed to limit the growth of unwanted microbes, but remember that unknown variables can always come into play. Bear in mind a few basic principles.

- Sugar, honey, vinegar, salt and alcohol are all excellent preservatives; oil, sometimes less so.
- The more a preservative substance is diluted with other non-preservative substances, the less well it will do its job. Note especially that the higher the water content in a substance, the less well it will keep. For example, the best syrups in terms of shelf life are those with a high ratio of sugar to water — equal parts, or more sugar than water by volume.
- The moisture content in plants can promote microbe growth. One way to reduce this moisture is to wilt the plants slightly before preserving them. And when making an infusion (as opposed to preserving whole parts of

a plant), be sure to strain out as much plant material as possible once the infusion is ready.

- When preserved food is unsealed, store it in the fridge or freezer.
- If you preserve your food in relatively small bottles or jars, you will reduce microbe growth overall as you are reducing exposure to oxygen and other substances.
- The most feared microbe invasion is that of *Clostridium botulinum* — the bacterium that produces botulinum toxins, which cause botulism, a very rare but potentially fatal paralytic illness. Bear in mind that *C. botulinum* can't thrive in oxygen and needs a pH above 4.6. Apples, pears, berries, stonefruits and citrus are generally all too acidic for it, as are wines and vinegars, and some honeys.
- Warm temperatures promote the growth of *Clostridium botulinum*, but refrigeration inhibits growth, especially if your fridge is at 3°C (37°F) or lower.
- When preserving food, it's important to maintain good hygiene and scrupulously sterilise all your implements and containers. To sterilise your equipment, place it in a stockpot full of water and boil for 10 minutes before use.
- Some people prefer to heat preserving jars and bottles in the oven at 121°C (250°F) — the temperature that kills spores of *Clostridium botulinum.*
- For more information about botulism, a good source is the Toi Te Ora Public Health website (see 'Resources' section, page 342).
- An alternative sterilisation method is to soak your equipment in cold water in which sterilising tablets have been dissolved. These are commonly available. Use them according to the manufacturer's instructions.
- There is no single authority on how long any given preserve will keep. Indeed, you'll find that people have conflicting experiences, and also that it's hard to untangle the variables that might be contributing factors. The storage times offered in the following methods are guidelines only, based on a mix of personal experience, other people's research and common wisdom. Check your preserves for mould before using them.
- When in doubt about how long something will keep, freeze or refrigerate it.

Tisanes

The simplest infusion you can make is a tea or, perhaps more correctly, a tisane (some people consider that the term 'tea' should be used only for infusions of the tea plant, *Camellia sinensis*).

Infuse fresh foraged plants for a delicious and healthy hot drink, or dry them to infuse later. If you're trying to give up your favourite caffeinated cuppa, try replacing it with wild tisanes. The experimentation and discovery involved can help take your mind off the mental pain!

You can also keep tisanes chilled in the fridge for a couple of days. To keep them longer, freeze them in a container or as ice cubes.

GOOD FORAGEABLES TO USE FOR TISANES

Plant part	Comment
blackberry leaves	Tart and astringent, good for diarrhoea and upset tummies, and a pleasant drink for its own sake
chamomile flowers	A classic tisane that has calming effects
chickweed leaves and stems	Soft and grassy-tasting, soothing to the throat and nutritious
citrus leaves, flowers or peels	Stunning, unusual tisanes can be made from any citrus
cleavers leaves and stems	Fresh and grassy-tasting, it will help cleanse the lymph system
dandelion flowers	A mild-tasting, bright yellow tisane best served in clear cups to make the most of the colour
elderberry flowers	Be sure to remove the mildly toxic green stems
fennel leaves or flowers	A strong aniseedy tisane that is supposed to help you break wind
jasmine flowers	The flavour will remind you straight away of Chinese jasmine tea, which is made with green tea leaves infused with jasmine
kawakawa leaves	Aromatic and delicious, antimicrobial and with a mildly anaesthetic quality

lavender flowers and leaves	Brimming with volatile oils, it can have a very strong flavour
mallow leaves	Mild, green-tasting and mucilaginously soothing
mānuka leaves	A pleasant, healthy tisane with a long and venerable tradition in Aotearoa
marigold flowers	Best served in clear cups to show off the brilliant orange of the infusion
nasturtium leaves, flowers or seedpods	A warming, mustardy tisane that can be good for alleviating the symptoms of a common cold
nettle leaves or tops	Packed with nutrients, this tisane's deep, earthy flavour is an acquired taste, but once you have acquired it you may crave it
oat straw (the stems of oat grass)	Highly nutritious and said by some to have mild calming properties; best decocted (boiled) rather than steeped
parsley leaves or seeds	Aromatic and strangely delicious, but stick to half a teaspoon or less if using the seeds because they're strong; *avoid if you are pregnant*
pine, spruce and fir leaves	These plants don't always release their refreshing flavours quickly and can be steeped for longer than 5 minutes or decocted (boiled) instead
rosehips or petals	A gentle aromatic tisane; it's interesting to try different varieties of rose and compare flavours
scented pelargonium	Strong aromatic tisanes that vary in flavour according to the variety of pelargonium
tūtae kōau leaves and flowers	The flavour is similar to parsley; *avoid if you are pregnant*
yarrow flowers	In the same family as chamomile, yarrow doesn't taste quite as pleasant, but is considered just as useful medicinally, being a general tonic noted for its anti-inflammatory properties

Basic tisane

DF GF V

You can infuse pretty much any edible plant you find. Covering the liquid while infusing is important, partly so you don't lose any as vapour, but also because the molecules in some herbs such as yarrow and chamomile (especially German chamomile) change in valuable ways when they convert to steam and then recondense. This recipe makes a single serving.

1–1½ cups boiling water
1–2 teaspoons dried or 2–4 teaspoons fresh, chopped foraged treasure
honey or sugar to taste (optional)
a slice or squeeze of citrus (optional)

Pour water over the plant material in a cup, bowl or teapot.

Cover with a saucer or lid and leave to steep for about 5 minutes.

Strain into a jug or cup, or pour from the teapot, if using. Adjust flavour with honey, sugar or citrus, if desired.

Enjoy!

VARIATIONS

- Milks or creams aren't usually added to herbal tisanes, but I love either, plus honey with lavender and mānuka tisanes. Rose and elderflower tisanes are also delicious with milk or cream.
- Add lemon or lime juice to a tisane that's too bitter for your taste.

Fruit tisanes

Any fresh fruit can be made into a tisane. Cut or break the fruit up first to allow its flavours to permeate the hot water, and use a good handful. Fresh fruits make pleasant, refreshing and usually very mild tisanes.

Things to do with tisanes

ICED TEA

Take any foraged tisane, chill it and add a roughly equal quantity (more or less to taste) of fruit juice. Infusions of pine, fir, spruce, lavender, rose, fennel, jasmine, kawakawa, mānuka and scented pelargonium all hold their own when blended with fruit juice. Milder-tasting wild plants like chickweed, cleavers or dandelion flowers can work well, too.

BIRCHER MUESLI

For a satisfying and tasty breakfast, soak rolled oats in a bowl overnight in a tisane sweetened with a little juice or honey. In the morning, simply stir in milk, yoghurt or cream (dairy or non-dairy), then top with chopped nuts and/or fruits. Soaking the oats makes them gentler on your digestive system, and if you soak them in a tisane you get the extra nutritional benefit of the infusion ingredients.

WILD STOCK

A tisane can be used in any soup, casserole or gravy instead of stock. Try tisane stocks made from onion weed, tūtae kōau, parsley, wild celery, nettle, fir, spruce, pine, cleavers, chickweed, dandelion flowers, seaweed or a combination of these.

Mock rose water

DF GF V

True rose water is steam-distilled and lasts for ages because it becomes acidic through the distillation process. If you don't have a distiller, you can make a lovely mock rose water, but it will need to be refrigerated and won't last nearly as long as the real thing. You can, however, extend its shelf life if you add it to something with preservative properties, such as alcohol, vinegar or glycerine.

several handfuls of fragrant rose petals
2 cups water

Place rose petals and water in a small saucepan.

Bring them to a gentle simmer and then turn down the heat to barely simmering. Cover and continue simmering for 5–10 minutes.

Turn the heat off and leave to cool.

Strain the cooled liquid and decant the mock rose water into a jar or bottle. Store in the fridge.

Infused syrups

Syrups are not as quick to make as tisanes, but as the sugar used in them is a preservative, they last longer and are still an easy, versatile way to collect and save flavours. You can use syrups in myriad ways: add them to smoothies, use them in fruit-pie fillings instead of honey or sugar, pour them over ice cream, or use them to glaze grilled fruit kebabs, roasted vegetables or meats.

Simple infused syrup

GF DF V

You'll need a sieve and a clean muslin square to strain the syrup at the end of the process.

water
white sugar
foraged treasures

Place equal parts water and sugar in a saucepan over a medium heat and stir until the sugar has dissolved.

Bring to the boil and immediately remove from the heat.

Meanwhile, wash the foraged treasures and pick them over to remove foreign material.

Place the cleaned plant material into a bowl or jug, then pour enough hot syrup over them to cover.

Leave to infuse for 12–24 hours.

Strain the infused syrup through muslin into a bowl or jug. Transfer the syrup into a sterilised bottle or jar and seal. Keep refrigerated.

POSSIBILITIES

Chamomile flowers; citrus peel or flowers; elderflowers; fennel leaves, stems or flowers; kawakawa leaves or unripe berries; lavender flowers; mānuka leaves; pine, fir or spruce needles or tips; pink jasmine flowers; rosehips or rose petals; scented pelargonium leaves or flowers; sweet william flowers.

VARIATION

Try using honey in place of sugar. As heat destroys some of honey's health benefits, don't boil the honey and water but just heat it gently until the honey dissolves.

Simple fruit syrup

GF DF V

The main difference between this and the simple infused syrup is that the foraged fruit is simmered in the liquid. Some of the nutritional compounds in the raw fruit will be destroyed by the heat, but you'll extract more of the fruit flavour. The leftover cooked fruit is delicious with cereal or ice cream, or stirred through yoghurt.

This is a useful way to process windfalls of unripe fruit that might otherwise go to waste. Use equal parts by weight of fruit, sugar or honey, and water.

foraged fruits or berries
water
sugar or honey

Wash fruits or berries and pick them over to remove foreign material. Place them in a saucepan and add equal parts of water and sugar or honey — enough to cover the fruits.

Place over a medium heat and stir gently until it comes to the boil. Boil for 10 minutes. Remove the saucepan from the heat and set aside to cool.

Strain the infused syrup through a sieve and a piece of clean muslin into a bowl or jug. Transfer the syrup into a sterilised bottle or jar and seal.

If sugar is used and the bottle or jar is sealed well, this syrup should last 6–12 months in a cool, dark place. If honey is used, the results are more unpredictable. If you are unsure, keep the syrup in the fridge or freezer.

POSSIBILITIES

Apples and crab apples; blackberries; citrus fruit, peeled and sliced; coprosma berries; elderberries; fuchsia berries; ice plant fruit; kawakawa berries; pears; plums; quinces. If you're lucky, you may also be able to find kahikatea, rimu or tōtara berries.

FRUITS PRESERVED IN SYRUP

Ripe or unripe fruits can also be preserved in their entirety in sugar syrup. Prepare the fruit first to remove all the bits that you wouldn't want to eat, cut it into pieces if necessary, then simply follow the recipe for simple fruit syrup but skip the straining stage.

THE IMPORTANCE OF CITRUS

Lemon, lime, mandarin and orange all brighten and lift other flavours. The added acidity, especially of lemons and limes, can also extend shelf life. To add just a hint of citrus to an infused syrup, slice up a peeled citrus fruit and place it in the saucepan with the other plant material before infusing. You can leave the skin on, but it will probably impart some bitterness. Alternatively, simply add a squeeze of citrus to the infusion when you come to serve it. Elderflower syrup in particular benefits from the addition of lemon or orange, but other fruit syrups are also improved by a lift of citrus.

NO STRAIN, NO GAIN?

When it comes to straining syrups and other liquids, muslin is your best friend. If you don't mind a few bits in your products, then straining through a sieve alone is fine, but by lining the sieve with one or more layers of muslin first, you'll strain out all but the smallest bits. Sometimes this means leaving it to drip for a while over a bowl.

You can also strain without a sieve. Just bunch up the muslin with the pulp or boiled plant matter inside, then tie it, Christmas-pudding style, and hang it over your bowl to drip. If you're like me, you may sometimes get impatient and swish the pulp around in the sieve, or squeeze the muslin bundle to make it drip faster, but bear in mind that if you do so you will end up with a cloudy product.

Coffee filters also make excellent sieve liners and produce a truly clear, debris-free product.

Things to do with fruit syrups

CORDIAL

Use your syrup as a cordial drink. Try a ratio of 1 part syrup to 5 parts water to start with, then adjust this to your taste with more water or syrup. If you can't get the balance right and it feels like it needs something extra, try adding a few squeezes of citrus juice, especially lemon or lime. You could also try adding a little vanilla essence.

ICED TEA

Make a jug of black, green or white tea and set it aside to cool. Mix the tea in equal parts with cordial (see above) and pour it over ice cubes. Serve with a slice of citrus.

ICE BLOCKS

Make ice blocks with cordial (see above). Use commercial moulds or pour into ice-cube trays, then add wooden ice-block sticks. To stop the sticks falling out, stretch plastic food wrap over the top of the tray and make small slits in the plastic above each moulded cube. Slip a stick through each slit and into the liquid.

FIZZY

Instead of adding still water to your syrup as a drink, add soda water or carbonated water. Pour this over a scoop of ice cream to make an ice-cream soda.

FLAVOURED WATER KEFIR

Mix fruit syrup with some of your own freshly brewed water kefir. The tart flavour of water kefir is a perfect foil for a sweet syrup.

FRUIT SAUCE

Make a thicker syrup for pouring over ice cream or panna cotta (see recipes, pages 256 and 255) by adding 1 teaspoon of cornflour for each cup of syrup. Put a little of the syrup into a small cup or bowl, add the cornflour and mix to a runny paste. Warm the remaining syrup in a saucepan over a gentle heat and stir in the cornflour paste. Stir gently as it begins to simmer and remove from the heat after a couple of minutes or when the syrup has become transparent. Use the sauce hot or cold.

Country wine

DF GF V

Ferment your foraged cordial (see page 173) by harnessing the powers of local yeasts. This is the same principle that underlies making a sourdough starter. The addition of fresh fruit can speed up and strengthen the process, as the wild yeasts on their skins will help get the fermentation going.

cordial (see page 173)

a few unwashed grapes, plums, elderberries, or other berries or fruits (optional)

Place the cordial in a large, wide-mouthed jar. Add the unwashed berries and fruits, if using.

Cover the jug with a cloth or piece of muslin to keep dust and bugs out but let more wild yeasts in.

Leave the mix in a warm place for several days, stirring well twice a day, or more if possible.

When the mix begins to bubble, remove the berries or fruits and transfer the mixture to a clean jar or bottle.

You want to keep air out but allow pressure to be released, so put a lid on the fermenting mix only loosely, or use an airlock (you can buy these from a home-brew supplier). Some ingenious folk stretch a balloon over the mouth of the jar or bottle.

Leave until the bubbling slows – probably 2–4 weeks. Drink straight away or seal the wine and age it for anything from a week to a year. If you age the wine, try it from time to time to see how it's going.

VARIATION

Relying on wild yeasts when making wine or other fermented products can be unpredictable. For some people that's part of the fun, but for others – even die-hard foragers – it can be more important to ensure a strong, reliable ferment. If you feel that way, by all means add a bit of commercial yeast at the start of the process. A pinch of baker's yeast will give you a rough and ready result, but winemaker's yeast is likely to taste better and give you a higher alcohol content. There are many winemaker's yeasts available, suited to different wines – ask your closest home-brew supplier what they recommend.

Infused vinegars

Vinegar has strong antimicrobial and, therefore, preservative properties. This means that infusing vinegar is one of the best ways to preserve foraged foods and their flavours for a long time. Any vinegar will work, and each brings its own unique attributes to an infusion. Tangy apple cider vinegar, with its widely touted health benefits, is a popular choice. White wine vinegar is milder in taste, and the flavours of the infusion will therefore shine through more brightly. Infusing balsamic vinegar makes a rich, sweet, complex vinegar that is a delicious addition to many cooked dishes.

Simple infused vinegar

DF GF V

There are many possible combinations of plant and vinegar. You may want to add a sprig of the infused plant to the final product for decoration as well as an identifier. Note that with very strongly aromatic plants, such as rosemary or lavender, you may only need a sprig or two.

foraged treasures
vinegar of your choice

Wash the foraged treasures and pick them over to remove foreign material. Pat them dry with a paper towel.

Cram your treasures into a jar or bottle, breaking them up if you need to, and pour in the vinegar. Make sure no bits of plant material are sticking out above the surface, as there's a small chance they may grow mould. Store the jar in a cool, dark place for a week or two, giving it a shake now and then.

If, at the end of that time, your vinegar is not as strongly infused as you would like, repeat the process to make twice-infused vinegar.

Strain the liquid through clean muslin and pour into sterilised bottles. Infused vinegars can generally be stored for a year or more in a cool, dark place.

POSSIBILITIES

Chamomile flowers; coprosma berries; crab apples; elderflowers or elderberries; fennel flowers, leaves and/or stems; fuchsia berries; horopito leaves, torn up;

ice plant leaves or fruit; kahikatea, rimu or tōtara berries; kawakawa leaves or fruits; lavender flowers or leaves; mānuka leaves, flowers and seedpods; marigold flowers; nasturtium leaves, flowers and/or seedpods; nettle leaves and/or tops; oat straw or milky oats; onion weed bulbs, leaves and/or flowers, as well as other wild alliums; parsley leaves, stems, flowers and/or roots; pine, spruce and fir leaves or tips; pink jasmine flowers; rose petals; rosemary leaves and/or flowers; scented pelargonium leaves and flowers; tūtae kōau leaves, stems and/or flowers; wild celery leaves, stems and/or flowers.

Things to do with infused vinegars

- Add 1 teaspoon of infused apple cider vinegar to a glass of iced water for a healthy, refreshing and oddly moreish drink.
- Whisk or shake together 1 part infused vinegar to 3 parts oil to make a salad dressing.
- Add 1–2 teaspoons of infused vinegar to soups, sauces or gravies. Note that vinegar in bone stocks helps extract the gelatine from the bones.
- Use a dash of infused vinegar to deglaze a roasting pan before making gravy.
- Use infused vinegar as the base for a mayonnaise (see recipe, page 213).
- Mix 2 parts infused vinegar with 1 part oil, plus a little salt and sugar and a crushed garlic clove (optional), to make a marinade for meats or tofu.
- Make a delicious shrub, or drinking vinegar, using 2 parts infused vinegar to 1 part water. Usually these are made with fruit-infused vinegars, but you can also use herb or floral vinegars. Gently heat your infused vinegar and sugar, stirring to dissolve the sugar. Remove the shrub from the heat and let it cool before using it straight away, or storing it in the refrigerator. Tightly sealed in a sterile container, it can last up to 6 months. To serve, add to soda water and ice cubes or use as a drink mixer in other ways.

Luxury butters

If you don't eat dairy products, you can use a dairy-free butter substitute for either of the methods given here. Try a commercial butter substitute, or consider using virgin coconut oil. For enfleuraged aromatic butter, you'll need something that's relatively solid at cooler temperatures, such as virgin coconut oil.

A lot of people choose an unsalted butter if they're planning to use their luxury butter to make or serve with sweet dishes. Personally, I'm a bit of a salt fiend and prefer salted butter in almost every situation.

Enfleuraged aromatic butter

DF GF V

This works with strongly aromatic plants that ooze scent and flavour. If the scent of a plant lingers on your fingers after you've brushed them across its foliage, then it's likely to be a good candidate for this process. For more on enfleurage, *see page 306.*

250 g (9 oz) block of butter or butter substitute
aromatic foraged treasures

Choose a container large enough to hold the block of butter and line it with your aromatic plant material.

Place the butter on top, then cover it with a thin blanket of more aromatics – you may also want to tuck some down the sides.

Let the butter nestle there for 12–24 hours, keeping it in a cool, dark place. In warm weather the best option may be the fridge.

After 24 hours, remove the block of butter from the aromatic plants, and carefully remove any stray bits of plant stuck to the surface – these can go mouldy if you leave them there.

Wrap the now aromatic butter in baking paper or put it in a container, and store it in the fridge or freezer as you would with any other butter.

POSSIBILITIES

Citrus flowers; fennel leaves and/or flowers; lavender sprigs; pine twigs and needles with a strong scent; rosemary sprigs; scented pelargonium leaves; wild jasmine flowers.

Blended butter

DF GF V

Blended butter is ideal for plants that have a slightly less powerful scent than the highly aromatic plants used to make enfleuraged butter. These plants should also be soft enough to eat raw.

You can either make a savoury butter or one that's good in desserts. There are no hard and fast rules about the ratio of plant material to butter – a handful or two of foraged treasures to 250 g (9 oz) of butter is about as precise as I'd get, and even that seems slightly too prescriptive! As ever, be creative and work to your own tastes.

250 g (9 oz) block of butter or butter substitute
a handful or two of one or two foraged treasures

Soften the butter and then beat it in a bowl until pale and well creamed.

Wash your foragings, pick them over to remove foreign material, and then finely chop them.

Add your chopped foragings to the butter and cream it some more.

To store the blended butter, form it into small patties and place these on a tray lined with baking paper. Place in the freezer and, when the patties have frozen, transfer them to a container or freezer bag and return to the freezer until required.

Alternatively, you can spread a sheet of baking paper on a bench and arrange the butter in a 3–4 centimetre-diameter (1¼–1½ inch) log. Roll the paper around the log and twist the ends to seal. Store in the fridge or freezer and cut off slices as required.

POSSIBILITIES

Some of these ingredients, such as borage and marigold flowers, are added more for colour than for flavour: borage flowers; chamomile flowers or leaves; citrus peel, finely zested; fennel leaves, flowers or pollen; harakeke pollen; kawakawa leaves; marigold petals; nasturtium flowers or leaves; onion weed flowers or leaves; parsley leaves; pine, fir or spruce tips; pink jasmine flowers; rose petals; scented pelargonium leaves; sweet william flowers; tūtae kōau leaves; wild celery leaves; wood sorrel flowers or leaves.

Things to do with enfleuraged and blended butters

- Spread on hot bread, toast or scones.
- Make shortbread (see recipe, page 247).
- Use in a foraged fruit crumble (see recipe, page 262).
- Use to make popcorn in a pan on the stove (a 50:50 mix of butter and rice bran oil works well), or melt over popped popcorn. To prevent popcorn becoming soggy when the butter is added, clarify the butter first by melting it over a gentle heat in a pot on the stove. Then pour only the golden oil off the top, leaving behind as much of the white residue as possible.
- Serve with hot corn cobs.
- Melt over hot, boiled or steamed vegetables just before serving.
- Add to root vegetables just before mashing.
- Daub over roast vegetables or meat.
- Use to fry an omelette.
- Use with an equal quantity of oil to caramelise onions.
- Use in tea sandwiches, with or without another filling (see recipes, pages 227–229).
- Use to make butterscotch sauce (see recipe, page 259).
- Use to make aha tortoni (see recipe, page 263).
- Use to make buttercream icing (see recipe, page 248).

Infused oils

My two favourite oils to infuse are extra-virgin olive oil, for its nutritional value and delicious taste, and rice bran oil, for its high smoke point and bland taste, which gives other flavours their time in the limelight. Lately, I've also fallen in love with avocado oil. But any oil will do, so choose one you enjoy and can afford.

Some ingredients, like marigold and borage flowers, are more for colour, so try combining a colourful flower with some of the more highly flavoured forageables. Mould is one of your biggest enemies when making infused oils, so take precautionary measures during the entire process and reduce the moisture content of your foraged treasures as much as possible.

Simple infused oil

DF GF V

You can use fresh or dried foraged ingredients to infuse oil. It's a bit of extra effort to dry the ingredients first (see page 194), but if you want to be able to store your oil for a while then it can be worth it — the trade-off is a reduced risk of mould.

foraged treasures — enough to fill your jar

oil — enough to cover

Wash the foraged treasures and pick them over to remove foreign material. Pat dry, and either dry fully or leave them flat in a dry place for a few hours to wilt and reduce their water content.

Crush the plant material slightly, or cut or tear it into pieces. Cram it into a sterilised jar, then pour the oil over it. Be scrupulous about filling the jar as near to the top as you can, to reduce the amount of oxygen that will be sealed inside the container when the lid is on.

Make sure no plant material is sticking above the surface, poking down any exposed bits.

Place the infusing oil, tightly covered, in a cool, dark place. Give it a shake now and then, and keep an eye on it to make sure no plant material has bobbed above the surface.

Infuse for 1–3 days, then strain through muslin, very gently pressing the

plant material to get as much of the oil out of it as possible without causing it to disintegrate.

If you'd like a stronger infusion, recharge with a new batch of plant material for another 1–3 days. Repeat this as many times as you like, until the infusion is as strongly aromatic as you want.

When you're happy with your infused oil, strain it very well, remembering that any plant pieces left in the oil may encourage mould growth. Decant it into a sterilised bottle and store in the fridge.

An optional step that may help the oil keep longer is to let it stand for a few days, then decant it again, leaving behind any sediment that has settled.

POSSIBILITIES

Borage flowers; chamomile flowers; fennel leaves, stems and/or flowers; horopito leaves; kawakawa leaves and unripe fruits; lavender flowers and/or leaves; mānuka leaves; marigold flowers; nasturtium leaves, flowers or seedpods; onion weed leaves and flowers; parsley leaves, stems and/or roots; pine, fir or spruce needles, tips and/or twigs; pink jasmine flowers; rose petals; rosemary leaves and/or flowers; scented pelargonium leaves and flowers; tūtae kōau leaves.

Things to do with infused oils

- Whisk or shake up 1 part vinegar to 3 parts infused oil to make a salad dressing.
- Use to fry or sauté meat, vegetables or tofu.
- Use to pop popping corn.
- Drizzle over cooked meat.
- Use with equal parts butter for caramelising onions.
- Use to make mayonnaise (see recipe, page 213).
- Use to fry fritters, chips and schnitzels.
- Mix 1 part infused oil with 2 parts vinegar or citrus juice, a little salt and sugar, and a crushed garlic clove to make a marinade for meats or tofu.
- Use aromatic infused oils as a massage or body oil (see page 294).

Infused honeys

Every honey has its own distinct and delicious aroma, depending on where the bees have been collecting nectar, so it's fun deciding which wild plant to combine with which honey, then testing the result.

Any runny honey is good for an infusion. The best possible honey you can use is raw honey from a local beekeeper, but it isn't always possible to get hold of this. If you don't have a honey that is sufficiently runny, you could add a little water to a solid honey and stir well to combine, or very gently heat the honey whenever the recipe requires it to be runny (see 'Heating honey', page 185).

Aromatic honey

DF GF

Herbs and flowers with robust flavours are best for infusing honey, since the honey has a strong flavour of its own. To ensure foraged flavours shine through strongly, consider using a mild-tasting honey like clover honey.

- foraged treasures
- honey of your choice

Wash the foraged treasures carefully and pick them over to remove any foreign material. Cut or chop your foraged finds.

Half-fill a sterilised jar with the plant material.

Pour the runny honey over the top, adding enough to fill the jar. Make sure the lid is on tight and is leakproof.

Leave it in a cool, dark place for 2 weeks, turning the jar upside down every second day.

After that, pour the honey through a fine sieve into another sterilised jar – the amount of time it takes to drip through will depend on how viscous the honey is. You may have to be patient! If you want to speed things up, place the jar in a bowl of warm water to heat the honey just enough to improve the flow, stirring it gently as it warms.

When all of the honey has been strained into the clean jar, put the lid on the jar and store in a cool place or the fridge.

POSSIBILITIES

Citrus flowers or peels; elderflowers; fennel leaves, flowers and/or seeds, or pollen; horopito leaves; kawakawa leaves and fruits, ripe or unripe; lavender flowers and/or leaves; pine, fir or spruce needles and tips; rose petals; rosemary leaves and/or flowers; scented pelargonium leaves, stems and/or flowers; wood sorrel leaves and flowers.

HEATING HONEY

The biggest challenge when working with honey is its viscosity. Heat will make it flow more easily, but the more it heats up, the more of its goodness is destroyed. Pure, raw honey has strong preservative and antimicrobial properties and contains many health-giving compounds, but even at 37 °C (99 °F) the effectiveness of these declines. That's why it's good to use honey that's as runny as possible to start with, especially if you're using raw honey and want to hold on to its qualities.

Of course, it's not the end of the world to lose some of the honey's benefits. Whatever honey you use and however you heat it, you'll still have a delicious infused product with extra nutrients gained from your foraged ingredients. And, if you're using commercial supermarket honey as your base rather than raw artisan honey, it's probably lost goodness already through processing and filtering methods.

Berry honeys

DF GF

In this recipe, an equal ratio of honey to berries works well, but there are no hard and fast rules – you could alter it one way or the other and still end up with a delicious product. The higher the ratio of honey to fruit, the longer it will generally keep. You can also use plums in place of berries.

foraged berries
honey

Put the berries in a saucepan over a gentle heat and mash them with a fork as they begin to soften. Continue heating until the berries become pulpy.

Push the pulp through a sieve over a large bowl to remove any large seeds and stubborn bits of skin, then leave to cool.

When the pulp has cooled slightly, add the honey and stir together until combined.

Transfer the mixture to a sterilised jar and store in the fridge. It should last at least 2 weeks and probably more, but keep an eye out for mould. Much depends on the fruit used, the fridge temperature, how often the jar is opened and what other material gets into the honey.

POSSIBILITIES

Blackberries; cherries; coprosma berries; fuchsia berries; kahikatea, rimu or tōtara berries; kawakawa fruits; plums.

Things to do with infused honeys and berry honeys

- Spread on bread or scones.
- Use to glaze meat or tofu — try mixing the honey with soy sauce, ginger and garlic or onion weed for a savoury flavour.
- Drizzle over ice cream, panna cotta or a scoop of mascarpone (see recipes, pages 256, 255 and 222).
- Add to a fruit pie or crumble filling (see recipe, page 262) instead of sugar.
- Spread on dainty sandwiches.
- Eat a spoonful straight from the jar.

Infused alcohols

The first time I made my own liqueur — a simple mix of vodka and sugar syrup infused with 'Black Doris' plums — I was thrilled with the product. I wanted to shout to the world: 'Make liqueurs! Now! At home! With whatever you can find!'

Making wild infused alcoholic drinks is an exhilarating pastime, and not only when you test the results frequently. Using the methods below, it's almost unbelievably easy to concoct a profusion of infusions — a vast array of delectable and distinctive beverages that you and your friends and family will appreciate. It makes you feel generous and clever and, yes, occasionally drunk.

Infused spirits are strong and delicious. Add sugar syrup, and spirits become liqueurs. You can also infuse red and white wines and fortified wines such as sherry.

Wild herbs, fruits and flowers are all great to use for infusing. Kitchen spices can also be added — a particularly delicious combination is a single cinnamon quill and a single vanilla bean pod, left for at least a week to infuse.

Infused spirits

DF GF V

Vodka and gin are both popular spirits to use for infusing, as their flavours are quite neutral, allowing the other ingredients to shine. However, many people enjoy working with stronger-flavoured spirits such as whisky, and infusing them with equally charismatic plants. Make as big a batch as you like, as you'll have no trouble giving away any excess.

foraged treasures — enough to fill your jar
spirit of choice — enough to cover

Wash the foraged treasures carefully and pick them over to remove any foreign material. Pack the plant material into a sterilised jar.

Pour your spirit over the top, making sure the foraged plant material is completely covered to prevent the growth of mould.

Leave the infusion for as long as it takes to produce the flavour you want — this could take anything from 24 hours to 4 weeks, depending on the ingredient (see 'Tips for infused spirits', page 188). Shake it now and then if you remember.

Once you think your infused spirit is tasting as lovely as can be, strain it through a sieve lined with muslin into a sterilised bottle, or through a coffee filter if you want to make sure you remove all the bits.

Leave your delicious spirit to mellow for a while or start drinking it straight away. Well-sealed and stored in a cool, dark place, it should keep for a year or more. Once opened, keep it in the fridge.

Tips for infused spirits

- Your best gauge of readiness is your own tongue. Taste a little of your spirit every day to see how it's going. When you decide the flavour is right, it's time to halt the infusion.
- Flowers and fresh herbs are best left to infuse for only 24 hours.
- Try infusing dried herbs for a week or two, although longer is also fine.
- Fruits often need to be left to infuse for at least a week, but leaving them for longer will produce a stronger, richer flavour.
- Dried kitchen spices can be left to infuse for many weeks.
- If you're using several ingredients that require different infusion times, it may be best to infuse them separately, one at a time.

Infused wines and fortified wines

To infuse wine and fortified wine, follow the same method as for wild spirits.

Infused liqueurs

DF GF V

When making an infused liqueur, you can choose your preferred ratio of spirit to sweet syrup, as well as your preferred ratio of water to sugar in the sweet syrup. The recipe here is a good starting point, but I admit that I love even stronger, sweeter liqueurs, using about 1 part very strong sugar syrup to about 2 parts spirit. My favourite way to drink infused liqueurs, especially in summer, is as a shot poured over a glass full of ice cubes.

foraged treasures
sugar or honey syrup (see recipe, page 170)
spirit of choice

Wash the foraged treasures carefully and pick them over to remove any foreign material. Pack the plant material into a sterilised jar.

Mix equal quantities of syrup and spirit, then pour into the jar, ensuring the foraged treasures are well covered.

Leave the infusion for as long as it takes to produce the flavour you want — this could be anything from 24 hours to 4 weeks or more, depending on the ingredient(s) (see 'Tips for infused spirits', page 188).

Once your liqueur is tasting delicious, strain it through a sieve lined with muslin into a sterilised bottle. If you want to be sure that you get rid of all the bits, strain it through a coffee filter.

Leave your infused liqueur to mellow for a while, or start drinking it straight away. Well-sealed and stored in a cool, dark place, it should keep for a year or more. Once opened, keep it in the fridge.

POSSIBILITIES

Apples and crab apples; blackberries; chamomile flowers; cherries; citrus fruits, peels, leaves and/or flowers; coprosma berries; dandelion flowers — new; elderflowers or elderberries; fennel leaves, flowers and/or pollen; fuchsia berries; kahikatea, rimu or tōtara berries; kawakawa leaves and fruits — ripe or unripe; lavender flowers; mānuka leaves; pears; pine needles, twigs and/or tips; pink jasmine flowers; plums; rose petals; scented pelargonium leaves or flowers; sweet william flowers; walnuts — green or ripe and shelled.

THE EFFECT OF TIME

It's fascinating to have two or three batches of the same alcoholic infusion going at once, and to stop each one and strain out the plant material at a different time so you can compare the flavours. Sometimes you may worry that you've missed an infusion's peak deliciousness, or you may find it begins to take on a flavour that you don't like so much. If you have at least two batches going, you can stop one straight away and leave the other(s) for longer to see if the flavour starts to change again and becomes even better with a little extra time — this happens quite often.

Things to do with wild spirits, liqueurs and wines

- Add to melted chocolate (about 1 part alcohol to 2 parts chocolate) to make an incredible dessert sauce.
- Drizzle over ice cream or panna cotta (see recipes, pages 256 and 255).
- Mix into jelly, ice cream or panna cotta (see page 250 for the wild fruit jelly recipe, and remember that you may need a little extra gelatine to set an alcoholic jelly).
- Add to water to poach fruit.
- Add to eggnog instead of brandy.
- Use instead of wine in a pasta sauce (see recipe, page 242).
- Use to soak oats for cranachan (see recipe, page 260).
- Use instead of sherry in aha tortoni (see recipe, page 263).

Things to do with leftover alcohol-saturated fruits after infusion

- Serve as a dessert with custard, cream, pavlova or ice cream (see recipe, page 256).
- Use as a filling for a fruit pie or crumble (see recipe, page 262).
- Add to a cooked casserole.

The art of freezing

Unpredictability, serendipity and the seasonal ebbs and flows of supply are par for the course when foraging. Freezing is a great way to prolong the supply of some of your foraged foods, and also an easy and satisfying process.

Freezing breaks down the cell structure of plants, so when using this process keep in mind the end uses of your foraged treasures. If it doesn't matter to you that they emerge from their Antarctic sleep a bit mushier, then all's well. However, it's a good idea to chop or slice things ready for use before you freeze them because, once they thaw, their mushiness will make them harder to cut up.

If you have the time and inclination, blanching some foods before freezing is a good idea, as it hinders enzyme action and ensures they stay in good condition for as long as possible. Leafy greens are good candidates for blanching, as are vegetables such as fern fiddleheads, tī kōuka shoots and parsley roots. Frozen foods usually last at least 6 months. It's a good idea to keep track of how long they've been frozen by writing the freezing date on the container or bag.

Oversupplies and undersupplies

The freezer is a good friend to the forager. It comes in handy if you've gathered too much of something to be able to deal with it all straight away, but it's also good if you haven't been able to collect enough of a favourite forageable to make something worthwhile. In that case, you can throw your gatherings into a bag or container in the freezer until you've built up a large-enough supply. This works especially well with foragings that are in short supply in any given location — for example, berries, onion weed bulbs, nasturtium seedpods and dandelion buds. I throw these small gatherings into containers or freezer bags and put them in the freezer as is — there's no need to blanch them first.

Freezing vegetables

Fill a large bowl with ice-cold water and bring a large saucepan of water to the boil.

Meanwhile, clean and prepare the vegetables as if you were going to use them straight away.

Drop the prepared vegetables into the boiling water in small batches – the water needs to come back to the boil quickly. Boil for 2–3 minutes.

Lift vegetables from the water with a slotted spoon or scoop them out with a sieve so that you can continue to use the same water for each batch. Drop the hot vegetables into the bowl of icy water as quickly as possible to stop them cooking.

When all the vegetables have cooled in the water, drain them and get rid of as much excess water as possible. The easiest way to do this is to spread them in a single layer on a tea towel to dry.

When all the vegetables are very dry, transfer them to a container or freezer bag and place them in the freezer. Alternatively, lay out the pieces on a tray, oven tray or plate lined with baking paper so they aren't touching, and put in the freezer. Once they're frozen, you can bag them up together.

Freezing leafy greens

Prepare as for vegetables, but blanch the greens for only 1–2 minutes before scooping them out and dropping them into icy water.

Lift the greens from the water in handful-sized clumps and gently squeeze the excess water from them. Press into patties and arrange on an oven tray or plate lined with baking paper and place it in the freezer.

When the patties are frozen, transfer them to a container or freezer bag and return to the freezer until required.

Freezing herbs and berries

Small, flavourful plants can be chopped as for cooking and frozen as is without blanching. These include parsley, tūtae kōau, wood sorrel, rosemary, rose petals, lavender, onion weed, kawakawa leaves and horopito leaves.

Small berries and berry-like fruits can be frozen as is, although it's a good idea to pick them over carefully first to remove all foreign material.

Freezing larger fruits

Wash, peel, pit, core and slice fruits, removing any bruised or damaged bits.

To inhibit browning on pale fruits like apples, pears and quinces, fill a bowl with cold water and mix in the juice of a lemon. Dip the sliced fruit in briefly. Alternatively, use 1 teaspoon of salt dissolved in 8–10 cups of water. Drain and dry the pieces thoroughly once you are ready to freeze them.

Spread the slices of fruit in a single layer on a tray, plate or oven tray lined with baking paper and place in the freezer.

Once frozen, transfer the frozen fruit to a container or freezer bag, pushing out the air, and return to the freezer until required.

For fruit that's too overripe to slice easily, consider simply cooking it to a purée and then freezing this in portions in ice-cube trays.

Freezing citrus fruits

Citrus fruits don't need to be blanched before freezing, but as with vegetables it's a good idea to cut them up first into pieces suited to different recipes. For example, slice the fruits with their skins on if you anticipate adding them that way to punch, or zest the rind and squeeze the juice if that's the form you're likely to need once they have thawed.

The art of drying

Lots of flavourful wild herbs, flowers and greens respond well to drying. People sometimes say that the best-flavoured leaves for drying appear just before a plant flowers, but I gather and dry all sorts of plants at different times of the year and am happy with the results.

Dehydrators are great, but you don't need one: you can air-dry and oven-dry most things. You can also dry herbs in a microwave.

Store your dried foraged goods in an airtight jar or container, and keep them as whole as you can so they retain their flavour and active compounds for as long as possible. If you want to use them powdered or crumbled, prepare them in this way just before you use them.

Air-drying

Air-drying needs to be done in a dry environment. If the weather is humid or your house is damp, you'll have more success with a different drying method. There are three basic ways to air-dry plants; choose whichever seems most appropriate and manageable.

Option 1: Spread the plants out in a single layer in a dark, dry place. Turn them regularly to ensure even drying. You may want to spread them on a rack.

Option 2: In a dry room with good air circulation, suspend swathes of muslin from your ceiling like small hammocks, and place your plants in them to dry.

Option 3: Bunch plants together at the stem ends and tie them together. Hang them in a dry place with good air circulation, and with the stems up and the leaves or flowers down. You may want to tie paper bags around bunches of flowers or leaves that you're hanging to dry, to protect them from light and dust, and to catch any bits that fall off.

Oven-drying

Oven-drying can be harsh. The trick is to keep the temperature extremely low – you want the herbs to become dry and crumbly, not burnt. Every oven is different and the plants themselves are another variable. For these reasons it's always a good idea to do a test-run on one or two samples before you fill your oven.

If you can get your oven to stay at 60°C (140°F) or even lower, you should be able to successfully dry most plants. If your oven gets too hot, you might want to heat it up then turn it off before you put your plants in to dry. If the plants need a bit more drying, you may find you need to turn the oven on again after it has cooled. Leaving the oven on with the door slightly open may also help regulate the temperature.

Lay the plant material in a single layer on an oven tray or sheet. You may want to line it with baking paper, although this is not necessary. Place the tray or sheet in the oven. Keep an eye on the plants to make sure they don't burn, and adjust the temperature as required.

When the plants are brittle and crumbly, remove them from the oven and leave to cool.

Transfer the dried material to an airtight container, and store in a cool, dark place until required.

Microwave-drying

Spread the plants between 2 sheets of baking paper and microwave on high for 1 minute. Check to see if the herbs have dried. If some have and some haven't, take out only the dried ones.

Move the remaining herbs around a bit and give them another 20-second blast. Repeat the process until all of the herbs are dry.

Sun-drying

Just as the sun fades your curtains, so it mutes the colours, aromas and other active components of foraged plants as it dries them. However, some people do like to start the drying process in the sun, letting just a bit of moisture evaporate before moving on to air-drying or oven-drying.

POSSIBILITIES

Blackberry leaves; Brassicaceae leaves, flowers and seedpods; citrus peels and flowers; eucalyptus leaves; horopito leaves; jasmine flowers; kawakawa leaves and unripe fruits (see 'tākawa peppercorns', page 124); lavender flowers; mānuka leaves; marigold flowers and seeds; nettle leaves and tops; onion weed leaves and stems; parsley leaves, flowers, seeds and roots; pine, spruce and fir tips; rose petals; rosemary leaves and flowers; scented pelargonium leaves; seaweeds; tūtae kōau leaves and flowers; wild celery leaves; wood sorrel leaves and flowers.

Making your own herb and spice mixes

Every culture has flavours that help define its cuisine. Local ingredients and methods of preparation are combined and recombined to form a kaleidoscope of dishes that are very different from one another yet recognisably of their place.

Just as every culture has characteristic flavours, so every enthusiastic cook develops favourite methods, ingredients and ways of combining them that add up to an individual culinary personality. I love the way people use foraged ingredients in their cooking to express themselves and their place in the world, finding the plants growing wild around them that they like and using them in creative ways. Through adventure and experimentation, you will find your own house flavours and style.

It's easy to go to the shop and buy a herb or spice mix containing a popular representation of a culture's time-honoured flavour combinations. But developing your own favourite dried spice and herb mixes by combining foraged finds from your local area is both challenging and rewarding.

Dry foraged herbs according to the instructions on pages 194–196. Dry each plant separately, as they may require slightly different drying conditions and times.

When combining your dried foraged herbs, invent, experiment and adapt! Store your prepared mixes in airtight jars ready to use. You can use any of the dried herbs in the list of possibilities. A few ideas for starters:

- 1 part fennel seeds or pollen to 9 parts parsley, wild celery or tūtae kōau leaves
- 1 part fennel seeds to 4 parts orange zest
- 1 part lavender to 3 parts fennel seeds or pollen
- 1 part lemon zest to 1 part fir tips and 1 part lemon pelargonium leaves
- 1 part lemon zest to 2 parts jasmine flowers
- 1 part mānuka leaves to 1 part kawakawa leaves
- 1 part onion weed leaves to 2 parts wood sorrel leaves
- 1 part parsley leaves to 1 part kawakawa leaves and 2 parts onion weed leaves

- 1 part parsley leaves to 1 part onion weed leaves and 4 parts nettle leaves
- 1 part rose petals to 4 parts wood sorrel leaves
- 1 part rosemary leaves to 1 part Brassicaceae seeds

Things to do with herb and spice mixes

- Sprinkle onto Parmesan crisps before baking (see recipe, page 215).
- Use to flavour mayonnaise (see recipe, page 213).
- Sprinkle on baked potatoes.
- Use to flavour a plain yoghurt dip.
- Add to soups, sauces, casseroles and gratins.
- Use to coat vegetables or meat before roasting (cover while roasting so they don't burn).
- Add to bread dough before baking.
- Add to meat, lentil or bean patties.
- Add to baked fish: place a whole fish or fillets on a piece of baking paper or cooking foil and add a knob of butter. Sprinkle with herb mix and fold the paper or foil to make a parcel. Bake at about 240°C (465°F) for about 4 minutes per centimetre (10 minutes per inch) thickness of fish.

The art of pickling

Pickles come in many forms — quick uncooked pickles for instant gratification, cooked pickles that keep for longer, and fermented pickles that corral wild microbes and set them to work.

Pickles generally require quite a bit of salt. For the best results, use sea salt or pickling salt. It's especially important not to use iodised salt for fermented pickles, as the iodine inhibits the fermentation process. If you include seaweed or ureure in a pickle, note that you will want to use less salt than the recipe states as they are both salty already.

Pickles — served with cheese and bread or crackers — have long been a Kiwi kitchen staple. Sweeter pickles are great served on the side with curries and barbecued foods.

Cooked pickle

DF GF V

Practically anything goes, but you'll need a combination of bulky and flavoursome plants for a well-balanced pickle.

foraged treasures, roughly or finely chopped depending on how chunky you want your pickle
salt — enough to coat the plant material
apple cider vinegar — enough to cover the plant material in the saucepan
sugar — half as much by volume as you use of cider vinegar
freshly ground black or tākawa pepper to taste (see recipe, page 124)

Wash the foraged treasures carefully and pick them over to remove any foreign material. Chop them as finely as you like and place them in a bowl.

Sprinkle with salt — enough to cover the lot. Stir the salt through the plant material and cover. Set aside for 12–24 hours — overnight is ideal.

Rinse the plant material under cold running water. Drain well. Put the vinegar and sugar in a saucepan over a medium heat and stir until the sugar has dissolved. Bring to the boil.

Add the plants and pepper, then reduce the heat. Continue simmering for 10 minutes.

Take the saucepan off the heat and set aside to cool. Transfer the cooled pickles to a sterilised jar and seal.

Store in a cool, dark place for up to 12 months. Refrigerate once opened.

THICKER PICKLES

Some pickles are better thickened. A thickened pickle needs a warm colour, so if the pickle doesn't look as appetising as you'd like, add something colourful like turmeric or paprika. Follow these simple instructions to thicken pickles.

Use the cooked pickle recipe, but when the pickle mixture comes to the boil, add some cornflour paste as follows. Put the cornflour in a small bowl — I usually allow 2–3 teaspoons per cup of cider vinegar used in the recipe. Add a little extra vinegar to the cornflour and blend to form a thin, smooth paste.

Pour the paste into the simmering pickle mixture and bring it back to the boil. Boil for a couple more minutes, until the cornflour is cooked — the pickle should look shiny and clear. Take the saucepan off the heat and set aside to cool a little, then transfer the cooled pickles to a sterilised jar and seal.

Uncooked refrigerator pickle

DF GF V

This is the easiest way to make pickle. However, the finished result doesn't last as long as its cooked counterpart and needs to be kept in the fridge. It's worth making if you know you'll eat it up quickly.

foraged treasures — enough to fill your jar

TO COVER

4 parts vinegar

4 parts water

1 part salt

1 part sugar (optional)

Wash the foraged treasures carefully and pick them over to remove any foreign material. Pack them into a sterilised jar.

Put the vinegar and water in a saucepan over a medium heat, then add the salt and sugar, if using. Stir until the salt and sugar have dissolved.

Let the liquid cool and pour it over the foraged goods.

Cover and refrigerate.

This pickle will be softer and nicer after a day or two, so let it sit if you can. It will keep for a week or so.

Lacto-fermented pickle

DF GF V

The beauty of lacto-fermenting foraged treasures is that you're doing double the foraging, as you're also harvesting the wild lacto-bacteria that fill the air around us to preserve your food. This recipe is based on the sauerkraut method popularised by fermentation master Sandor Katz.

Like the cooked pickle on page 199, you need a mixture of bulk and flavour. A glass or ceramic jar is best for the fermentation process, but some people do use plastic — just be sure to avoid reactive metals.

foraged treasures
salt (roughly 1 teaspoon per 250 g [9 oz] of plant material)

Wash the foraged treasures carefully and pick them over to remove any foreign material. Chop them as finely or chunkily as you like and arrange them in layers in a bowl, sprinkling each layer liberally with salt.

When everything is chopped and salted, stir to mix the salt in well. Pack the salted plant material into a large-mouthed sterilised jar, pressing down as you go. The salt will begin to draw water from the plant material immediately, forming a brine — pushing down on the mix will aid this process.

When all the plant material has been packed into the jar, sit a smaller jar or glass into the mouth of the larger jar and fill it with water. This acts as a weight, holding the plant material below the surface of the brine.

Cover the whole thing with a tea towel to keep out insects and dust. Over the next 24 hours, press down on the weight from time to time to force more water from the plant material.

If the brine hasn't risen well above the base of the weight within 24 hours, add a little extra salt water to make sure the plant material is fully submerged. Once the brine level is permanently above the plant matter, remove the weight.

Leave your jar of pickle covered or lidded in a cool, dark place to ferment —

somewhere it can't be knocked over. Check on it once a day. A bit of mould may form on the surface of the brine. As long as the plant material remains submerged, this isn't a problem and you can simply skim it off.

You may want to taste the pickle from time to time. When you're happy with the taste, seal the jar and store it in a cool, dark place until required. It should last 2–3 months, and possibly more. Refrigerate once opened.

POSSIBILITIES FOR THE BULK OF PICKLES

Apples; borage leaves; Brassicaceae leaves; chamomile flowers; chenopodium leaves; chestnuts; chickweed leaves and stems; clover flowers; dandelion and other DYC buds; dead-nettle leaves; fern fiddleheads; harakeke seeds (fleshy white seeds); ice plant leaves; kōkihi leaves and berries; mallow leaves and seedpods; miner's lettuce leaves; nasturtium leaves, buds and flowers; onion grass fruits; onion weed bulbs and leaves; pears; plantain leaves, finely chopped; plums; purslane leaves; quinces, finely chopped; seaweed; tī kōuka shoots; ureure; walnuts — green or ripe and shelled; yarrow leaves.

POSSIBILITIES FOR FLAVOURING AND COLOURING PICKLES

Borage flowers; Brassicaceae flowers; citrus zest; fennel leaves, flowers and pollen; harakeke pollen; kawakawa leaves, fruits and dried peppercorns (see page 124); marigold petals; nasturtium flowers and stems; onion weed; pine, fir or spruce tips; rosemary leaves and flowers; tūtae kōau leaves and flowers; wild mustard leaves, flowers and seedpods; wood sorrel leaves, flowers and stems.

NON-FORAGED FOODS TO ADD TO PICKLES

It's satisfying to make a pickle almost entirely from foraged foods, but you might want to add a few bought or home-grown vegetables. Here are some ideas:

- Add garlic and/or chopped onion if you don't have onion weed or another wild allium in the mix.
- Add traditional ingredients such as chopped cucumber, cabbage, cauliflower or broccoli.
- Add raisins and currants for extra sweetness.
- Add parsley, bay leaves, fresh or dried chilli and cumin, cloves and cinnamon, either whole or ground, for extra flavouring.

Curing olives

This is an easy method and ideal if you've gathered only a few ripe olives, although it can be scaled up for bigger hauls. You'll need a sterilised jar, large enough to hold the olives, and a clean muslin square to cover the jar.

2 cups salt, plus extra for bottling
2 cups freshly picked, unblemished, fully ripe black olives

Mix the salt and olives together well in a large bowl, then pour or spoon the olives and salt into the sterilised jar. Pour extra salt over the top so the olives are well covered. Cover the jar with muslin.

After a week, pour the olives out into a bowl and give them a quick mix or shake. Place the olives back into the jar and add a layer of new salt over the top. Cover with the muslin again.

Repeat this every week for 4–6 weeks until the olives are edible (note that they will always be a little bitter). When you're happy with the taste, pour the mix into a sieve and shake to get rid of the excess salt. Lay the olives out to dry at room temperature for 12–24 hours.

To store the olives, mix them with a little more salt and then cram them into a sterilised jar. They should keep for 3–4 weeks in a pantry, or up to 6 months in the refrigerator.

You can eat the olives straight or use them in cooking. For eating as is, you may want to rinse off the salt and soak them generously in oil and herbs — perhaps foraged.

ALTERNATIVE

You can also cure olives in brine (roughly 1 part salt to 10 parts water). Usually, people change the brine every week or two, but to be honest I've changed it much less frequently and the olives have still been delicious. Let them cure for 3–6 months, trying them now and then to see what you think. Many people slit the olives at the start of the process.

Recipes

Foraging throws open the doors to a pantry of ingredients that are often new and exciting yet also have reassuringly familiar qualities. That gives you plenty of scope for trying out ideas and inventing recipes, but those familiar aspects of each plant — flavour, texture or some other resemblance to an ingredient you already know — can give you a solid foundation to work from.

The recipes in this section are simple and streamlined, and are intended to be used as templates that allow you to swap ingredients in and out. You can stick to them closely or diverge from them wildly, and you can use them with varied wild plants, adapting the ingredients and methods to suit your tastes. At the end of each recipe is a list of suggestions for foraged ingredients. You can also look up the main entry on any of those ingredients to get more tips for using them. Some of the recipes use freshly foraged plants, while others use preserves from the previous section of the book as building blocks.

When life is busy, you have to be efficient to incorporate foraging into your cooking. The non-foraged ingredients in these recipes are cheap and accessible, while the methods are quick, with simple measurements. That means the recipes are easy to memorise for added speed, and also simple to scale up or down, as foraging can be unpredictable and you don't always know how much of any given ingredient you're going to find. Where possible, I've also tried to ensure the recipes either don't use any fancy kitchenware, or allow you to improvise.

The adventure is as much about discovering what you can do with wild plants as it is about heading out and gathering them.

The dietary-requirements key on page 164 applies throughout this section.

Creative cooks are by nature foragers, they forage for ideas as they do for great ingredients.

— SALLY SCHNEIDER, *THE IMPROVISATIONAL COOK*, 2006

Flavour combinations

Foraged plants give you a wide palette of flavours to work with. Many cooks prefer to star just one interestingly flavoured foraged ingredient in an otherwise simple dish so the flavours don't muddy one another. However, there are a few tried-and-true combinations and starting points for experimentation.

- Mānuka, or a sparing addition of soft-scented lavender, adds nuance to a range of fruits and berries, from lemons and plums to blackberries. Beware that lavender readily overpowers. If in doubt, use much less than you think to start with.
- Rose infusions are delicious with both plums and apples.
- In general, you can't go far wrong if you blend one flower flavour with one fruit flavour.
- A citrus flavour will go with almost any other, making it sparkle. For starters, fennel and orange is a popular combination.
- Pine, fir and spruce all have citrus notes and, like citrus, they will go with all sorts of other flavours. *Some* pine has an overbearing flavour, so treat it as you would lavender.
- Ingredients like nettle and jasmine have a rough earthiness to them that sometimes doesn't work as well on its own as it does combined with more smoothly or brightly flavoured ingredients.
- A hot flourish of horopito can be added to many other infusions, in the same way you might add chilli to various sweet or savoury dishes for extra bite.
- In savoury herb combos, onion weed or one of the other alliums will go with pretty much anything.
- Kawakawa, parsley, nasturtium, wood sorrel and tūtae kōau can be combined interestingly with one another.

Combining simple tisanes is one way to try out new flavour combinations without investing too much time or effort or wasting too many non-foraged ingredients.

Many of the same hints for combining apply to both cookery and perfumery. For example, both cooks and perfumers find inspiration in pondering the subtle background flavours or aromas that they like in an initial ingredient, deciding what they are reminiscent of, then finding a second ingredient that has those qualities in greater quantity to bolster them (see 'Found perfumes' section, page 293).

Super-salads

You can toss a few foraged treasures into a salad of cultivated greens or make a whole salad from your harvest. Either way, it'll pack a health punch: wild-growing foods are often more dense with nutrients than cultivated foods, which tend to have been bred for sweetness, size, appearance, shelf life and uniformity.

Mixing and matching flavours

To make a wild salad, always choose the lushest, healthiest bits of plant and serve them while they're still fresh. Think about the individual flavours of your pickings. Blend foraged ingredients that have a variety of tastes, choosing from two or more taste groups, then, if you like, add a complementary dressing.

It's a good idea to make sure bitter greens don't make up more than about one third of your salad. You can manage the bitters by adding something crisp, fatty and/or salty — this explains the traditional popularity of dandelion leaf and bacon salads. Sundried tomatoes or delicious roasted nuts are just as good for balancing bitter greens, as is well-seasoned oily fish.

Bitterness comes from alkaline chemicals, which can be neutralised with sour acidic ingredients such as lemon juice, lime juice and vinegar. However, if you use an acidic dressing on a salad of bitter leaves, you'll still taste the bitterness strongly when you bite into the leaves. You may prefer to pound a good harvest of bitters and sours together — for example, in a pesto.

Below is a list of foraged salad ingredients, divided into taste groups. Note that some plants appear on more than one list.

MILD GREENS AND FLOWERS

- borage leaves and flowers
- chenopodium leaves
- chickweed leaves and stems
- cleavers leaves
- clover flowers, broken up
- dead-nettles
- mallow leaves and flowers
- miner's lettuce leaves
- young plantain leaves (finely chopped)

MUSTARDY GREENS AND FLOWERS

- Brassicaceae leaves and flowers
- nasturtium leaves, flowers, buds and seedpods

BITTER GREENS AND FLOWERS

- Brassicaceae leaves and flowers
- fuchsia flowers, well chopped
- pūhā, dandelion and other DYC leaves

SOUR GREENS

- kōkihi
- purslane
- wood sorrel

AROMATIC GREENS AND FLOWERS

- fennel leaves or stalks, finely chopped
- jasmine flowers
- kawakawa leaves, well chopped and used sparingly
- mānuka flowers
- parsley leaves
- rose petals
- rosemary flowers
- scented pelargonium flowers
- sweet william petals
- tūtae kōau leaves
- wild celery leaves

CRUNCHY, JUICY GREENS

- fern fiddleheads
- kōkihi berries
- onion grass fruits
- purslane
- sea lettuce and other delicate seaweeds
- tī kōuka shoots, chopped and raw, or pre-cooked
- ureure

SALTY GREENS

- kōkihi leaves and berries
- sea lettuce and other delicate seaweeds
- ureure

ONIONY GREENS AND FLOWERS

- onion weed leaves and flowers, and those of other wild alliums

COLOUR

- borage flowers
- clover flowers, pulled apart
- dandelion and other DYC flowers, pulled apart
- elderflowers, stalks removed
- fennel pollen
- fuchsia flowers, chopped finely
- gorse flowers
- jasmine flowers
- mallow flowers
- mānuka petals
- marigold petals
- nasturtium petals
- onion weed flowers
- pansies and violets
- pelargonium flowers — scented and unscented
- rosemary flowers
- sweet william flowers
- wood sorrel flowers

FRUIT TO ADD, CHOPPED OR WHOLE

- apples
- blackberries
- citrus fruits
- coprosma berries
- fuchsia berries
- kahikatea, rimu or tōtara berries

- kawakawa fruits
- pears
- plums
- tātarāmoa berries

DELICIOUS EXTRAS

- chestnuts, boiled or roasted and chopped up
- fennel pollen
- harakeke seeds or pollen
- pine pollen
- walnuts
- wild mustard seeds

Shred or tear?

You can shred your ingredients to make a weedslaw or you can roughly tear them into pieces to make a light, bouncy green salad (don't make the pieces too small). For a green salad to be attractively light and bouncy, there should be gaps between the leaves. Cultivated salad greens have curves, frills and wrinkles that help with airiness, but with foraged greens you have to make more effort to achieve that effect. Use the youngest, tenderest leaves you can find so that you can leave them whole, and even leave some stems on to add shape. Include miner's lettuce and/or chickweed, if you can. They're great salad volumisers.

Check the hairiness or stringiness of all ingredients. If they're stringy, be sure to chop them finely; if they're hairy, chop them finely and don't use too much.

Dressings

The right dressing can make a salad. Adding sweetness, saltiness or strong, bright flavours like citrus zest to your dressing helps cut through the taste of bitter greens in a salad and balances out mustardy greens. On the other hand, if your salad is full of salty plants, you may not need any added salt.

Basic vinaigrette

DF GF V

Use this vinaigrette plain, or add strong, delicious flavourings, such as crushed garlic, citrus zest, a dash of soy sauce or miso, extra balsamic vinegar, a dab of nut butter, a few pinches of sugar or some fine gratings of Parmesan cheese. You can also raid your store of dried foraged ingredients (see page 194).

1 part vinegar
3 parts oil
salt and pepper, to taste

Put your dressing ingredients in a screw-top jar or bottle and shake to combine.

Pour just enough dressing to coat the salad into the bottom of the salad bowl. Put the salad on top.

To toss, use forks or your very clean hands. Reach down the sides of the bowl to the bottom, gently lifting and turning the greens to coat them with dressing. Tossing the salad from the bottom helps retain its lightness and each manoeuvre brings up a little of the dressing at a time.

VARIATIONS

- Use a wild infused vinegar or oil (see pages 175 and 181).
- Use a mucilage extracted from wild ingredients instead of oil (see page 103).

Basic mayonnaise

DF GF

I could rarely get mayonnaise to emulsify until I discovered this technique, which works just about every time.

2 egg yolks
1–2 teaspoons vinegar
1 cup rice bran oil
1–2 teaspoons lemon juice
salt and pepper, to taste

Put a cloth over the top of a saucepan and place your mayonnaise-making bowl into that. This will prevent it from spinning as you whisk.

Put the yolks and vinegar into the bowl and whisk until well combined.

Add the oil, a dribble at a time, to the eggs, whisking continuously. If it gets hard to do both, rest your pouring arm and just keep whisking.

The mixture will become paler and creamier when it emulsifies.

Continue until all the oil has been added.

Once the oil is in and emulsified, you can relax a bit. Add the lemon juice and salt and pepper, to taste.

Store in an airtight container in the fridge. It should last at least a couple of days.

VARIATIONS

Add 2–3 heaped teaspoons of finely chopped foraged herbs.

POSSIBILITIES

Good foraged herbs to add include: Brassicaceae flowers; fennel leaves or pollen; harakeke pollen and citrus zest; kawakawa leaves; lavender or rosemary flowers; nasturtium leaves or flowers; onion weed (all parts); parsley; pine spruce or fir tips; scented pelargonium flowers; tūtae kōau; wild celery; wood sorrel.

SALAD ACCOMPANIMENTS

A large serving of wild salad makes a satisfying meal when served with a baked potato or kūmara, or an egg, or both. The potatoes themselves can be garnished with wild herbs or finished with a knob of blended butter (see page 179).

Omelettes offer more opportunities for throwing in foraged ingredients or some wild herb cottage cheese (see page 220). Everyone has their favourite way of cooking an omelette, but mine is Julia Childs' fast and furious method, which you can see in several different videos on YouTube. Omelettes cooked this way never come out too dry, and once you master the method, or even nearly master it, you'll be able to churn out omelettes for a large group of people in double-quick time. It's true that you'll have best results with the size and shape of pan Childs specifies, but it's also possible to do so without, as long as you use a pan with sloping sides. At a pinch, you can even use a wok.

Snacks

Parmesan crisps

GF

A few of these crisps with a substantial wild salad makes for a light summer lunch. They're also ideal to serve with drinks. If you can, grate the cheese so it's in long, thin threads. Makes a big plateful, enough for 4 or more people.

1 cup finely grated Parmesan or tasty cheese
1 teaspoon standard plain flour
around 2 tablespoons very finely chopped fresh foraged greens, herbs or flowers, or 1 tablespoon dried and crumbled foraged herbs

Preheat the oven to 200°C (400°F) and line an oven tray with baking paper.

Use a whisk or fork to mix all of the ingredients together lightly but well.

Using a teaspoon, drop small piles of the mix onto the oven tray, pressing down on them a little with the back of the spoon.

Bake until they are bubbly and browning slightly around the edges. This won't take long if your oven is preheated: check them after 3 minutes, then every 30 seconds or so after that.

Remove from the oven and carefully slide the paper with the crisps onto a wire rack to cool. Note that they won't crisp up until they have fully cooled.

Store the cooled crisps in an airtight container until required. They last for only a day or so before losing their crispness.

POSSIBILITIES

The following are all good additions to these tasty crisps: Brassicaceae flowers, leaves and/or seeds; citrus zest; fennel leaves, flowers or pollen; harakeke seeds or pollen; kawakawa leaves; nasturtium leaves; nettle leaves; onion weed; parsley; pine pollen, and pine, spruce or fir tender young tips; rosemary leaves or lavender flowers; tūtae kōau; wild celery; wood sorrel.

Rice crackers

DF GF V

These homemade crackers are free of additives. Makes a snack for 4.

1 cup rice flour
1½ teaspoons baking powder
1 teaspoon salt
⅔ cup water
soy sauce

Preheat the oven to 180°C (350°F) and line 2 oven trays with baking paper.

Whisk together the rice flour, baking powder and salt. Pour in the water and mix quickly with a wooden spoon.

Using a teaspoon, place small, evenly-sized dollops of mixture onto the oven trays. Spread them into thin puddles with the back of the spoon. They will spread a little while cooking, so place them a reasonable distance apart.

The crackers cook around the edges faster than in the middle. To help them cook evenly, make a small dip in the middle of the uncooked mixture with the back of the teaspoon before placing them in the oven.

Bake until they've begun to brown all over — start checking after 5 minutes.

Remove from the oven and place the trays on cooling racks. Working quickly, brush each cracker lightly with soy sauce and leave to harden.

Store them in an air-tight container, but preferably eat within a few hours because they don't store well.

POSSIBILITIES

Add 2–3 teaspoons of finely chopped foraged greens, flowers or seeds to the mixture. Try one or more of: Brassicaceae flowers, leaves and seeds; citrus zest; fennel leaves, flowers or pollen; harakeke seeds or pollen; kawakawa leaves; nasturtium leaves; nettle leaves; onion weed; parsley; pine, spruce or fir tips; rosemary flowers or leaves; tūtae kōau; wild celery; wood sorrel.

TIP

The trickiest bit to these crackers is catching them at the precise moment when they have browned enough to be crisp and lose their bland raw taste, but haven't yet become so brown that they're bitter. Start with a small test batch.

Forager's damper

DF V

Add anything from 1 tablespoon to 1 handful of the finely chopped foragings, fresh or dried, according to your preference and how strong the wild flavours are. This makes 8 good slices.

3 cups standard plain flour, plus extra for dusting
4 teaspoons baking powder
1½ teaspoons salt
90 g (3¼ oz) butter or butter substitute, chopped
½ cup milk or milk substitute, plus a little extra for brushing
½ cup water
finely chopped foraged herbs or greens

Preheat the oven to 200°C (400°F). Grease an oven tray or line with baking paper.

Sift the flour, baking powder and salt into a bowl. Rub in the butter or butter substitute until the mixture looks sandy.

Add the milk and water, sprinkle in the foraged herbs or greens, and mix together very lightly.

Turn out onto a floured surface, knead gently into a 15 centimetre-diameter (6 inch) circle and place onto the oven tray.

With a sharp knife, make four cuts across the dough in a star shape, about 1 centimetre (½ inch) deep. Brush the top of the dough with the extra milk.

Bake for 10 minutes or until golden brown, then reduce the temperature to 180°C (350°F) and bake for another 15 minutes.

POSSIBILITIES

Great additions to damper include: borage leaves and flowers; chenopodiums; cleavers, young leaves; clover flowers, broken up; dandelion and other DYC greens and flower petals; dead-nettles; fennel leaves, flowers and pollen; fern fiddleheads; harakeke seeds or pollen; kawakawa leaves; kōkihi; lavender flowers; mallow leaves; marigold petals; nasturtium leaves, flowers, buds and seedpods; nettle; onion weed; parsley; pine pollen and pine, spruce or fir young, tender tips; plantain, young leaves; pūhā; rosemary leaves and flowers; scented pelargonium flowers; tūtae kōau; wild celery; yarrow, young leaves.

Wild herb pesto

DF GF V

Chickweed is the most beloved of foraged pesto ingredients because it's an especially creamy plant when pounded or puréed. However, there are many other wild-growing herbs you can also add. If you're using bitter ingredients such as dandelion leaves, consider pre-boiling them for 5–10 minutes in a large saucepan of water, but remember to drain them well. This is also a good time to use lemon or lime juice to reduce bitterness. Because the bitters are crushed and their juices released, added lemon juice will do a good job of neutralising some of the bitterness. This recipe makes more than 1 cup of pesto.

1 clove garlic
2 big pinches of salt
2 cups foraged greens, torn up and loosely packed
¼ cup olive oil
½ cup cashew nuts
⅓ cup dried breadcrumbs or grated Parmesan cheese

Pound the garlic and salt with a mortar and pestle. Gradually add the greens, continuing to pound.

Gradually add the oil and nuts, until you have a smooth, thick paste.

Stir in the breadcrumbs or Parmesan.

Alternatively, use a blender for all the ingredients except the Parmesan or breadcrumbs, stirring these through the pesto by hand.

POSSIBILITIES

Among the many wild greens you can include in pesto are: borage leaves and flowers; Brassicaceae leaves, especially cress; chenopodiums; citrus flowers; dandelion, pūhā and other DYC leaves; dead-nettles; fennel leaves, flowers and pollen; harakeke pollen; kawakawa leaves (sparingly); mallow leaves; miner's lettuce; nasturtium leaves, flowers and seedpods; nettle leaves (briefly pre-cooked to remove the sting); onion weed leaves and flowers or other wild alliums; parsley; tūtae kōau; wild celery; wood sorrel. If you can gather enough borage petals to use them alone, you can make an amazing blue pesto – use it up as soon as you make it, though, as the colour fades.

TIPS FOR SERVING PESTO

- Dollop onto raw or cooked vegetables.
- Stir through pasta as a quick and easy sauce.
- Add to vinaigrette or mayonnaise (see recipes, page 213).
- Mix with sour cream or yoghurt to make a creamy dip.
- Use in sandwiches (see page 227).

Three easy cheeses

On the following pages are three simple cheese recipes that make a fantastic canvas for foraged flavours. The very best milk or cream to use for these are unpasteurised products bought direct from the farm gate. If you can't get these (and many of us can't), try full-fat milk that hasn't been homogenised.

To make a firmer cheese, use a cheese press or create your own makeshift version. Wrap the cheese tightly in muslin to form a little package. Sandwich the wrapped cheese between 2 chopping boards, and weigh down the top of these with something heavy. Bit by bit, add more weight over the next 2–3 hours. Increasing amounts of whey will seep out, until the curd holds together strongly. This doesn't work as well as a proper cheese press, but it's quite adequate.

There are many uses for these cheeses in your other foraged dishes: as toppings for pizza, added to soup or pasta before serving, or served with crackers and a foraged pickle (see page 199).

Wild herb cottage cheese

GF

If you're tossing up between using citric acid or citrus juice, bear in mind that the juice may not curdle the milk quite as strongly but it will add a pleasant taste. Makes about 2 cups.

2 litres (3½ pints) mik
juice of 2 lemons or limes or ¼ teaspoon citric acid
¼–½ cup foraged treasures, finely chopped
salt to taste

Place the milk in a saucepan and heat over a medium heat until bubbles begin to form on the surface around the edge.

Remove the saucepan from the heat and add the lemon juice or citric acid. Leave to cool and curdle.

When cool, strain through muslin and let drip for half an hour or more.

Place the cheese in a bowl. Stir in finely chopped foraged greens and a little salt to taste.

Cover and store in the fridge until ready to use.

POSSIBILITIES

Good foraged herbs to add include: Brassicaceae flowers; fennel leaves or pollen; harakeke pollen and citrus zest; kawakawa leaves; lavender or rosemary flowers; nasturtium leaves or flowers; onion weed (all parts); parsley; pine spruce or fir tips; scented pelargonium flowers; tūtae kōau; wild celery; wood sorrel.

Mascarpone

GF

Soft, rich mascarpone is a hugely versatile cheese that can be used in both sweet and savoury dishes. You can serve sweet mascarpone as a dessert in its own right, or as an accompaniment to a pie or pudding. Makes about 2 cups.

1 litre (1¾ pints) cream
juice of 2 large lemons or 4 small ones

Place the cream in a saucepan and heat over a medium heat until bubbles begin to form on the surface around the edge.

Remove the saucepan from the heat and add the lemon juice. Leave to cool and curdle.

When cool, strain through muslin and let drip for half an hour or more.

Place the mascarpone in a bowl, cover, and store in the fridge until required. It should last 3–4 days.

TO MAKE SAVOURY MASCARPONE

Stir in a little salt and some finely chopped foraged herbs (see 'Possibilities' for wild herb cottage cheese and use as you would cottage cheese).

TO MAKE SWEET MASCARPONE

- Stir in a little icing sugar and some finely chopped fragrant petals — try rose, lavender, rosemary, scented pelargonium or sweet william. Fennel pollen and finely grated citrus zest are also delicious.
- Stir in (or just pour over) some infused syrup or honey (see recipes, pages 170 and 184).

Crowdie

GF

This is a traditional Scottish cream cheese. As it uses rennet, you'll need a thermometer. Rennet – both the traditional and vegetarian versions – is available from any good cheesemaking supplies store. Makes 2 cups or more.

2 litres (3½ pints) milk
½ tsp rennet
100–300 ml (3½–10½ fl oz) cream
salt to taste
¼–½ cup finely chopped foraged treasures

Put the milk in a saucepan over a low heat and warm to 30°C (86°F). Remove from the heat and add the rennet. Leave to cool and curdle.

When cool, strain through muslin and let drip for half an hour or more.

Add the cream and salt, and beat or whisk until the mixture forms a paste.

Add the foraged greens and stir through.

Cover, cool, and store in the fridge for up to 3 days.

POSSIBILITIES

For starters, try: Brassicaceae flowers or seeds; chamomile flowers; fennel leaves or pollen; harakeke pollen or citrus zest; kawakawa leaves; marigold petals; nasturtium leaves and flowers; onion weed leaves and flowers; parsley; rose petals; rosemary flowers; tūtae kōau; wild celery; wood sorrel.

Meals — light and fresh

Souped-up weeds

All sorts of soup recipes from around the world can be adapted for use with your wild local foods. This section includes a couple of simple favourites.

Ready-to-go soup base

DF GF V

If you keep this base in the freezer, bagged into single or multiple servings, you'll always be ready to make a healthy vegetable soup in a flash with any foraged greens or other wild vegetables as you find them. If you have a nightshade allergy, replace the tomatoes and potatoes with 8 kūmara. Makes 8 servings.

- a slug of cooking oil and/or a large knob of butter
- 8 onions, chopped
- 8 carrots, chopped
- 8 potatoes or kūmara, chopped (optional addition for a more substantial soup)
- 8 tomatoes, chopped

Put the oil and/or butter in a saucepan over a low to medium heat.

Add the onions and cook gently until softened and browned. Remove from the heat and set aside to cool.

Blanch the carrots and potatoes or kūmara (see 'Freezing vegetables', page 192) and then pat them dry.

Gently mix the blanched vegetables with the onions and chopped tomatoes in a bowl until they're evenly distributed.

Divide the mixture into containers or freezer bags — the recipe makes eight servings of soup, so portion it out according to how you think you'll use these.

Place the bags in a single layer in the freezer until the contents have frozen. They can then be stacked for use later.

TO USE THE SOUP BASE

When you come home with wild greens or other treasures that would make a good soup, grab a bag of soup base and throw the contents into a saucepan.

Add a cup of water or stock per serving. Put a lid on the soup mix and simmer for around half an hour, then add your foraged greens and continue simmering until they're cooked as you like them. Add salt and pepper to taste, and perhaps a dash of balsamic vinegar, coconut aminos, soy sauce or miso.

Serve the soup on its own, with a dollop of mascarpone (see page 222) or wild herb cottage cheese (see page 220), or a sprinkling of Parmesan.

POSSIBILITIES

Wild edibles to add to your soup base include: borage leaves and flowers; Brassicaceae leaves, especially cress; chenopodiums; chickweed, chopped to lengths of 2 centimetres (1 inch) or less; cleavers, young leaves; dandelion, pūhā and other DYC leaves; dead-nettles; dove's-foot cranesbill; fennel pollen or finely chopped stalks; fern fiddleheads; kawakawa leaves (sparingly); kōkihi; mallow leaves and seedpods; miner's lettuce; nasturtium leaves, flowers and seedpods; nettle leaves; onion weed leaves and flowers or other wild alliums; parsley; plantains, young leaves; purslane; sea lettuce and seaweeds; tī kōuka hearts; tūtae kōau; ureure; wild celery; wood sorrel; yarrow leaves.

Miso soup

DF V

Miso is customarily made with dashi (see 'Making dashi', page 226), but a fish or chicken stock will also work well. Adding soba noodles makes this hearty enough for a lunch or dinner. As for foraged extras, there are plenty of options, but I particularly like melty mallow leaves in a thin broth like this. Serves 2.

- 1 helping of soba noodles (optional)
- 2–4 tablespoons miso paste, or to taste
- 3 cups dashi, other stock or water
- 1 cup cubed tofu
- 2 spring onions or onion weed plants, finely chopped (optional)
- finely chopped foraged greens

If using soba noodles, pre-cook them according to the packet instructions, then rinse under cold running water.

Stir the miso into a few teaspoons of the dashi, stock or water to make a thinner paste. Put the rest of the stock into a saucepan over a medium heat and bring to a gentle boil.

Add the tofu, the chopped spring onion / onion weed, if using, and the foraged greens to the liquid. Bring back to the boil and remove from the heat.

Stir the thinned miso paste into the soup and pour into serving bowls.

If using soba noodles, divide them among the serving bowls.

POSSIBILITIES

Some good foraged greens to include are: borage leaves and flowers; Brassicaceae leaves, especially cress; chenopodiums; chickweed, chopped to lengths of 2 centimetres (1 inch) or less; cleavers, young leaves; dandelion, pūhā and other DYC leaves; dead-nettles; dove's-foot cranesbill; fennel pollen or finely chopped stalks; fern fiddleheads; kōkihi; mallow leaves and seedpods; miner's lettuce; nasturtium leaves, flowers and seedpods; nettle leaves; onion weed leaves and flowers or other wild alliums; plantains, young leaves; purslane; tī kōuka hearts; tūtae kōau; ureure; wood sorrel; yarrow leaves. For an amazing bite, add a few horopito leaves to the boiling liquid and remove them at the last minute.

MAKING DASHI

Dashi is the stock used in Japan as a base for miso soup, giving it its distinctive taste. You can still make a delicious miso-based soup without it, or with a different stock. It is generally made with dried kelp and dried fish flakes — usually bonito but sometimes sardines, anchovies or other fish. It's also made with shiitake mushrooms.

When gathering kelp to make dashi, collect only the small, young straps. Cut or slice them thinly and dry-roast them gently at around 150°C (300°F) until crisp. They can then be stored until you need them, and will swell again once placed in water.

To make dashi, place pieces of dried seaweed — adding up to a surface area about the same size as your hand — in a saucepan with 5–6 cups of water over a medium heat. Heat slowly and take the stock off the stove just before it boils. Remove the kelp and add 1 cup of bonito flakes (available in most Asian food stores).

If using mushrooms instead of fish flakes, boil 1 cup chopped mushrooms first for around 10 minutes in the water, leave to cool, then add the kelp and proceed as above (shiitake are traditional, but button mushrooms work too).

Tea sandwiches with foraged fillings

DF V

Serve a varied selection of these dainty sandwiches at any one time.

- thinly sliced soft white or brown bread
- enfleuraged or blended butters (see recipes, pages 178–180)
- wild infused honeys (see recipes, pages 184–186)
- cheeses (see recipes, pages 219–223)
- mayonnaise (see recipe, page 213)
- wild mustards (see 'Harvesting wild mustard seeds', page 78)
- fresh foraged treasures and/or powdered dried wild herbs and greens (see 'The art of drying', page 194)

OPEN-FACED TEA SANDWICHES

Lay out the slices of bread and spread each with a thin layer of butter, honey, cheese, mayonnaise or mustard, making sure it goes right to the edges.

Sprinkle flower petals, small flowers, powdered herbs or greens, or citrus zest over them. Alternatively, lay decorative strips of shredded greens across them in even stripes, or use paper-thin fruit slices or crumbled walnuts.

Slice off the crusts, then cut each slice into fingers, squares or triangles.

CLOSED TEA SANDWICHES

Lay out the slices of bread in 2 rows and spread each with a thin layer of butter, honey, cheese, mayonnaise or mustard, making sure it goes right to the edges.

Sprinkle flower petals, small flowers or citrus zest over one row. Alternatively, scatter with shredded greens or crumbled walnuts, or arrange paper-thin fruit slices in strips. Place the remaining row of slices spread-side down on top.

Slice off the crusts, then cut each sandwich into small fingers, squares or triangles.

CLUB SANDWICHES

Lay out slices of bread in 3 rows and spread a thin layer of butter, honey, cheese, mayonnaise or mustard across the lower and middle rows, making sure it goes right to the edges.

Sprinkle flower petals, small flowers, shredded greens, crumbled walnuts, thin slices of fruit or citrus zest over the lower row. Then place the middle row, spread-side down, on top of the lower row.

Spread a layer of a different but complementary infused butter, honey, cheese, mayonnaise or mustard on the remaining row and place the slices spread-side down on the very top of the sandwiches.

Slice off the crusts, then cut each sandwich into fingers, squares or triangles.

PINWHEEL SANDWICHES

Lay out the slices of bread and spread each with a thin layer of butter, honey, cheese, mayonnaise or mustard, making sure it goes right to the edges.

Sprinkle flower petals, small flowers or citrus zest over the slices. Alternatively, lay strips of shredded greens across them, or paper-thin fruit slices in a single layer, or a scattering of crumbled walnuts.

Cut off the crusts and roll up the slices to form pinwheel logs (see 'Tips').

Slice the rolls into sections about 2 centimetres (1 inch) wide. Hold together with toothpicks, if required.

POSSIBILITIES

Below are some ideas for wild-treasures sandwich fillings:

- Small flowers such as borage, Brassicaceae, jasmine, mallow, scented pelargonium and rosemary, pulled from the sepals.
- Chopped or torn petals from flowers such as marigolds, roses, clovers, sweet william or chamomiles.
- Mild, chopped or shredded greens, such as chickweed, chenopodium, miner's lettuce, mallow and borage.
- More highly flavoured flora, chopped finely, such as the leaves and flowers of wood sorrel, onion weed, parsley, wild celery, tūtae kōau and fennel.
- Bitter greens such as pūhā, dandelion and other DYCs.
- Greens with an element of surprise, such as finely chopped numbing

kawakawa leaves, dried and powdered hot horopito, peppery nasturtium, cress or wild mustard seed.

- Harakeke pollen and seeds, fennel pollen and decorative slices of fern fiddleheads.
- Citrus zest.
- Paper-thin slices of firm foraged fruits, such as apples and pears.
- Fresh or roasted walnuts, chopped or crumbled.

TIPS

- You can add decorative edges to any tea sandwich by buttering one edge and dipping it into a bowl of very finely chopped fresh or dried wild herbs pounded to a powder.
- When making pinwheel sandwiches, wrap the logs in plastic wrap and put them in the fridge for an hour or so to make them easier to slice.
- It's easier to spread soft fillings onto semi-frozen bread.
- Using semi-frozen bread also makes it easier to avoid raggedy edges when removing crusts and cutting sandwiches into shapes.

Onion weed tempura

DF GF V

The key to good tempura is using ice-cold water in the batter and whisking it just before you're about to cook. The rice flour ensures a light-as-air batter. Test-cook a bit of batter first. If it's soggy, try hotter oil, colder batter or both, before cooking the rest. Allow 8–10 flowers per person if you're serving this as a snack, or a few more served alongside a salad for a light meal.

a few handfuls of onion weed flowers
1 egg or 1 tablespoon cornflour
1 cup icy water
1 cup rice flour
salt to taste
rice bran oil

Cut the flowers 1–2 centimetres (½–1 inch) below the point where they join the stalk. This holds the clusters together and gives you enough stalk to grip when you dip them in the batter.

If using an egg, whisk it in a bowl and then add the icy water and whisk some more. Add the rice flour and salt, and mix gently and briefly with a spoon.

If using cornflour, mix in a bowl with the rice flour and salt. Add the icy water, whisking as you go.

Don't overmix the batter and don't worry about lumps.

Put about 5 millimetres (¼ inch) of oil in a heavy-bottomed frying pan over a medium to high heat.

Once the oil is very hot, work quickly. Dip each flower into the batter and drop it into the oil. Don't cook too many flowers at once, as you don't want the temperature of the oil to drop.

When a battered flower is lightly browned on one side, turn it over — it won't take very long.

Remove each battered flower from the oil as soon as it's lightly brown on both sides, and place on a paper towel to drain.

Eat as is, or serve with a dipping sauce such as sweet horopito sauce (see recipe below).

POSSIBILITIES

Try making tempura from: whole borage leaves; new dandelion flowers; fern fiddleheads; whole kawakawa leaves; whole nasturtium flowers or leaves; clusters of pūhā flower buds; purslane leaves; sea lettuce; ureure stalks.

Sweet horopito sauce

Use this sauce as you would sweet chilli sauce. It's great with fritters.

¾ cup water
¼ cup vinegar
½ cup sugar
1 teaspoon salt
a good handful of fresh horopito leaves
3–6 cloves garlic, according to taste
¼ red capsicum
⅓ medium-sized carrot
1 tablespoon cornflour
10–15 centimetres (4–6 inches) cubed fresh ginger

Put the water, vinegar, sugar and salt into a saucepan and bring to a simmer.

Add the fresh horopito leaves. You may want to tear them up a little to help release their heat and flavour.

Simmer for 5–10 minutes.

Meanwhile, finely chop or mince the garlic cloves, deseed and chop the capsicum as finely as possible, and finely grate the carrot.

Strain the horopito from the liquid.

Add the garlic, capsicum and carrot to the liquid, and simmer for another 5–10 minutes.

Mix the cornflour with a little extra water and stir it into the hot liquid.

Simmer the mix for another minute or so until the cornflour is cooked. The liquid will be translucent.

Remove the saucepan from the heat.

Finely grate the fresh ginger and, by hand, squeeze the juice from the gratings into the saucepan and stir to combine.

Pour the hot sauce into hot, sterilised jars and seal.

The sauce should keep in a cool, dark place for up to 6 months, but refrigerate it to be certain.

Weedy pakoras

DF GF V

Chickpea flour (also called chana or gram flour) is full of protein, so this makes a sustaining snack for 2 people — or a light meal when served with a salad.

1 cup chickpea flour

1½ teaspoons curry powder or ground cumin

½ teaspoon baking powder

½ teaspoon salt

a big pinch of chilli powder or dried powdered horopito (optional)

2 cups finely chopped foraged greens, loosely packed down

2 tablespoons grated onion

water, if required

oil

Whisk the dry ingredients together. Add the greens and grated onion.

Mix to a very thick, dry batter. If necessary, add just enough water – a few drops at a time – to moisten the mixture so that it holds together.

Heat 1 centimetre (½ inch) of oil in a heavy-bottomed frying pan over a medium to high heat.

Dollop small spoonfuls of batter into the hot oil, or use wet hands to mould it into small patties and drop these in.

When the pakoras are golden brown on the underside, turn them over and fry on the other side.

When the patties have browned on both sides, remove them from the oil and place on a paper towel to drain.

Serve with yoghurt and/or relish.

POSSIBILITIES

The following foraged greens will work well on their own in pakoras, or in combination with one another: borage leaves and flowers; Brassicaceae leaves, especially cress; chenopodiums; chickweed, chopped to lengths of 2 centimetres (1 inch) or less; cleavers, young leaves; dandelion, pūhā and other DYC leaves; dead-nettles; dove's-foot cranesbill; fennel pollen or finely chopped stalks; fern fiddleheads; kawakawa leaves (sparingly); kōkihi; mallow leaves and seedpods; miner's lettuce; nasturtium leaves, flowers and seedpods; nettle leaves; onion weed leaves and flowers or other wild alliums; parsley; plantains, young leaves; purslane; sea lettuce and seaweeds; tī kōuka hearts; tūtae kōau; ureure; wild celery; wood sorrel; yarrow leaves.

TIP

If using very bitter greens, such as older dandelion leaves or wild mustard greens, you may want to reduce the bitterness by boiling them first for 2–5 minutes in a large pan of water, then leave them to drain well before chopping them and adding them to the batter. You'll need to squeeze some of the water out to avoid ending up with a batter that's too runny.

Stir-fried tofu and wild allium

GF DF V

This makes a tasty protein- and micronutrient-rich snack for 2, but can also be teamed with rice, noodles or a foraged green salad for a larger meal.

300 g (10.8 oz) packet of tofu, drained and cubed
a pinch or two of chilli powder
1 tablespoon rice bran oil
1 teaspoon grated fresh ginger
1 cup chopped onion weed or other wild allium
1 tablespoon tamari or shoyu
½ teaspoon sugar
½ teaspoon sesame oil or peanut oil
a dash of kecap manis or fish sauce (optional)

Pat the tofu dry and sprinkle with the chilli powder.

Preheat a wok or pan and add the rice bran oil. Add the grated ginger to the pan and fry for a few seconds.

Next, add the tofu and fry until browned on each side, then add the onion weed or other allium and fry until soft.

Add the tamari or shoyu, sugar, sesame oil or peanut oil, and kecap manis or fish sauce, if using. Stir gently to coat the tofu.

POSSIBILITIES

At the same time as you add the allium, add some wood sorrel, some finely chopped fennel stalks, or a few chopped nasturtium leaves, flowers or seedpods.

Ricotta panna cotta

GF

Savoury panna cotta is both delicious and satisfying. If you're using feta instead of ricotta, you may not need to add salt. With a salad, this serves 2–4 as a light meal.

4 leaves of gelatine

a handful or two of foraged greens or herbs, finely chopped

¾ cup milk

¾ cup cream

salt to taste

1 cup crumbled ricotta or feta

Put the gelatine leaves to soak in cold water (see 'Working with gelatine', page 252).

Put your foraged greens, milk, cream, salt and ricotta or feta into a saucepan over a gentle heat and stir until the cheese melts.

Take off the heat and leave to cool for 5 minutes.

Squeeze the water from the gelatine leaves and stir them into the warm mix until they're well dissolved and blended in.

Pour the panna cotta mix into a single bowl, or glasses or small ramekins for individual servings.

Cover and set aside to cool.

When cool, place in the fridge to set fully.

When set, serve the panna cotta as is, or unmould by gently running warm water on the back of the container, then upending it onto a serving plate or individual plates.

POSSIBILITIES

For your greens or herbs, try: borage leaves and flowers; Brassicaceae leaves, especially cress; chenopodiums; chickweed, chopped to lengths of 2 centimetres (1 inch) or less; citrus zest; cleavers, young leaves; dandelion, pūhā and other DYC leaves; dead-nettles; dove's-foot cranesbill; fennel pollen or finely chopped stalks; fern fiddleheads; kawakawa leaves (sparingly); kōkihi; mallow leaves and seedpods; miner's lettuce; nasturtium leaves, flowers and seedpods; nettle leaves; onion weed leaves and flowers or other wild alliums; parsley; plantains, young leaves; purslane; sea lettuce and seaweeds; tī kōuka hearts; tūtae kōau; ureure; wild celery; wood sorrel; yarrow leaves.

VARIATIONS

Vegetarians can use agar in place of gelatine — see 'Working with agar', page 253).

Meals — warming and filling

Potato-base pizza

DF GF V

If there's one thing pizza lovers take seriously, it's the thickness of their pizza base. Experiment until you find the exact thickness that works for you. You can use freshly mashed potatoes, but this is also a good way to use up leftovers. Makes a meal for 2 or a snack for 4.

1 cup mashed potatoes, made just how you like them
1 cup high-grade flour, but standard plain flour will do
salt to taste
tomato paste
1 clove garlic, crushed
a dash of balsamic vinegar, kecap manis or coconut aminos (optional)
foraged treasures for the topping
mozzarella or other grated cheese (vegan if desired)

Preheat the oven to 180°C (350°F) and grease an oven tray.

Mix the mashed potatoes and flour together, and add salt to taste.

Dollop the mixture onto the greased oven tray, and spread it in an even layer to cover the base. It should be around 5–8 millimetres (¼–⅜ inch) thick.

Place the pizza base in the oven and bake for around 10 minutes or until it begins to brown on top and feels as if it's forming a crispy crust when you tap it with a fork.

Mix together the tomato paste, garlic, and balsamic vinegar, kecap manis or coconut aminos. Spread this mixture evenly over the pizza base and scatter the foraged treasures over the top.

Finish with a scattering of grated cheese, and bake until the cheese is as melted or crisp as you like.

POSSIBILITIES

Below are just a few topping suggestions — pizza preferences are heartfelt and deeply personal!

- Blackberries with nuts and feta or another artisan cheese — perhaps your own wild herb cottage cheese (see recipe, page 220).

- Fern fiddleheads, lemon zest and sparsely scattered crumbs of lavender flowers.
- Fennel, onion weed and pickled nasturtium pods.
- Watercress and Parmesan.
- Kawakawa — a pizza topping par excellence, all on its own.
- Fennel and/or onion weed, slowly sautéed to caramelise it, with dabs of wild herb cottage cheese and some sliced almonds.

VARIATIONS

- Add yoghurt or leftover whey (see 'Three easy cheeses', page 219) to your mashed potatoes.
- Use mashed kūmara instead of potato, or a mix of the two.
- For a gluten-free base, use chickpea flour instead of wheat flour. You will need 1½ cups mashed potato and ½ cup chickpea flour.
- For a wholemeal base, use wholemeal flour and leave the flour and potato mixture to rest for several hours — this helps break down the fibres in the wholemeal flour so that it becomes more digestible. Using whey or yoghurt in the potato mix will aid the process further.
- In addition to your foraged toppings, try adding some finely chopped, strongly flavoured foraged foods to the base. Onion weed, kawakawa, nasturtium, wood sorrel, tūtae kōau, wild celery and parsley all work well.

TIP

If you find that some of the more delicate herb toppings dry and burn in the oven (this may happen if you don't use cheese or use it only sparingly), toss the greens in a bowl with a little vegetable oil before putting them on the pizza.

Scrounger's skirlie

GF DF V

Most of us are not used to thinking of oats as the basis for a savoury meal, but this traditional Scottish dish is a great way to use onion weed and other foraged greens. Serve it on its own, or make it more substantial by adding a poached egg, tofu or a vegetable mash. You can also serve it as a side dish with dinner instead of potatoes. Serves 2 as a light main or 4 as a side dish.

2 tablespoons olive oil
¾–1 cup finely chopped onion weed
1 teaspoon freshly chopped thyme or 2–3 chopped kawakawa leaves
1 cup rolled oats (gluten-free if required)
hot water
2 large handfuls of foraged greens, washed and torn up
salt to taste
black pepper or tākawa pepper (see recipe, page 124) to taste

Put the olive oil in a heavy-bottomed frying pan over a low to medium heat.

Add the onion weed and cook for 5 minutes until soft, stirring as it cooks.

Add the thyme or kawakawa. Reduce the heat and add the oats. Stir to combine.

Cook on a low heat for 5 minutes, until the oats have puffed up a bit and crisped.

Add a teaspoon or two of hot water to help the oats puff up more, and cook for another minute.

Stir in the foraged greens and cook until just wilted. Add salt and pepper, and serve warm.

POSSIBILITIES

Along with kawakawa and onion weed, the following foraged greens are great herbs for skirlie: borage leaves and flowers; Brassicaceae leaves, especially cress; chenopodiums; chickweed, chopped to lengths of 2 centimetres (1 inch) or less; citrus zest; cleavers, young leaves; dandelion, pūhā and other DYC leaves; dead-nettles; dove's-foot cranesbill; fennel pollen or finely chopped stalks; fern fiddleheads; kōkihi; mallow leaves and seedpods; miner's lettuce; nasturtium leaves, flowers and seedpods; nettle leaves; parsley; plantains, young leaves; purslane; sea lettuce and seaweeds; tī kōuka hearts; tūtae kōau; ureure; wild celery; wood sorrel; yarrow leaves.

Wild weed loaf

GF DF V

This delicious vegan loaf can be adapted to your taste. Serves 4–6.

2 tins of your favourite beans, well drained, or 3 cups of dried beans, cooked until very soft
2 medium onions
⅓ cup vegetable oil
3–4 cloves garlic, finely chopped
2 cups well-chopped foraged greens, packed lightly
100 g (3½ oz) tofu, chopped into 0.5 centimetre (¼ inch) cubes
3 tablespoons garlic salt or powdered stock
1 cup flour or breadcrumbs (gluten-free if required)
1 tablespoon tomato sauce

Preheat the oven to 180°C (350°F). Line a loaf tin with baking paper.

Mash the beans in a bowl, but not too thoroughly — you still want some interesting texture and a few bits.

Dice 1½ onions and set aside the remaining half.

Heat the vegetable oil over a low heat. Add the diced onion and fry gently for 10 minutes, stirring occasionally.

Add the garlic, and then grate in the remaining onion half. Keeping the heat very low, fry for another 5 minutes, stirring occasionally.

Add the chopped foraged greens and the tofu. Fry for another 5 minutes, continuing to stir.

Add the fried ingredients to the bean mix, along with the garlic salt or powdered stock and the flour or breadcrumbs, and stir well.

Pack into the lined loaf tin.

Spread the tomato sauce as a glaze over the top of the loaf.

Cover lightly with another sheet of baking paper and bake for around 45 minutes.

After taking the loaf from the oven, let it sit for at least half an hour to help it set. Serve it warm or cold, cut into slices and accompanied by a salad or vegetables.

POSSIBILITIES

Borage leaves and flowers; Brassicaceae leaves, especially cress; chenopodiums; chickweed, chopped to lengths of 2 centimetres (1 inch) or less; citrus zest; cleavers, young leaves; dandelion, pūhā and other DYC leaves; dead-nettles; dove's-foot cranesbill; fennel pollen or finely chopped stalks; fern fiddleheads; kawakawa leaves (sparingly); kōkihi; mallow leaves and seedpods; miner's lettuce; nasturtium leaves, flowers and seedpods; nettle leaves; onion weed leaves and flowers or other wild alliums; parsley; plantains, young leaves; purslane; sea lettuce and seaweeds; tī kōuka hearts; tūtae kōau; ureure; wild celery; wood sorrel; yarrow leaves.

VARIATION

In *The Trolls* by Polly Horvath, one of my favourite children's books, eccentric Aunt Sally encourages her nieces and nephew to eat their vegetables by making a surprise meatloaf with a different vegetable hidden in each section. It's fun to do this with foraged surprises, too.

For the surprises, try: dandelion buds and flowers; pre-boiled slices of ice plant; a small, plump piece of purslane; small, juicy kōkihi leaves or berries; a fern fiddlehead; a slice of tī kōuka heart; a nasturtium seedpod; a clover flower; a slice of sea lettuce; a strand of ureure; a mallow seedpod; a walnut; a piece of cooked sweet chestnut; an onion grass fruit; a blackberry; or a slice of foraged fruit.

TIPS

- Chop the greens as finely as you can, as this will help the loaf hold together.
- If you eat dairy products, substitute the tofu with feta cheese and cook the onion, garlic and foraged treasures in a 50:50 mix of oil and butter.
- If you have your own favourite vegan or vegetarian loaf recipe, use that and simply add in the gently fried foraged greens at the appropriate time – remembering to keep them chopped small.

Wild creamy sauce

GF DF V

Serve this stirred through cooked pasta as soon as it's ready. Top it with a sprinkling of finely chopped, freshly foraged herbs. This sauce also makes a moreish hot dip served with crackers, fingers of dense, toasted wholegrain bread or vegetable sticks. Serves 2–4.

- a splash of oil and/or knob of butter or butter substitute
- 2 large onions, peeled and grated or finely chopped, and/or 3 cloves garlic, crushed
- ½ cup wine or spirits (optional)
- 1–2 handfuls of foraged greens
- 1 cup soy or dairy cream
- salt and pepper to taste

Heat the oil and/or butter in a frying pan over a low to medium heat.

Add the onions and sauté until clear and beginning to brown. If using garlic, add just before the onions are ready. Add wine or spirits, if using, and simmer until evaporated.

Add the greens and simmer for a minute or two. Add the cream and simmer for another minute or two.

Season to taste and serve immediately.

POSSIBILITIES

Thinly sliced fennel stalks work really well as a foraged green in the recipe, and a scattering of sliced almonds on top at the end is a delicious final touch. Other especially flavoursome foraged items to use include: kawakawa leaves; kōkihi; nasturtium leaves and flowers; nettle leaves; onion weed or other alliums; parsley; rosemary flowers; sea lettuce; tūtae kōau; ureure; wild celery; wood sorrel. Other less highly flavoured greens will still be delicious, though.

VARIATIONS

- Turn it into a tomato cream sauce by adding tomato purée or diced tomatoes after the greens, and allowing to simmer before adding the cream.
- Use one of your own infused wines or spirits in the recipe.

Tasty breadcrumb pasta

DF V

Late winter and spring are the best times to make this recipe, as that's when onion weed is in full, lush bloom. Of course, if you dry onion weed you can have access to it all year round, but it's nicest fresh. If you're not blessed with a local patch of onion weed, you could use cultivated spring onion instead. Serves 2–4.

pasta — enough to serve everyone
½ cup olive oil
¾–1 cup finely chopped onion weed
¼ cup dried breadcrumbs
1–2 cups finely chopped foraged herbs and/or greens
salt and pepper to taste

Cook the pasta according to the packet instructions.

While the pasta is cooking, pour 2–3 tablespoons of the olive oil into a heavy-bottomed frying pan over a medium heat.

Add the onion weed and breadcrumbs, and sauté until the breadcrumbs are very crisp. Transfer the mixture to a bowl.

Meanwhile, pour the remaining oil into the chopped herbs and/or greens and toss together. Tip the well-drained hot pasta into the oil and herb mix, and stir through.

Put the tossed pasta into a warm bowl or individual serving bowls, and scatter the breadcrumb-onion weed mixture on top.

Serve immediately.

POSSIBILITIES

Flavoursome foraged items to use include: kawakawa leaves; kōkihi; nasturtium leaves and flowers; nettle leaves; parsley; rosemary flowers; sea lettuce; tūtae kōau; ureure; wild celery; wood sorrel. Other less highly flavoured greens will still be delicious, though.

PRINTED PASTA

If you like making pasta by hand, take your favourite recipe and adorn the pasta with foraged leaves and flowers. Suitable plants to use include onion weed flowers, cress leaves, small parsley or wild celery leaves, pot marigold petals, nasturtium petals, clover petals, nettle leaves, chamomile flowers, wood sorrel leaves or flowers, rosemary flowers, scented pelargonium flowers, borage flowers, sweet william flowers, chenopodium leaves and dead-nettle leaves.

Roll sheets of pasta dough through a pasta machine until they're as thin as possible. Sandwich the leaves and flowers between 2 sheets, and then put them through the roller once again. Use a clear butter- or oil-based sauce to show off the pasta.

Food writer Alessandra Zecchini makes miraculous creations in this way using all sorts of edible flowers. She simply cuts the pasta into shapes with a pastry cutter, cooks it in boiling water very briefly, then serves it with melted butter and a little Parmesan. Printed pasta also works well for ravioli.

Healthy wholemeal pasta

DF V

This is an unusual recipe for pasta, based on an idea that has been gaining support lately – that the healthiest and most digestible grains are wholemeal grains that have been fermented. Wholemeal flour with a particularly fine, even texture will give the best results. You may need to shop around to find it. Makes 4 large servings.

2 cups finely ground wholemeal flour, plus extra if the dough is too sticky
¼–1 cup very finely chopped foraged treasures
1 cup runny plain active yoghurt (use runny coconut yoghurt or kefir for a vegan pasta)

Sift the flour into a bowl. Add the finely chopped foraged treasures, and fork or whisk them through the flour.

Make a well in the middle of the flour and pour in the yoghurt.

Use a fork to stir the yoghurt, gradually incorporating the flour from around the edges. Switch to a wooden spoon, or just use your hands when it gets too hard to use the fork.

Lightly flour your bench and plonk the dough onto it. Begin to knead the dough, folding it over, pressing it down and turning it. Add extra flour if it's really sticky, but use as little as possible because the softer the dough is, the easier it is to knead.

Keep kneading until the dough feels smooth and a little silky. You may need to add an extra sprinkling of flour right at the end.

Let the dough sit back in its bowl and cover it with a damp tea towel or plastic wrap to stop it developing a crust.

Leave for about 24 hours.

Give it another quick knead, then use a pasta machine, according to the manufacturer's instructions, to roll out the pasta.

Use as you would use any other fresh pasta.

IF YOU DON'T HAVE A PASTA MACHINE

Shaping pasta by hand is an amazing art, and there are plenty of YouTube tutorials about it. Below are some suggestions to get you started.

- Roll the dough out and form it into little cupped shell shapes in your hands, or push over your thumbs to do so.
- Roll the dough between your fingers into tiny rice-grain shapes.
- Roll the dough out with a rolling pin until it is very thin and you can see through it slightly. Cut it into sheets to use as lasagne sheets, or cut it with a knife into tagliatelle or pappardelle noodles.

POSSIBILITIES

You can use all sorts of wild ingredients in this pasta. Find those with small, attractive leaves, flowers and petals.

Sweet treats

Many of these desserts and baked goods can be made using the infused butter, syrup and alcohol recipes in the previous chapter. Some recipes here also use infused milk or cream that is prepared fresh.

Foraged fruits make gorgeous desserts, and so do some foraged herbs. Wood sorrel's sour twang is nice in sweet dishes, and nettle can be an interesting and unexpected dessert green, too, if you balance it with vanilla.

Wild tea cake

DF V

My friend Wei Siew Leong (herself a keen forager) showed me the virtues of tea cakes. They're straightforward to make, delicious, filling, economical, convenient and very portable — whole or as slices.

2 cups extra-strong tisane of your choice
½ cup brown sugar or honey
3 cups mixed dried fruit
3 cups standard plain flour
3 teaspoons baking powder

While the tisane is still hot, stir a little of the sugar or honey into it. Pour the tisane over the dried fruit and leave to soak — overnight if possible.

When the fruit has softened, preheat the oven to 160°C (315°F) and grease a standard loaf tin.

Add the rest of the honey or sugar to the fruit and stir to combine.

Sift in the flour and baking powder, and mix to form a batter.

Pour the batter into the loaf tin and put into the oven, covered with a piece of baking paper or cooking foil.

Bake for around 45 minutes, or until you can insert a knife into the middle of the loaf and it comes out clean.

Remove the cake from the oven and stand on a cooling rack for a few more minutes before turning it out onto the rack.

Slice and serve warm with butter, a spread or on its own, or save to slice up cold for packed lunches.

Any-way-you-slice-it shortbread

DF GF V

Texture is everything when it comes to shortbread, and it's important to mix it as lightly as possible. Anything resembling kneading encourages the gluten in the flour to develop, and that works against the light texture you're after. Makes 8 very generous slices.

1 cup standard plain flour
¼ cup rice flour
a pinch of salt
⅓ cup caster sugar, plus a little extra for sprinkling on top (optional)
finely chopped foraged aromatics (see 'Possibilities' for quantities)
100 g (3½ oz) unsalted butter or butter substitute

Preheat the oven to 160°C (315°F) and grease or line a pie or flan dish or a baking tin that is around 25 centimetres (10 inches) in diameter.

Sift the plain flour, rice flour and salt into a bowl. Add the caster sugar and foraged aromatics.

Cut the butter into cubes and add to the dry ingredients.

Rub the butter into the flour between your thumbs and forefingers. When the mix looks mostly sandy with some bigger lumps, start scooping up handfuls and pushing them together into clumps — make sure you clump the mixture together and don't squish it.

Press the mixture into the dish or tin. Ensure the mix is a roughly even depth all over.

Bake for 15–20 minutes or until the shortbread is just faintly browning — it should still feel soft.

Stand it on a wire rack in its dish or tin and let it rest for 10–15 minutes.

Using a sharp knife, cut the shortbread into slices in the dish or tin. If you have a round dish, cut through the centre of the circle and divide into 16 pieces in a bicycle-spoke pattern.

Leave it to cool completely in the dish or tin. It will be brittle by then, but the slices should lift out easily.

Serve sprinkled with extra caster sugar, if using. Alternatively, serve it warm with sudden comfort ice cream (see recipe, page 256).

POSSIBILITIES

Use any of these foraged aromatics: fennel leaves, flowers or pollen; fir, pine or spruce tips; kawakawa; lavender flowers; mānuka or kānuka; finely chopped nettle plus a teaspoon of vanilla; rose petals; rosemary flowers; scented pelargonium flowers. You could also add citrus zest alongside any of these items. If using lavender, fennel pollen or a strong pine, add only 1–2 teaspoons. With any of the other plants you can add 1–2 tablespoons. Once you've made the recipe, you'll know if you'd like to add more aromatic treasures next time.

VARIATIONS

- For a gluten-free shortbread, use equal quantities of rice flour and cornflour.
- For a dairy-free shortbread, use virgin coconut oil instead of butter.
- Use a wild infused butter instead of plain butter (see recipes, pages 178–180).
- Add chopped, peeled chestnuts, or crushed or chopped foraged walnuts.

Buttercream icing

DF GF V

Make this icing using any enfleuraged or blended butter or butter substitute that's flavoured with citrus, fennel, kawakawa, lavender, jasmine, pine, fir, spruce, rose, scented pelargonium, sweet william or wood sorrel, all of which work well in sweet dishes.

Buttercream icing can be used to ice cakes, served with scones, spread between two biscuits or used as a filling for chocolates.

200 g (7 oz) softened butter or butter substitute
2½ cups icing sugar
5–6 teaspoons milk or milk substitute

Whisk or beat the butter until pale and fluffy.

Add the icing sugar a little at a time, beating well after each addition.

Dribble in the milk at the end, adding just enough to thin the mixture to the desired texture, which should be even lighter and fluffier.

Flower or fruit fritters

DF GF V

Elderflower and dandelion fritters are classic forager's fare — dandelion flowers make particularly cute, round, juicy fritters. However, you can use many other flowers or fruits. Serves 4 or more as a sweet snack.

Follow the tempura recipe on page 229, but replace the onion weed with less pungent flowers and pieces of fruit (see 'Possibilities', below).

Dip larger flowers into the batter and fry them individually. A mix made with small flowers can be spooned into the oil, much like making pancakes. Don't cook too many fritters at once, as the oil needs to hold its temperature.

When each fritter is golden brown on the underside, turn it over.

When it has browned on both sides, remove it from the oil and place on a paper towel to drain.

POSSIBILITIES

- Borage flowers; Brassicaceae flowers; chamomile; whole clover flowers or pieces of flowers; new dandelion or other DYC flowers; elderflowers (see 'Tips', below); pot marigold; rose petals; sweet william; wild jasmine.
- If using fruit, try peeled apple slices, peeled pear slices and firm, unripe plum slices. Batter them fresh or marinate them first in an infused liqueur or honey (see recipes, pages 188 and 184), or in butterscotch sauce (see recipe, page 259).
- Kawakawa fruits, blackberries and the choicest fuchsia berries also work well.

TIPS

- It's usual to remove stems from flowers and, if possible, sepals before dipping them in batter. But, if you like, you certainly can leave the stems on dandelion flowers, other DYCs and chamomile flowers as a handle to hold them as you eat them.
- Some people like to make elderflower fritters by dunking a cluster of flowers in batter, stems on, then frying the clusters, stem end up. To eat, you nibble the battered flowers off the stems. Other people prefer to snip the stems off while the fritters cook. However you do it, get rid of as much stem as possible.

The green bits of elder are indigestible and mildly toxic, although most people seem to be able to tolerate a small amount.

Fruit jelly

DF GF V

As I discovered at my daughter's birthday picnic one midsummer day, homemade jellies can melt if they get too hot! Keep them cool until you're ready to serve them — it's worth the effort to capture the fresh fruity flavours of real food. In the following recipes you can use gelatine powder instead of leaves (see 'Working with gelatine', page 252). You can also use agar as a vegan alternative (see 'Working with agar', page 253). Makes 2 medium or 4 small jellies.

2 cups cordial, made how you like it (see recipe, page 173)
4 gelatine leaves
water to soak gelatine leaves

Pour the cordial into a saucepan over a gentle heat. Meanwhile, soak the gelatine leaves in cold water.

Remove cordial from the heat just before it begins to simmer. Squeeze the water out of the gelatine leaves and stir them into the warm cordial until dissolved and mixed through.

Pour the liquid into a large bowl or 2–4 smaller glasses for individual servings. Cover, cool and place in the fridge to set.

When set, serve the jelly or jellies as is, or gently run warm water on the backs of the bowl or glasses before turning them out onto a serving plate or small plates. If in doubt about whether or not to turn out a jelly, leave it in the bowl!

To make a firmer jelly you can be certain will hold together, add an extra leaf of gelatine.

Snow pudding

DF GF

The secret to snow pudding lies in folding the beaten egg white evenly into the partially set jelly. This can be tricky, but if it goes wrong you can always call it sleet pudding – it'll be just as delicious. It could also be an excuse to make more, and further practise your folding skills. Makes 4 medium or 6 small puddings.

1 fruit jelly, made with 3 gelatine leaves (see recipe, page 250)
2 egg whites
¼ teaspoon cream of tartar
½ cup sugar

Prepare the fruit jelly (see recipe, page 250) using only 3 gelatine leaves – this creates a softer jelly.

When the jelly is partially set, beat the egg whites until frothy.

Add the cream of tartar to the egg whites and beat some more.

Add the sugar to the egg whites bit by bit, beating after each addition to the soft-peak stage. The mixture should be glossy.

Gently fold the egg white through the partially set jelly until combined.

Put the bowl back in the fridge or spoon the mixture into glasses for individual servings. Store in the fridge until ready to serve.

Gummy lollies

DF GF

If you like firm, chewy gummies, use 6 leaves of gelatine. This recipe makes a medium plateful of lollies for treats, but you can easily double the quantities.

1 cup cordial, made how you like it (see recipe, page 173)
4–6 gelatine leaves
water to soak gelatine leaves

Pour the cordial into a saucepan over a gentle heat. Meanwhile, soak the gelatine leaves in cold water.

Remove the cordial from the heat before it boils. Squeeze the water out of the gelatine leaves and stir them into the hot cordial until dissolved and mixed through.

Pour the cordial jelly into ice-cube trays, chocolate moulds or another container in which the mixture will be about 1–2 centimetres (½–1 inch) deep.

Cover, cool and place in the fridge to set.

When set, unmould the lollies by gently running warm water on the back of the moulds.

If the jelly is in a single block, turn it onto a board and carefully slice it into small squares or oblongs.

Eat the lollies as is, or use them to garnish cakes and other desserts.

WORKING WITH GELATINE

Gelatine can be bought as leaves or powder — each form has its pros and cons. The leaves are much easier to use and don't have the slightly unpleasant aftertaste of gelatine powder. On the other hand, gelatine powder can be easier to find in shops.

USING GELATINE LEAVES

To use the leaves, simply soak them in cold water for a few minutes, so they turn from brittle and crackly to soft and squishy. Next, squeeze as much of the water out of the leaves as you can and add them to any hot liquid you want to set, stirring until dissolved.

The ratio of gelatine leaves to liquid depends on how firm or soft you want the jelly. Two leaves per cup of liquid will make a firm jelly, and 1½ leaves per cup will make a soft one. For a very firm jelly such as the gummy lollies (see recipe, page 251), use up to 6 leaves.

USING GELATINE POWDER

To use any gelatine powder, follow the ratios on the packet and remember to soak it in cold liquid to soften and swell before adding this to the hot liquid you want to set. The instructions on gelatine powder packets don't always tell you this, but it's an essential step.

You can either soak the powder in a little of the liquid that you want to gel before heating it, or use a very small amount of water. Sprinkle the gelatine powder over the surface of the cold liquid and leave it to stand while the gelatine swells. Then, as with the gelatine leaves, add the softened gelatine to the hot liquid you want to set. Use more or less powder, depending on how firm you want the jelly.

EXTRA TIPS FOR WORKING WITH GELATINE

- Don't boil the liquid once the gelatine has been added.
- To allow gelatine to reach its maximum holding power, chill for at least 8 hours, but preferably 24 hours if possible.
- Uncooked pineapple, figs, kiwifruit and ginger contain bromelin, an enzyme that can stop gelatine from setting. If you want to use these in a jelly, cook them first as this denatures the enzyme.
- You may need a little extra gelatine if you have alcohol in the mix or an unusually large amount of sugar. Both sugar and alcohol inhibit gelatine's action.

WORKING WITH AGAR

Gelatine is made from the collagen in animal skin and bones, and so is not suitable for vegetarians or vegans. For vegan jellies, agar — also called agar-agar and made from seaweed — can be used instead. Follow the instructions on the packet. An agar mix needs to be heated to boiling point, boiled gently for 5 minutes while stirring or whisking, and then put into the fridge to cool and set. A mix made with agar powder sets more strongly than one made with flakes, so you need less if using the former — around 2½ teaspoons to 4 cups of liquid.

TIPS FOR BEATING EGG WHITES

USING A BEATER

Some people like to use a copper bowl for the best set, while others are more comfortable with stainless steel or glass. If you have a stand mixer you probably won't have a choice. Whichever bowl you use, make sure there's no oil or fat on the beaters or in the bowl.

Use eggs at room temperature and separate them carefully, making sure there's no yolk in the whites. Start beating on the lowest speed and gradually build up to the fastest.

When the egg whites are frothy, add ⅛ teaspoon cream of tartar per egg to help them retain their structure. 'Soft-peak stage' is reached when the peaks of the beaten whites have droopy tips at the top. To prevent the egg whites splitting, use them immediately after you have beaten them.

USING A HAND WHISK

Sometimes I like to prove to myself that I can survive in the kitchen without electricity. The first time I tried beating egg whites without the aid of modern technology, I ended up with an occupational overuse syndrome relapse and a broken whisk – but they were pretty nicely beaten.

Perhaps you're one of those amazing people who routinely whisks their egg whites by hand, or perhaps, like me, it's only an occasional discipline for you. I reckon most people should try it once, but be sure to have a strong whisk!

The basic instructions are the same as for using an electric beater. Use small, fast, constant movements to start with, never letting your whisk leave the eggs. As the eggs begin to foam, gradually build up the size of your movements.

THINGS TO DO WITH LEFTOVER EGG YOLKS

- Add to a smoothie.
- Use to make eggnog.
- Use to make custard.
- Use to make ice cream.
- Use to make hollandaise sauce.
- Use in homemade pasta instead of whole eggs.
- Mix through hot, cooked pasta with herbs and seasonings.

Basic sweet panna cotta

DF GF V

Panna cotta is often flavoured with vanilla, but if you are using herbs like kawakawa you may not need it. The best panna cotta I've ever eaten — a light, refreshing, fennel-flavoured offering gleaming in syrup — was cooked by foraging chef Anthony North. Makes 2 large servings or 4 small ones.

- 4 gelatine leaves
- water to soak gelatine leaves
- foraged herbs or flowers
- 1 cup milk
- 1 cup cream
- ¼ cup sugar or honey
- a few drops of vanilla essence (optional)

Soak the gelatine leaves in cold water (see 'Working with gelatine', page 252).

Place foraged ingredients, milk, cream and sugar or honey into a saucepan over a low to medium heat. Heat gently until nearly simmering.

Remove from the heat and set aside, with the lid on, for half an hour while the foraged ingredients continue to infuse.

Strain through muslin or a fine sieve, and return the liquid to the saucepan. Reheat to hot but not simmering. Stir in vanilla, if using.

Squeeze the water from the gelatine leaves and stir them into the warm infused liquid until they're well dissolved and mixed in.

Pour the panna cotta mixture into a single bowl, or individual serving bowls or glasses. Cover, cool and place in the fridge to set fully.

When set, serve the panna cotta as is, or unmould it by gently running warm water on the back of the bowl or individual serving containers.

POSSIBILITIES

For a deliciously fragrant panna cotta, add any of these foraged aromatics: citrus blossoms; elderflowers; fennel leaves, flowers or pollen; fir, pine or spruce tips; jasmine flowers; kawakawa; lavender flowers; mānuka or kānuka; finely chopped nettle plus a teaspoon of vanilla; rose petals; rosemary flowers; scented pelargonium flowers; sweet william flowers; or a combination of nettle and vanilla.

VARIATIONS

- For a dairy-free panna cotta, use coconut milk instead of milk and cream.
- Make a yoghurt panna cotta by omitting the cream and using just 1 cup of milk. After the mix has cooled to lukewarm but not yet started to set, stir in 1 cup of yoghurt. Don't add the yoghurt to the warm milk or the mixture may separate. You may also need to add a little extra sugar or honey.
- For a vegan panna cotta, use agar instead of gelatine (see 'Working with agar', page 253).
- You can serve a plain vanilla or an infused panna cotta with wild infused syrup, a fruit or berry syrup, a runny infused honey or a berry honey (see the recipes in the previous chapter).

Sudden comfort ice cream

DF GF V

Although I love making ice cream using homemade custard, this indulgent alternative is the quickest, easiest ice-cream recipe I know, and it doesn't need an ice-cream maker. Condensed milk is the secret – it stops the ice cream from freezing hard, instead creating an ice-free perma-cream. Make as little or as much of this recipe as you would like.

1–2 parts foraged treasures, depending on how strong you would like the flavour
1 part milk
1 part cream
2 parts condensed milk
½–1 teaspoon vanilla essence per part (optional)

Place the foraged ingredients, milk and cream into a saucepan over a low to medium heat. Heat gently until nearly simmering.

Remove from the heat and set aside, with the lid on, for half an hour while the foraged ingredients continue to infuse.

Strain through muslin or a fine sieve.

Stir in the condensed milk and vanilla, if using, until well combined, and pour the mixture into a freezeproof container.

Freeze, stirring every hour or so to break up and aerate the mix as it freezes.

The ice cream will keep in the freezer, covered, for at least 1 week.

POSSIBILITIES

Try adding the following: citrus blossoms; elderflowers; fennel leaves, flowers or pollen; fir, pine or spruce tips; jasmine flowers; kawakawa; lavender flowers; mānuka or kānuka; finely chopped nettle plus a teaspoon of vanilla; rose petals; rosemary flowers; scented pelargonium flowers; sweet william flowers; or a combination of nettle and vanilla.

VARIATIONS

- Omit the cream and, after the mix has cooled, stir in 1 part yoghurt. Don't add the yoghurt to the warm milk or the mixture may separate. You may also need to add a little extra sugar or honey with this.
- For a dairy-free and vegan soy ice cream, use 1 part soy condensed milk, 1 part soy milk and 1 part soy cream.
- For a dairy-free and vegan coconut ice cream, omit the cream and milk and simply use condensed coconut milk (see homemade condensed milk recipe, 'Variations', page 259). I've found that in order to make a creamy coconut milk ice cream that doesn't form ice crystals, you can't add any regular coconut milk. Using all condensed coconut milk makes it very sweet and rich, so moderation is called for!

TIPS FOR SERVING

- Serve with wild infused syrup, a fruit or berry syrup, an infused honey or a berry honey (see recipes in the previous chapter).
- Serve with butterscotch sauce (see recipe, page 259) and a sprinkle of chopped foraged nuts.

Peking dust

GF

Peking dust is a simple, classic, delicious Chinese dessert. Serves 4–6.

1¼ cups cream
4 tablespoons caster sugar
chestnut dust (at least ½ cup, but more is better — see 'Note')

Whip the cream and sugar until thick. Divide between individual dessert bowls or glasses, and sprinkle a thick layer of chestnut 'dust' over the top.

NOTE

Make the chestnut dust by pushing well-boiled, peeled chestnuts through a sieve. As with peeling, it's easiest to do this when they're warm and soft. Alternatively, grate the chestnuts or chop them very finely.

VARIATIONS

- Add a splash of vanilla essence or brandy to the cream.
- Garnish each individual dessert with a sugared walnut.
- Place the cream on top of the 'dust' rather than vice versa.

Homemade condensed milk

GF

Whether you like to make things from scratch or want to use your own raw or organic milk, or you simply prefer not to support the companies that make condensed milk, it's simple to make your own.

2 cups whole milk
¼ cup sugar

Put the milk and sugar in a saucepan over a medium heat and bring to a gentle boil, stirring to dissolve the sugar.

Reduce to a simmer. Continue to simmer, stirring every now and then until the liquid has reduced by half and turned a pale yellow. Remove from the heat.

The resulting condensed milk won't be quite as thick as the store-bought version at first, but it will thicken as it cools.

VARIATIONS

- To make condensed soy milk, replace the whole milk with soy milk. It will turn milky brown rather than a pale yellow — almost the colour of a latte.
- To make condensed coconut milk, replace the whole milk with coconut milk. It will turn grey, but don't let the colour put you off — it's delicious!

Butterscotch sauce

GF

You can use this butterscotch sauce recipe in myriad ways — with raw or cooked fruit, or as an accompaniment to panna cotta, ice cream or a steamed pudding, or all three together. The sauce is delicious instead of honey or sugar on porridge in the morning, and is perfection served with your own foraged walnuts scattered over it.

50 g (1¾ oz) butter
1 cup packed brown sugar
¾ cup cream
1 teaspoon vanilla essence
½ teaspoon salt

Melt the butter in a saucepan over a low heat.

When it has nearly melted, add the sugar. Turn the heat a little higher and stir until the mixture begins to bubble.

Add the cream. Boil for 5–10 minutes, whisking occasionally. The longer you leave the sauce, the thicker it will be, but make sure it doesn't catch on the bottom of the saucepan.

Remove from the heat, leave it to cool slightly, then stir in the vanilla and salt.

VARIATIONS

- Try making butterscotch sauce using a butter infused with rose, lavender or scented pelargonium (see enfleuraged aromatic butter recipe, page 178).
- A blend of 50:50 butterscotch sauce and infused or fruit honey is delicious (see the aromatic honey recipe, page 184).
- Try adding a dash, according to taste, of spirits or wine infused with wild fruits or flowers to your butterscotch sauce.

TIPS FOR USING BUTTERSCOTCH SAUCE

The butterscotch sauce recipe can be used with foraged fruits to make many different sweet treats. Here are some of my favourites.

- Cut a selection of raw fruit into pieces and thread onto kebab sticks. Drizzle thick butterscotch sauce over the kebabs and serve immediately.
- For a more manageable or delicate snack, try mini-kebabs, with just 2 pieces of fruit threaded onto toothpicks.
- For a richer treat, use peeled fruit for the kebabs, then coat them in butterscotch sauce and fry them in butter until they're heated through. Serve immediately. (Note that plums don't need peeling.)
- Add butterscotch sauce to a fruit crumble instead of sugar (see recipe, page 262).
- Use the sauce to make gooey toffee apples. If you have very small apples, set out a bowl of cooled thick butterscotch sauce, push ice-block sticks or the handles of teaspoons into the apples, and let children make their own gooey toffee apples by dipping the apples into the butterscotch sauce. For extra foraging points, use sturdy apple tree twigs instead of ice-block sticks or spoons. As a colourful extra, set out one or more bowls of finely chopped foraged flower petals to sprinkle over the caramel.

Create-your-own cranachan

DF GF

The great beauty of this Scottish dessert, traditionally made with whisky and raspberries, is that it provides the ultimate choose-your-own-adventure recipe for both you and your guests — there are as many methods to make cranachan as there are cooks.

Before you begin, decide when you want to add the alcohol. Some people add it to the cream as they whip it, some add it to the honey, some cook the fruit in alcohol, and some soak the oats in it the night before. It's up to you, so add it as you go wherever you think it will work best. Make as little or as much of this recipe as you would like — ingredients are listed per serving.

alcohol (optional)
2–3 tablespoons rolled oats (gluten-free if required)
1 tsp brown or white sugar (optional)

1–2 cups foraged fruits or berries, fresh or lightly cooked or marinated
50–60 ml cream
a dash of vanilla essence (optional)
2 tablespoons runny honey

Put the rolled oats in a heavy-bottomed frying pan over a low heat and gently toast them until they're crunchy and browned but not burnt. You may like to add a little sugar as you do this.

Remove the oats from the heat, transfer to a bowl and set aside to cool. If you want to cook or marinate the fruits or berries, do so now.

Strain cooked fruits to remove seeds and skins, if necessary.

Place prepared fruits in a serving bowl.

Whip your cream with a dash of vanilla, if using, to the stiffness you like, and transfer to a serving bowl.

Place your runny honey in a bowl or jug to serve.

HOW TO SERVE

Give each of your guests their own glass bowl or tall glass and long spoon. Bring all the serving bowls to the table, with serving spoons, and let your guests layer up the ingredients however they like.

POSSIBILITIES

Slightly tart fruits are best for this recipe, such as coprosma berries, blackberries, and the tartest apples and plums. If you're cooking sweet fruits, you could add a bit of lemon juice or chopped wood sorrel.

VARIATIONS

- For dairy-free cranachan, make a cream substitute by whizzing soft tofu with a little bit of icing sugar to taste in a food processor until smooth and creamy.
- Use one of your own wild infused alcohols or wild infused honey (see recipes, pages 187 and 184).
- If your honey is too thick, stir in a tiny bit of an infused spirit or a tisane to make it runnier.

Scrumper's crumble

DF V

Crumble is a great way to use freshly gathered fruits or berries, or those that have been lingering in the fridge for a while. It's also fun to add other splashes of foraged flavours. This is a simple crumble recipe; if you have your own favourite, feel free to use that or any of the variations below. Serves 4–6.

1 cup standard plain flour
125 g (4½ oz) butter or butter substitute, diced
¼ cup brown sugar
3 cups foraged berries and/or chopped fruit
2–3 teaspoons extra brown or white sugar (optional)
juice of 1 citrus fruit (optional)
a handful of oats

Preheat the oven to 180°C (350°F) and grease or line a baking dish.

Sift the flour into a bowl. Add the butter or butter substitute, and rub into the flour between your thumbs and forefingers.

When the crumble mix looks mostly sandy with some bigger lumps, lightly stir in the sugar. Put in the fridge until required.

Sprinkle the fruit with the extra sugar and the citrus juice, if using, and spread evenly in the baking dish.

Sprinkle crumble mixture over the fruit and scatter the oats on top.

Bake for around half an hour or until the crumble is crispy and golden brown, and the fruit juices are bubbling up around the edges.

POSSIBILITIES

You can also add to the filling: elderflowers (shake them off their stems); fennel pollen; jasmine flowers; rose petals; rosemary flowers; scented pelargonium flowers; sweet william petals; finely chopped wood sorrel. Rose and rose-scented pelargoniums are especially versatile and team well with almost any fruit. As ever, experiment and find the combinations you like.

VARIATIONS

- For a dairy-free crumble, consider using virgin coconut oil as your butter substitute.

- Try adding citrus zest or very finely chopped pine, fir or spruce tips to the crumble mix.
- Let the fruit marinate in a little wild infused syrup or alcohol (see recipes, pages 170 and 187) before adding to crumble.
- Serve with sudden comfort ice cream (see recipe, page 256).

Aha tortoni

GF DF

This is a coming-out party for a heavenly dessert recipe that my small family has tried to keep secret for more than 45 years. As a teenager, my mother, Mary Knox, visited her auntie Jean in Canada, who gave her this recipe. My mother brought it back to Aotearoa and began serving it at dinner parties. People begged her for the recipe many times, but she would only give it to good friends who were leaving the country. It was also our special dessert for birthdays and Christmas.

Auntie Jean called it sherry tortoni, as did we, and there are quite a few recipes around with this name. Yet our family version is quite different from any other I've seen, so to publish it I've altered the name to reflect the excitement this dish generated in me and my sister, Andrea, when we were children. Andrea recalls that, as a small child, she came to believe the dish was called 'Aha!', because whenever Mum was making it and we asked what was for dessert, that was all she would reply.

I'd like to thank Mum and Andrea for allowing me to include this recipe, breaking the code of silence we've shared for as long as I can remember! But now we're curious. This recipe must have come from someone before Auntie Jean. Perhaps someone reading this might have clues as to its origins? Serves 4–6.

1 packet vanilla wine biscuits
3 eggs, separated
1 cup caster sugar
½ cup unsalted butter or butter substitute, softened
¼ cup sherry

Make sure all the ingredients are at room temperature.

Crumb the biscuits in a food processor or put them in a plastic bag and use a rolling pin to pound or grind them to crumbs.

Whisk the egg whites until fairly stiff, beating in a little of the caster sugar so that they hold their shape while you prepare the other ingredients.

Without washing the beaters, use them to cream the butter thoroughly. Add the remaining sugar and cream well again. Add the egg yolks and beat until fluffy and pale.

Add the sherry and beat until combined. Gently fold in the whisked egg whites.

Arrange this mixture and the biscuit crumbs in thin alternating layers in a glass dish or individual serving dishes, starting and ending with crumbs.

Cover and chill overnight.

POSSIBILITIES

- Use a wild infused butter (see recipes, pages 178–180).
- Use a wild infused sherry or other spirit (see recipe, page 187).

VARIATIONS

- For a dairy-free tortoni, use an unsalted butter substitute.
- For a gluten-free tortoni, use gluten-free biscuits instead of wine biscuits.

TIP

Eggs are easier to separate when they are cold, straight from the fridge, so do that ahead of time. Leave the separated eggs covered on the bench to allow them to reach room temperature before you use them.

Aromatic junket

GF

Soft, creamy, delicious junket is a favourite invalid recipe that you can delicately infuse with many wild aromas and medicinal herbs. It's helpful to have an accurate thermometer when you make it. Serves 2–3.

2 cups milk (preferably raw, whole milk)
2 teaspoons honey or sugar
a handful of foraged treasures
a few drops of vanilla essence, to taste
2–3 drops vegetable rennet mixed with 1 teaspoon water

Put the milk, honey or sugar, and foraged treasures in a saucepan over a medium heat, stirring to mix in the honey.

Heat until small foamy bubbles appear around the edges. Take the mix off the heat, and leave to cool to 31°C (88°F). Strain to remove the plant material.

Add the vanilla and stir in, then add the rennet mixed with water and stir through the milk for 15 seconds or so.

Pour the junket into a single bowl or individual serving dishes and leave to set. Don't move it while it's setting as the curd could break.

Once it's set, transfer it to the fridge until required.

TIPS FOR SERVING

- Serve junket plain, or sprinkle on a little nutmeg or cinnamon. Cinnamon is full of antimicrobial compounds and is considered a very healing spice.
- Just before serving, sprinkle caster sugar over the surface of the junket. Eat it straight away before the sugar turns to syrup. The granulated texture of the sugar is a particularly delicious addition to a floral-infused junket.

POSSIBILITIES

The following can all be used sparingly to provide a delicate flavour: a sprinkling of citrus zest; elderflowers; one or two kawakawa leaves; a small sprig of lavender; mānuka leaves; pine, spruce or fir tips; rose petals; a scented pelargonium leaf; sweet william flowers.

Solar cooking

If you're using wild plants in recipes or to make medicines, cosmetics and dyes, and are consuming foods cultured with wild microbes, you might as well harvest wild energy, too. Your first solar-cooked meal is always thrilling. To put something into a container in the sun and come back a few hours later to find it cooked feels little short of miraculous.

There's no one right method of solar cooking, and there are many types and designs of solar cooker. You can whip one up in half an hour out of corrugated cardboard and cooking foil. Others involve wood and mirrors, sawing and hammering.

While solar-cooking enthusiasts are always experimenting with variations, most solar cookers have certain features in common: a black or very dark sealed vessel to hold the food or liquid and absorb heat; something transparent that covers or surrounds the container, often an oven bag or lidded glass bowl, to let heat in but not out, like a mini-greenhouse; reflective surfaces that collect the sun's rays and focus them on the dark container.

One of the easiest solar cookers you can make at home is the panel cooker developed by Malaysian engineer Teong Tan (although there are many other panel cooker designs as well). See 'Solar-cooking resources' on page 344 for links to more information and instructions.

The black vessel

As mentioned above, your cooking vessel should be black or dark. It should also have a tight-fitting lid, otherwise vapour escapes and steams up the greenhouse part of your cooker.

It's often said that you'll get best results using a thin metal vessel that heats up quickly and conducts heat rapidly, but I know people who've solar-cooked beautiful meals in sturdy cast-iron cookware. It can be tricky to find thin metal lidded cookware, but you can improvise by using two identical black oven pans or non-stick pans, secured together with bull clips. You can also use a piece of cooking foil painted black as a lid, or paint a light-coloured lidded container.

When to solar cook

According to US writers Lorraine Anderson and Rick Palkovic in their book *Cooking with Sunshine* (see page 344), the best solar-cooking days are when your region is at a 45-degree angle to the sun for 4 hours or more. Here in Aotearoa, that means your prime solar-cooking days begin sometime in October and run through until sometime in March, depending on how far north or south you are. However, with a very powerful solar cooker it's possible to get good results outside this prime period.

For best results, you need little or only intermittent cloud cover during the hours you're cooking. Wind can be another challenge. If it's gusty, you may have to use ingenious methods to weigh down your cooker (a strategically placed brick or two can work).

Tips for solar cooking

- Cook during the hours that the sun is highest in the sky.
- If possible, move the cooker from time to time to follow the sun.
- Think of your solar cooker as a slow cooker — put the meal out in the sun mid-morning or very early afternoon, and open it up at dinner time.
- The fuller your cooking vessel, the longer the food will take to cook.
- Avoid the urge to peek as this will let the heat out.
- It's important to set the container of food on a rack of some sort to lift it off the base of the cooker. This allows the sunlight to reflect up into the bottom of the container as well as onto the top and sides. If you don't do this you may end up with a dish that's cooked on top but not at the bottom.

What to cook in your solar cooker

- For guaranteed first-time success, start with something simple like boiled eggs, corn on the cob or a basic tisane (see recipe, page 168).
- With many homemade solar cookers, you won't achieve a rolling boil inside your container, so use recipes that lend themselves well to being slow-cooked at a low temperature, and chop ingredients into small pieces.
- Use much less fluid than you would in an oven- or stove-cooked recipe.
- Lentil, tofu and root vegetable casseroles all work well — perhaps with plenty of foraged greens.

- Rice grains and most pastas present a challenge, and you need a very efficient solar cooker to cook them well. Try bean threads (cellophane noodles) or rice noodles instead. They're easier to cook at low temperatures, and not as inclined to go squidgy as wheat pasta does when slow-cooked. All the same, you may need to do a bit of experimenting.
- When it comes to desserts, try poached fruits or fruit compotes.
- You can also use a solar cooker for baking, but with most recipes you won't achieve browning on the outside.
- A solar-cooked pavlova is a gooey delight — it's not crisp like an oven-baked pavlova but has a charm all its own.

Natural healing and well-being

Medicine from nature

When I arrived at Te Wānanga o Raukawa in 2019 to study rongoā, I imagined I would be learning a catalogue of plant properties and medicinal recipes all year long, and I think a few of my classmates did too. But our pūkenga — Whaea Rita Tupe, Whaea Maudy Tupe and Whaea Mate Tihema — soon instilled in us that there was infinitely more to rongoā than that.

Rongoā Māori is an all-encompassing, holistic approach, and there are vital things to get right before working with people or crafting medicines: wairuatanga, aroha, kaitiakitanga, kotahitanga, respect for the whenua and the ngahere, an understanding of the role of karakia, and a clear, free, receptive mind as you work.

There are also issues of history and politics to grapple with. Ideally, you don't work with rongoā unless you understand how it has been colonised and how it needs to be restored to its rightful place as the first healing practice of Aotearoa. This means recognising that rongoā is not an adjunct to the current government health framework — a form of 'complementary medicine'. Rather, it's a system and a body of knowledge that needs to be (at least) sitting right alongside the Western health system, and accorded equal respect and value. That was among the many guarantees in Te Tiriti o Waitangi and, as with the others, it remains to be honoured.

If you feel a calling to rongoā, do find a teacher. There are some courses listed on page 346, or there may be someone in your community who will mentor you.

Learning to practise rongoā is a lifetime's worth of work, or more. I've only scratched the surface and only ever will. I will only ever make rongoā for my own family, and I'm pleased and grateful to be able to do that. Nonetheless, since studying at Te Wānanga o Raukawa, my practices around working with nature's healing qualities have slowly but surely deepened, and continue to do so. I'm getting to know some plants better and appreciating new things about them. I work with both native and introduced plants, which have very different whakapapa and, for me at least, entail different ways of doing and being. I continue to work a lot with ideas from the Western tradition of herbalism as well.

I try harder now to approach plants with a clear mind and spirit, and I work to set my intentions carefully. Why am I picking this plant? Who is it for? What is it for? I think I might be starting to get it right when a meditative sense of flow takes over, and I lose track of time and place, focusing only on the life and lives around me, and the conversations I realise I'm having with them.

> **HARVESTING WITH RESPECT**
>
> Greet the ngahere and ask for permission or invitation to harvest its plants. Look for signs as to what exactly you should gather, and give thanks. Show respect by using every part of your gathered materials if you can, and return unused leftovers to the place they came from — or as close to that as possible.

Some simple remedies

Listed through this section are basic remedies that can be prepared easily with foraged plants that are both common and widespread. Follow the instructions for making and using them with care.

Healing kawakawa oil or salve

Kawakawa has powerful skin-healing properties and can be used to make an oil or salve for eczema, bites and dry-skin conditions, which you can apply frequently.

- 10–15 kawakawa leaves, torn up
- 2 cups healing oil such as extra-virgin olive oil, avocado oil or sweet almond oil

Place everything in a pot, and infuse the leaves in the oil over a low heat for 5–6 hours. Aim to keep it just below simmering point. You can use a slow cooker if you have one, or a solar cooker (see page 266).

Let the oil cool fully then strain into a sterile bottle.

Stored in a cool dark place, this will last up to a year.

TURNING IT INTO A SALVE

To make a kawakawa salve, add beeswax to the oil as you heat it. Use 1 part beeswax to 5 parts oil for a smooth, soft ointment. If you prefer a slightly harder ointment, use 1 part beeswax to 4 parts oil. Use the same method as above, and pour into sterile jars before it sets.

Healing woundwort oil or salve

Woundwort oils and ointments are good for injuries and inflammation. Make them using the same method as for kawakawa (see page 271). Use two big handfuls of field or hedge woundwort leaves, stems and flowers per 2 cups of oil.

Cooling chickweed compress or poultice

Use a chickweed compress or poultice to ease bites, itches and inflamed skin. To have it at the ready, keep a lush patch of chickweed growing in your garden all year round or nurture one nearby in your neighbourhood. Alternatively, always keep a container of chopped chickweed in the freezer.

a few handfuls of chickweed
water

CHICKWEED COMPRESS

First make juice from a few handfuls of chickweed. You can do this in a juicer if you have one. Alternatively, whizz up the chickweed in a blender or food processor with a little water, or pound it with a mortar and pestle.

Strain the processed mixture through muslin.

Finally, lay a piece of clean cotton on a clean towel and pour the chickweed juice over it.

Place the juice-soaked cotton on the affected area, or wrap it around it tightly. Leave it on for as long as is convenient and comfortable.

CHICKWEED POULTICE

Pound a large handful of chickweed with a mortar and pestle.

Spread the chickweed over the area you want to treat, and bind it on with a strip of cotton bandage or plastic food wrap, or a layer of each, beginning with the cotton bandage.

Chamomile tisane

This tisane is useful to calm nerves and aid digestion, and to aid sleep (although remember that a few people find chamomile indigestible — see page 69). To have it at the ready, pick German chamomile, Roman chamomile or rayless chamomile flower heads regularly during spring and summer. The more you harvest, the more flowers the plant will produce. Dry or freeze any excess for use during autumn and winter when the main flowering period has passed.

2–3 teaspoons freshly picked chamomile flowers or 1–2 teaspoons dried chamomile flowers
boiling water

Place the flowers in a cup and pour the boiling water over them.

Cover with a saucer and leave to steep for 5–10 minutes, depending on how strong you like it.

Strain and drink. If using this as a sleep aid, drink it just before you go to bed.

Hot lavender bath or shower

To ease tension headaches, treat yourself to a lavender bath or shower. To have it at the ready, use lavender fresh while it's flowering and gather bunches of stems to dry.

2–3 handfuls of fresh or dried lavender

LAVENDER BATH

Place the lavender in the centre of a piece of muslin and tie together in a bundle.

Place in the tub as you run a hot bath.

Leave it there as you sink into the bath and relax, inhaling the calming lavender scent.

LAVENDER SHOWER

Tie sprigs of lavender into 2 or 3 bunches.

Place the bunches on the floor of the shower cubicle. The hot water pounding onto it will send up clouds of lavender scent as you shower.

Plantain or yarrow poultice

To treat wounds, apply a poultice or compress of plantain or yarrow leaves or flowers. This will help coagulate blood and staunch bleeding. Plantain also contains allantoin (the same substance for which comfrey is valued — see page 74), which stimulates new tissue growth. If you're using plantain, broad-leaved plantain generally has the most pharmacological activity, but narrow-leaved plantain is also fine.

To have the ingredients at the ready, gather yarrow early in the flowering season to dry, and keep a lush supply of plantain growing in your garden or nearby all year round.

a large handful of yarrow or plantain leaves and/or flowers

Pound the leaves and/or the flowers with a mortar and pestle.

Spread the plant material over the wound, and bind it on with a strip of cotton bandage or plastic food wrap, or a layer of each, beginning with the cotton bandage.

Blackberry leaf tisane

This tisane can be drunk to ease diarrhoea. To have it at the ready, gather new, young blackberry leaves during spring and summer — they will be a much lighter green than the older leaves and may have a reddish blush. Use them fresh, then dry some to store as well.

a few fresh, young blackberry leaves or 1–2 teaspoons dried young blackberry leaves
boiling water

Place a few fresh, young blackberry leaves in a cup and pour boiling water over. If using them fresh, tear or cut them up a bit first.

Leave to steep for 10 minutes.

Drink slowly, and take up to 3 times a day.

VARIATION

You can make a stronger treatment by decocting (boiling) the leaves in water for 5–10 minutes.

Eucalyptus steam inhalation

Use this remedy to ease colds or a blocked nose or sinuses. To have it at the ready, keep an ice-cream container or two full of dried eucalyptus leaves in your store cupboard or hang a bunch of leaves somewhere to dry.

a few fresh, dried or semi-dried eucalyptus leaves
boiling water

Put the leaves in a heat-resistant bowl and pour boiling water over them.

Place a plate on the bowl and leave to infuse and cool slightly (no more than 5 minutes).

Sit at a table with your head lowered over the bowl and make a steam tent by draping a towel over both your head and the bowl. You may wish to blow your nose first, to clear your nasal passages and improve uptake.

Keep your face at a comfortable distance from the bowl.

Inhale the steam, breathing through your nose for as long as you can or until the water has cooled.

VARIATIONS

- If you're treating a child who feels uncomfortable using the towel tent, simply let them sit beside the bowl and breathe the steam in.
- If you or your patient is sick in bed, you can simply put the bowl in a corner of the room to fill the space with vapour — in this case, you can use it without first leaving it to cool.

Kawakawa or blackberry leaf gargle or tisane

To ease a sore throat, make a gargle or tisane with kawakawa or blackberry leaves, which have antimicrobial properties. Kawakawa leaves are also anaesthetic, while blackberry leaves are particularly astringent, helping soothe inflammation.

To have the ingredients at the ready, gather new, young blackberry leaves during spring and summer – they will be a much lighter green than the older leaves and may have a reddish blush. Gather kawakawa leaves at any time of year, preferably those with the most holes (see page 123). Use them fresh or dry them to store.

5–10 torn-up kawakawa leaves or young blackberry leaves (fresh or dried)
1 cup boiling water

Make a strong tisane with the leaves (see the blackberry leaf tisane recipe, page 274). Use as a gargle, or sip to soothe your throat.

Elderflower or elderberry tisane

Try an elderflower or elderberry tisane to decrease the severity of flu during its onset. To have the ingredients at the ready, harvest elderflowers around November. Hang them to dry in a bag to catch all the flowers as they fall off. Remove the stalks once the flowers have fallen. Elderflower dries quickly and easily, and can be stored for up to a year. Elderberries can be gathered in summer and keep well in the freezer.

2 teaspoons fresh elderflowers or 1 teaspoon dried elderflowers, or 1 teaspoon elderflower berries
boiling water

Place the flowers or berries in a cup and pour boiling water over them. Leave to infuse for 10 minutes.

Drink up to 3 times a day.

VARIATION

You can use elderflower or elderberry syrup as a cordial drink in place of the tisane (see cordial recipe, page 173). Freeze the syrup in ice-cube trays to ensure you always have some to hand.

Cleavers spring tonic

'Tonic' is a loose term for any mixture that invigorates you and nurtures your health and well-being in a general way. 'Spring tonics' make use of the season's new growth and often use detoxifying plants. The idea is to give your body a spring clean after a long winter. Cleavers is known as one of the best detox herbs, gently stimulating your lymphatic system. The juice can be taken regularly in myriad ways: for example, added to fruit juice, cordial, iced tea, punch or an infused syrup.

2–3 cups cleavers stems and leaves

2–3 tablespoons water, if required, to help processing

Wash your cleavers haul well, and pick it over to make sure there are no bits of other plants caught up in it.

Chop the leaves and stems, then put them through a juicer. If you don't have one, put them in a blender and whizz them up. You may need to add the water at this stage. After whizzing, pour the pulp into a muslin-lined sieve and let the juice drain out. You can help it along by bunching up the muslin a bit to squeeze it through.

This should make at least a quarter of a cup of juice — enough for one to three 'doses' when mixed into another drink. (There are no hard and fast rules here.) What you don't use can be frozen in ice-cube trays for another day.

VARIATIONS

You can also juice and use chickweed (see page 80) in this way. See also the infused syrup recipes on pages 170–173 for ideas for drinks to blend with cleavers or chickweed juice.

Natural body care

Factory-made cosmetics have been around for just a fraction of the time humans have existed. We've been using cultivated and wild plants to look after our hair and skin for much longer. This section includes a few recipes using readily forageable ingredients.

> *You don't need the cosmetic industry. The cosmetic industry needs you. Your face supports an industry worth billions.*
>
> — ELIZABETH FRANCKE, *MAKE YOUR OWN COSMETICS AND FRAGRANCES*, 1988

Mallow hair conditioner

*To make this hair conditioner, you need to use herb mallow (*Malva *species), not tree mallow (*Lavatera *species). This makes one application if your hair is long, but if it's shorter, you'll be able to get more from it.*

2 cups boiling water
a handful of freshly foraged herbs
2 cups mallow leaves

Make 2 cups of strong tisane by pouring the boiling water over your foraged herbs. Leave it to sit until it cools.

Strain the infusion through a sieve or piece of muslin.

Roughly chop the mallow leaves and pour the infusion over them.

Stir well or squeeze the leaves with your hands.

Strain out the mallow leaves, pressing them to extract every bit of mucilage from them. The infusion should now be thick and silky.

Use this as a conditioning rinse. It will keep in the fridge for a couple of days or in the freezer for several months.

POSSIBILITIES

For the foraged herbs, try the following, either individually or in combination: chamomile flowers; cleavers leaves and stems; lavender flowers; nettle leaves; pot marigold flowers; rose petals; rosemary sprigs.

HERBS FOR HAIR CARE

- Nettle, rosemary and cleavers have long been known as hair-conditioning and scalp-care herbs par excellence.
- Rosemary adds gloss to dark hair.
- Marigold adds highlights to medium auburn hair.
- Chamomile lightens blonde hair.
- Lavender and rose are all-round favourites for body-care products, including for hair care.

Wild aftershave

You will need an alcohol tincture made with vodka and wild herbs for this. After that, it couldn't be simpler.

½ cup wild vodka tincture (see recipe, page 303)
½ cup distilled water
1 teaspoon glycerine

Mix the ingredients together well and decant into a sterilised spray bottle.

Spray on after shaving. This will keep for several months in a cool, dark place.

Wild powder deodorant

Baking soda is often used as a minimally processed, odourless deodorant, but you can add fragrant herbs to it as well. On very hot days or when you're very active it may not do the job as effectively as some store-bought products, but for regular wear it works well. You can use fuller's earth (an antimicrobial clay) in place of baking soda, which many people find gentler on the skin.

½ cup baking soda or fuller's earth (bentonite clay is a good choice for deodorant)
crisp, well-dried fragrant herbs

Crumble or pound the herbs into a powder and mix with the baking soda or fuller's earth. Apply to the underarms with a powder puff, or just with your hands.

TIPS

- Carry a small container of the deodorant around with you and reapply as necessary.
- If you have sensitive skin, try the baking soda on its own first without adding any fragrance. If you don't react to it, add your fragrant herbs one at a time. If your skin reacts with any addition, drop the offending herb or try a different one.

POSSIBILITIES

Use well-dried fragrant herbs that are gentle on the skin, such as elderflower, jasmine, lavender, rose petals and scented pelargonium.

VARIATION

To make a fragrant baking-soda deodorant that will last longer on your skin than a powder, mix the baking soda to a paste with a pomade (see page 306). Mix in as much baking soda as the pomade will take.

Deodorising foot powder

Use the same recipe as the wild powder deodorant (see page 280).

Sprinkle a thin layer of powder into your shoes every day for a week, tipping out the old powder and adding new.

POSSIBILITIES

Use herbs with strong antimicrobial actions, such as kawakawa and rosemary.

Infused face wash

Many wild herbs have a long history of use in skin-care products – take your pick!

a few freshly picked foraged treasures
boiling water

Make a strong tisane using the plant(s) of your choice (see page 166).

Use as a face wash to cleanse and tone your skin. It will keep in the fridge for a couple of days.

POSSIBILITIES

Chamomile flowers; chickweed leaves and stems; cleavers leaves and stems; elderflowers; jasmine flowers; lavender flowers; nettle leaves; pot marigold flowers; rose petals; yarrow flowers.

Chickweed or cleavers juice face wash

These herbs are said to be good for soothing and smoothing skin.

several handfuls of chickweed or cleavers leaves and stems

Whizz the plant material in a food processor, then strain and squeeze the pulp through muslin.

Splash on your face to cleanse, then gently rinse off and pat dry.

Glycerine moisturiser 1

1 part mock rose water (see page 169) or infused face wash (see page 281)
1 part glycerine

Mix the rose water or face wash and glycerine in equal parts.

Glycerine moisturiser 2

1 part glycerine extraction (see page 305)
1 part distilled water

Make the glycerine extraction with one or two changes of fresh plant material. Dilute the mixture in an equal quantity of distilled water.

Both these moisturisers keep quite well at room temperature, but store in the fridge if you want to be sure. You don't need to use much at a time, so depending on how much you make, these can last weeks or months.

POSSIBILITIES

For either moisturiser, try: chamomile flowers; chickweed leaves and stems; cleavers leaves and stems; elderflowers; jasmine flowers; lavender flowers;

nettle leaves; pot marigold flowers; rose petals; yarrow flowers; or any pairing from this list.

Exfoliating face and body scrub

1 teaspoon coarse chickpea flour or ground almonds
½ cup glycerine moisturiser (see page 282)

Simply mix the ingredients together and store in a jar.

To use this exfoliating scrub, rub it over your skin in a gentle circular motion, then rinse off with lukewarm water. You can then splash your face with cold water. This will make 10 or more applications of face scrub. For a whole body scrub, use it in the shower.

Mallow face and body scrub

1 cup infused face wash (see page 281)
1 cup herb mallow (*Malva* species) leaves, chopped or torn
1 teaspoon ground almonds or chickpea flour

Pour the cooled infused face wash over the chopped mallow leaves. Stir until the mix is silky and mucilaginous.

Strain the mallow leaves out, pressing to get every last bit of mucilage into the mixture.

Mix in the ground almonds or chickpea flour.

Use as for the exfoliating scrub above. It will keep in the fridge for only 2–3 days, so use it lavishly.

Oat bath 1

Oat baths soften and soothe skin, and are particularly good for irritable skin and rashes. Some eczema sufferers swear by them. They can also be relaxing – or invigorating. These recipes are each for one bath's worth, but you could make a larger quantity and store it for a few months.

¼ cup oats
a large handful of fragrant foraged herbs of your choice, fresh or dried

Bundle up the oats and herbs in muslin, and tie together, steam-pudding style.

Fix the bundle under the tap so that, as the water runs through, it carries the fragrant oat milk out into the bath water. Alternatively, swish the bundle around in the bath to release the milk.

Once the bath is ready, you can use the bundle a bit like a wash cloth.

By the end of the bath, the bundle will be filled with fragrant porridge, so discard the contents into the compost and wash the muslin to use again next time.

Oat bath 2

½ cup oat flour or rolled oats, ground as finely as possible in a blender
a handful of fragrant foraged herbs of your choice, fresh or dried

Mix together the ingredients, sprinkle into the bath and enjoy a long, soothing soak.

POSSIBILITIES

For either oat bath, try: chamomile; fennel; jasmine; kānuka; kawakawa; lavender; mānuka; rose petals; rosemary; scented pelargonium. Different herbs have different effects on your mood – lavender and jasmine are often relaxing, while rosemary is energising. But do experiment as you may react differently from other people.

Sea salt bath

This recipe is quoted directly from Jeanne Rose's classic Kitchen Cosmetics *(see page 345). With its salts and seaweed, it brings the ocean to your bathtub and makes for a very relaxing, soothing soak.*

equal quantities of salt, powdered dulse (see 'Possibilities', below), baking soda and Epsom salts

Mix together the ingredients.

Pour a good quantity (at least 1 cup) in a warm bath. Soak and let the healing salts release the toxins and poisons from your skin.

POSSIBILITIES

Dulse (*Palmaria palmata*) is a red seaweed. It can be found around Aotearoa shores and is sold commercially, but you don't have to use it in this recipe. Almost any kind of seaweed you find will be lovely and mucilaginous, and add ocean ambience to your bath. Instead of adding dried, powdered seaweed to the mix, you could go a step further and add a little fresh seaweed to the bath water.

Making soap with foraged finds

Melt-and-pour soap kits are a good way to start, especially if you want to focus on adding extra ingredients. For Aotearoa suppliers, see page 345.

THE PALM-OIL QUESTION

The only problem with melt-and-pour soaps is that most formulas rely on palm oil. This vegetable oil is used extensively in commercial food and body-care products, but is associated with wide-scale environmental destruction. If you want to use ethical ingredients in melt-and-pour soaps, there are two options: use a melt-and-pour product that is free of palm oil, or choose one that uses sustainably produced palm oil. Palm oil is a high-yield crop compared to other options, so transitioning to other oils could be more damaging to the environment in the long run.

Making cold process soap from scratch is beyond the scope of this book, but I highly recommend it, as ultimately it gives you much more control over your ingredients and you can choose whatever oils you like.

Wild purée soap

a handful of aromatic foraged treasures
a small quantity of nourishing oil
melt-and-pour soap, chopped (see method for quantity)

Place your gathered plant material in a blender or food processor, and add just enough oil so that the plant is easily whizzed to a pulp.

Place your melt-and-pour soap pieces in the top of a double boiler (or a pot suspended in boiling water).

Once the soap has fully melted, add 1 part purée to 19 parts melt (pour it by weight). The plant purée should be about 5 per cent of the mixture.

Stir well and pour immediately into moulds. There's no need to keep stirring after that, and often it's better not to.

Unlike cold process soaps, melt-and-pour soap doesn't need to cure, so you can use it as soon as it has set, which takes several hours. I usually leave my soaps overnight to be safe, and so that I'm not tempted to keep prodding them.

POSSIBILITIES

- Any of the more strongly scented members of mint family will add a noticeable fragrance, including rosemary, lavender, mints, sages and thyme.
- Strongly scented members of the carrot family will also add a bit of scent, particularly fennel and coriander.
- You could experiment with scents from pine tips (the pale green tips that pine trees grow in spring). Hunt to find especially aromatic pine trees for this.
- Other plants that are less scented but are wonderful for skin care include kawakawa leaves, rose petals and pot marigold petals. All of these can also add beautiful colour to your soap.

Enfleurage soap

Enfleurage is another lovely way to scent soap. Soap is ideal for this method because the fats and oils it contains absorb scent readily.

strongly aromatic foraged treasures
bar of plain melt-and-pour soap

Simply nestle your soap in the plant material. The longer you leave your soaps in with the scented plants, the stronger the scent will be. You can change out the plants for fresh ones every couple of days or so to allow the soap to keep absorbing more and more scent.

POSSIBILITIES

Scented pelargonium leaves are especially good for this method, as are sweet broom flowers, fennel, pink jasmine flowers, and many of the strongly scented members of the mint family, including lavender, rosemary, mint, sage and thyme. You can also try mixing scents.

TIP

Melt-and-pour soaps tend to sweat — more romantically referred to as glycerine dew. To minimise this, keep the soaps in a non-humid environment at room temperature. You can also wrap them in beeswax wraps or keep them in an airtight container.

Mental health

You don't have to read much media to see that around the world there is soaring collective stress, anxiety and sadness. Some of us are feeling an acute disconnection from the natural world. In parallel, we know that the Earth herself is in massive trouble, and is feverishly trying to fight off a sickness of industrialisation's making.

Indigenous cultures generally recognise that our mental, physical and spiritual health are unbreakably entwined with the health of the land, the waters, the sky and all the life around us. Meanwhile, people from industrialised cultures who feel they've become severed from their own long ancestral traditions are looking to find ways back.

Ecotherapy

In the United States and other parts of the Western world, a new therapeutic discipline called ecotherapy has sprung up. This sees reconnection with nature as vital to mental health. In one way, it seems unbearably sad that what should be a normal part of everyone's life — simple connection with the natural world — has had to be codified into a structured discipline, complete with textbooks and training courses. But if this is what it takes for the world's industrialised societies to come home to their life source, then why not?

If you're interested in this healing discipline, I recommend you read *Ecotherapy: Theory, Research and Practice* by Martin Jordan and Joe Hinds, and *Ecotherapy: Healing with Nature in Mind* by Linda Buzzell. Also, prominent Californian ecotherapist Ariana Candell runs the Earthbody Institute, which offers online distance courses for therapists and community workers that explore ecotherapy's many facets.

You may also want to look at 'The Work that Reconnects', the teachings of Joanna Macy, detailed in many books, videos and websites. It's not for the faint-hearted, and involves facing up to the state of our world in order to move through fear and grief, while celebrating that this grief springs from our love for the natural world. The idea is that through this we begin to heal and then try to make change. For more information on all these resources, see page 344.

Western natural-healing movements have suffered from a pervasive tendency to appropriate Indigenous cultures, but lately I've seen many people within those movements having conversations about this, trying to weed out this tendency and turning more strongly to their own traditions instead. This feels exciting and full of possibility.

Sitting with nature

In this country we're lucky: most of us live close to fields, forests and waters. We can spend time — alone or with others — taking in the natural world with all our senses, feeling ourselves as part of a greater whole, and allowing whatever presents itself to soothe us.

If we have specific troubles we can look for messages or teachers here, watch the stories unspooling slowly around us and greet the players — animal, vegetable and mineral. We can look for metaphors in the way they move, grow and interact with the world around them.

Sometimes, something in your surroundings may be trying to get your attention but it won't be immediately obvious. Tuck it away in your mind or your pocket (if it feels right), or take a photo. Look it up when you get home. Perhaps when you find out more about it you'll understand the message or the teaching. Or perhaps you won't. If not, let it sit; it'll likely come to you eventually.

Found perfumes

Perfumes blended from whole natural extracts are a world away from most modern mainstream commercial perfumes, which are cocktails of synthetic lab-developed fragrance compounds. With their quirks and quiet complexity, natural fragrances are beguiling.

Making natural perfumes is a heady, addictive activity. However, it can be expensive. Purchasing essential oils and other botanical extracts from around the world — such as frankincense from Oman, vetiver from Haiti and pink lotus from India — is costly. The prices for such precious ingredients are volatile, as the market rocks on the changeable ocean of the global economy. And there is enormous privilege involved in buying these materials, which are still farmed, harvested and processed by hand, often by people working for very low wages and in poor conditions.

Luckily, getting into natural perfumery doesn't have to be this way. Increasingly, artisan perfumers are foraging locally for plants from which to extract scent or are growing them themselves. There are simple, infinitely adaptable ways a creative forager can make perfumes.

Handmade fragrances can be liquid, stored in bottles with lids, atomisers or roll-on tops, and they can have a water, alcohol or oil base. Alternatively, they can be solid perfumes, made from oils, butters and waxes, and usually presented in a jar or compact — some perfumers use antique powder compacts.

Many natural perfumers branch out into making items that can be less intensely fragrant, including body oils and butters, and aftershave.

A brief history of natural perfumery

The oldest tradition of perfumery in Aotearoa belongs to Māori, and there are still expert practitioners working with this mātauranga. Elsewhere around the world, humans have sought to become more intimate with nature's scents over the millennia, using them in rituals, as adornment or to lift spirits. The world's oldest known perfumes were found on Cyprus in 2003 and date back 4000 years. It wasn't until the late nineteenth century that synthetic fragrance ingredients were developed and, from then on, the art of perfumery moved away from its natural roots.

At first these modern perfumes contained just a few synthetic substances, but as the decades passed, the ratio of synthetic to natural ingredients grew. Today, perfumery is big business, and most commercially produced perfumes are almost wholly synthetic.

Parallels to industrialised food are unavoidable. Humans crave sugar, salt and umami flavours. Industrially created food gives us what we want in larger quantities than we'd ever be able to find in nature. Likewise, modern fragrance technology gives us unnaturally strong, sweet, consistent and long-lasting perfumes.

It's also about economics. Fast food means using the cheapest factory-processed ingredients to create maximum profit for company owners. The late British artisan perfumer Alec Lawless asserted that, in the same way, most of the dollars you spend on a mainstream perfume these days go towards marketing and packaging.

Store-cupboard staples for perfumery

Basics

- vodka or gin
- good-quality extra-virgin olive oil
- vanilla beans
- mango butter (available from soapmaking suppliers)
- extra-virgin coconut oil (solid when cool)
- glycerine (available from soapmaking suppliers)
- baking soda
- bottles and jars of varying sizes
- muslin

Nice to have

- pure perfumer's alcohol (available from soapmaking suppliers)
- benzoin resin
- other skin-nourishing oils such as apricot kernel oil
- oils with an extra-long shelf life — the best are jojoba oil and fractionated coconut oil

The good oil

Extra-virgin olive oil is my favourite for natural perfumes. It's gentle on the skin, and if your skin is sensitive you'll be able to feel the difference between a good oil and one of a lower quality — some of the cheap supermarket brands feel horrible on the skin. Many small Aotearoa olive oil presses make excellent oils, perfect for homemade skin-care products.

Bought botanicals — a primer

If you do want to incorporate bought botanicals into your natural perfumery work, here's a quick primer. Four main types of fragrant extract are available. Look for fair trade and organic products, or at least local ones.

Essential oils

These are the volatile compounds of a plant extracted through distillation. Only some plants are suitable for this process — the plant's fragrance and physical structure need to be able to withstand heat and water or steam. For example, it's extremely rare for essential oils to be processed from jasmine and certain other flowers. Instead, you'll generally find their fragrance captured in absolutes or carbon dioxide extracts.

Absolutes

To create an absolute, the volatile oils of a plant are extracted with solvents and then separated out. Absolutes are very concentrated and some also have a thick, sticky consistency that's challenging to work with. Warming them gently makes them runnier and easier to deal with.

You can often buy absolutes ready diluted in jojoba oil or fractionated coconut oil. However, many perfumers prefer to buy them neat and do their own dilution using carrier oils or pure alcohol. Any absolute you buy should state on the bottle whether it is diluted, what with, and at what percentage.

Carbon dioxide extracts

This process has recently been developed for extracting botanical aromas. Carbon dioxide, under such high pressure that it acts like a liquid, is pumped through plant material, pulling out resins and volatile oils as it goes. It releases them when it returns to a gas. This process produces an aroma that is very true to nature, and is generally more environmentally friendly than the production of absolutes.

Hydrosols

These are by-products of essential-oil distillation. They're the fragrant distilled waters left after the essential oil has been skimmed off. Hydrosols are acidic and therefore keep well, and they have many uses in natural cosmetics and perfumery.

Where to buy good-quality botanical extracts

If you want only one or two commonly available extracts, your best bet is to buy them from a reputable local company (see 'Aotearoa suppliers of body-care ingredients', page 345). If you're looking to buy larger quantities or want to try samples of diverse and rare botanicals, consider ordering from an overseas supplier with a scaled range of wholesale discounts. Even taking into account freight costs and currency conversion rates, this may be a more economical option.

However, it is a case of buyer beware! Corruption is rife in the world of natural botanicals. Many products that are sold as 'natural', both here and overseas, are adulterated with synthetics, or are mélanges of cheaper naturals made to imitate the fragrance of the extract they're being sold as. (Again, for reputable dealers, see 'Aotearoa suppliers of body-care ingredients', page 345.)

If you buy from a reputable and experienced supplier, you have the best chance of getting a pure, honest product. Even so, some dodgy specimens can slip through as the supply chain is sometimes long, and there are several points along the way where an excellent product might be adulterated before it reaches the purchaser.

So, what signs should you look for that a product may not be genuine? One is price. If it seems too good to be true, it probably is. On the other hand, that's not to say that an expensive price guarantees authenticity.

Colour is another indicator. A few plant extracts are completely clear, but many are not. For example, if you come across a rose absolute or a vanilla essential oil that's thin and clear, it must be synthetic. Sometimes, the best indicator is your own sense of smell. With experience you can often sniff out fakes, although you'll likely make mistakes along the way as you train your nose.

All in all, if you want to know for sure what's in your botanical extract, you'll need to obtain it from someone you know and trust, and whose process is transparent — or make it yourself.

Your brilliant nose

Top perfumers usually have a highly sensitive nose and have honed their olfactory skills through years of training. Just as people with ability in the visual arts see things the rest of us don't and interpret what they see in exciting ways, so those with exceptional olfactory skills perceive and appreciate tastes and smells with a clarity and a sense of wonder that elude others. You might have raw olfactory talent or maybe, like most of us, you weren't born with a particularly extraordinary nose. Either way, as in many areas of human endeavour, hard work and practice count for a lot, too.

Developing your skills

It's possible for most people to improve their olfactory ability. Perfumers talk about a scent memory and say that it's a key skill to develop. It's not about getting better at smelling, but at recalling and thinking about what you smell. Below are some scent-memory exercises you can do — like olfactory isometrics. They can easily be incorporated into your daily life and, over time, they'll improve the way your brain comprehends fragrance.

Scent-memory exercises

Do these as often as you like, with as many repeats as you like and in any order or combination. If you practise them regularly, you'll notice a definite improvement in your olfactory skills.

EXERCISE 1

Wherever you are, become deliberately aware of the shifting smellscape around you. Tune your nose into your surroundings. How many different smells can you discern? What do you think they are?

EXERCISE 2

Imagine a food, plant, place, person, piece of clothing or other item and try to recall its smell in 'your mind's nose'. Think hard to remember it as vividly as you can.

EXERCISE 3

See how many different smells you know that you can clearly imagine. Start a mental list. Notice how you can conjure some smells quite clearly, while others you can only vaguely recollect.

EXERCISE 4

Notice how, when you try to imagine a smell, you breathe in, as if sniffing something. Try imagining the same smell without breathing. Notice how much harder this is. A related challenge is to try imagining certain smells in your mind when there are other strong smells around that you can't help breathing in.

EXERCISE 5

Sniff something, then move it away from your nose and try to remember the smell as clearly as possible. Repeat this as many times as you like. Later in the day, after you haven't smelled the item for a while, try to remember its smell again.

EXERCISE 6

Try to imagine how two scents that you know well might smell if combined. If you can do that, try imagining three scents combined with one another. This is very hard for a lot of people. The tendency is to run through the different smells in your mind very quickly one after the other, rather than imagine them all at once.

Interior and exterior smelling

We smell things in two different ways: we sniff from the outside up through our nostrils, and we smell from the inside of our mouths, as the aromas of what we're eating or drinking rise up through the back of our nose and are exhaled. In other words, we sniff external smells by inhaling and internal smells by exhaling. (Have you noticed how, when you have a cold and can't smell or taste much, you can sometimes intensify the aromas of food just enough to detect them by exhaling through your nose very hard?)

As most people know from school science experiments, what we usually refer to as taste or flavour is a mix of the basic sensations we detect with our taste buds (usually categorised as sweet, salt, sour, bitter and umami), along with the rich variety of aromas that rise up through our olfactory cavity. Studies have shown that our brains perceive the same scent molecules slightly differently depending on whether they reach it by interior or exterior sniffing. Nonetheless, the art of cooking and the art of perfumery are closely linked, and people who are skilled at combining flavours are often just as good at perfumery and vice versa.

A note about notes

The word 'note' is used in two different ways to describe perfume. The first definition of note is a single scent that your nose detects. Most plant extracts contain many notes. For example, a scented pelargonium may contain a complex of rose, lemon and musk notes.

The word is also used to group particular scents together according to their role in a perfume. In this case, each may be described as a top note, middle note or base note. A perfume often has several top, middle and base notes.

TOP NOTES

These are the flyaway parts of a perfume, contributing strongly to first impressions. Their molecules are the most volatile, hitting your nose first and giving lift and sparkle to a perfume. They vanish quickly, leaving the middle and base notes to shine. Citrus peel extracts are among the most common top notes in artisan natural perfumery.

MIDDLE NOTES

These are made up of less volatile molecules that take longer to evaporate after the perfume is applied. Many floral extracts provide middle notes.

BASE NOTES

These are the least volatile parts of a perfume. They create the lingering scent that you can still smell hours later. They can also act as fixatives, clutching on to parts of top and middle notes so that they, too, last longer.

Getting started

Here are four age-old ways to extract plant fragrances that can be used at home — you don't need any elaborate equipment. There's also advice on how to mix extracts together to make creative, fragrant blends.

Alcohol tinctures

You can use either a pure perfumer's alcohol, or a low-odour drinking alcohol like vodka. You will also need some sterilised jars and a fine sieve, clean muslin or coffee filter papers to make a tincture.

fragrant foraged treasures

alcohol

Carefully pick over the foraged plants to remove foreign material. Cram your ingredients into a sterilised jar and pour in enough alcohol to cover them.

Seal the jar and leave it covered in a dark place to infuse for 24 hours or more.

Check the scent often to gauge how the extraction is changing — different scent compounds take different lengths of time to extract. You may find you prefer the scent compounds that are extracted in the first few hours or days.

When your first infusion is complete, strain the alcohol into a new jar through several layers of muslin, or through a coffee filter, to ensure all bits of plant material are removed. Sometimes, one infusion gives a strong enough tincture, but with most ingredients you need to carry out several rounds of infusion.

If your tincture isn't strong enough, recharge the alcohol with fresh plant material and leave it for another 24 hours or more and strain. Repeat this process until your tincture is as strong as you want it. Don't be alarmed if you have to do 10 or more recharges to get a strong fragrance.

Decant the tincture into sterilised bottles, seal and store in a cool, dark place. Stored well, alcohol tinctures can last years.

POSSIBILITIES

Fragrant broom flowers; all kinds of citrus flowers and leaves; fennel leaves, flowers and seeds; lavender; mānuka leaves; parsley; pine, spruce and fir bark, resin, needles and cones; rose petals; rosemary; scented pelargonium leaves, stems and flowers; dried tākawa peppercorns (see page 124) or hard, unripe green tākawa (kawakawa fruit); tūtae kōau; wild jasmine.

TIPS

- Don't despair if you can't gather enough of a plant to recharge the tincture sufficient times to create a strong fragrance. A weak tincture can be frozen and stored for up to a year, or until you have a new supply of the plant material. Alternatively, a weak tincture can be made into an aftershave (see recipe, page 280).
- You could also continue an infusion with a different, complementary ingredient. Experiment with just a small amount of the tincture to make sure the scents you're working with combine well, rather than clashing with each other or turning the tincture 'muddy'.
- If using flowers, make sure you've removed as much greenery as possible, including sepals, stems and so on. You want only the scent of the petals, unless you're using a plant like fennel that also has aromatic greenery.
- Flowers and leaves are generally tinctured for 24 hours or less, because as the plant material quickly degrades the tincture may begin to absorb some off notes. Drier plant material, like conifer cones and dried tākawa, can be tinctured for a week or more and the tincture will become increasingly stronger over that time. Before tincturing, some perfumers leave their aromatic plants in a dry place for a few hours to wilt and reduce their water content.
- Try pouring off some of the tincture at intervals and keeping it, to compare and contrast its changing scent over hours or days. You may find that although you liked a particular extraction after 1 day, it was even better after 4 days; equally, it may be worse after 7 days. Only by experimenting will you know how to time different extractions to achieve the results you like best.

BLENDING WITH ALCOHOL TINCTURES

- Tinctures made with drinking alcohol like vodka, which is generally 50 per cent or more water, can be mixed only with other tinctures made from either drinking alcohol or pure perfumer's alcohol, glycerine extractions or hydrosols (see page 297).
- Tinctures made with perfumer's alcohol are more versatile than those made with drinking alcohol. Mix them sparingly, little by little, into a fragrant oil

or pomade. Add essential oils, absolutes or carbon dioxide extracts to them sparingly, drop by drop — they can easily overpower a tincture.

- Alternatively, dilute essential oils, absolutes and carbon dioxide extracts in alcohol at a strength of 5–10 per cent before adding to a tincture so that it's easier to control the effect. Even once they're diluted, add them only drop by drop and mix and check between each addition.
- Once you've mixed a pure alcohol tincture with any essential oils, absolutes or carbon dioxide extracts, you cannot mix it with a glycerine extraction or a drinking alcohol tincture, or it will separate.

Glycerine extractions

Glycerine works by sucking the fragrant juices from plant material. With this method, use only the freshest plants.

fragrant foraged treasures
glycerine

Carefully pick over the foraged plants to remove foreign material. Cram your ingredients into a sterilised jar and pour in a small amount of glycerine — there's no need to cover the plants.

Use a chopstick or similar implement to stir things up, making sure all the plant material is thoroughly coated with glycerine. Add a little more glycerine if there doesn't seem to be quite enough — the plant material needs to be well coated but not swimming in it. Over the next 24 hours or so, the glycerine will suck the aromatic water from the plants. You don't have to be quite as scrupulous about changing the plant material as you do with alcohol tinctures, as glycerine is such a good preservative.

Over time, the glycerine will become more watery, the plants will relax and the liquid level will rise. After 24 hours or more, strain the glycerine through a sieve into a clean jar and add fresh plant material, again making sure it's thoroughly coated. Leave for another 24 hours and then strain again.

Repeat this process until your extract is watery but strong-smelling. Strain it really well through several layers of muslin or a coffee filter to remove stray plant material. Decant the extraction into sterilised bottles, seal and store in a cool, dark place. This will keep for a year or more.

POSSIBILITIES

Citrus flowers and leaves; fennel leaves, flowers and seeds; jasmine; unripe fresh kawakawa fruit or leaves; lavender flowers; mānuka leaves; pine, spruce or fir needles; rose petals; rosemary leaves and flowers; scented pelargonium leaves and flowers.

BLENDING WITH GLYCERINE EXTRACTIONS

- Glycerine extractions will mix with perfumer's alcohol tinctures, vodka tinctures, hydrosols and other glycerine extractions.
- Glycerine extractions won't usually mix with oils, fats, butters, essential oils, absolutes or carbon dioxide extracts. That said, if you dilute any of those substances in pure perfumer's alcohol at a strength of 5–10 per cent, you can sometimes coax a little to mix with a glycerine extraction, adding them drop by drop. However, this may give your blend a cloudy look, and don't experiment with this unless you're happy to risk failure. Mix and check the fragrance after each addition.

Pomades

A pomade is produced using the classic French perfumery technique of enfleurage. It's essentially a fragrance-saturated fat — fats love to absorb smell. You'll need an enfleurage 'frame' of some kind, which can be quite makeshift (see 'Your enfleurage frame', page 309).

odourless or pleasant-smelling solid oil, fat or body butter
heavily scented foraged treasures

Smear a thin layer of solid oil, fat or body butter — roughly 5 millimetres (¼ inch) thick — across the surfaces of your enfleurage frame that will face each other.

Arrange your plant material in a layer over the fat on the bottom half of the frame. Don't worry too much if some greenery is still attached to the flowers. It can be helpful to retain the green bits that hold the flowers together so you don't have such a fiddly time removing them all from the fat when the enfleurage is complete.

Close the frame and secure the top and bottom together. If they don't fit together, firmly wrap them with elastic or a sheet of plastic food wrap.

Leave in a cool place for 24 hours.

Open the frame and remove the flowers. Try not to leave any little bits behind, as they will rot and go mouldy.

Carry out the process repeatedly, changing the flowers every 24 hours, until the fat smells as strong as you would like it. To test it for odour strength and longevity, take a little out with each recharge and try it on your skin.

Once you're happy with your pomade, scoop it out into a small jar or other airtight container, and keep it in a cool place. Stored well, these will keep for a year or more, although the fragrance will very slowly fade over time.

If your pomade is very strong, you can use it as a perfume on its own or blend it (see 'Blending with pomades', below). If it's subtler, it will make a great massage or body butter.

POSSIBILITIES

Fragrant broom flowers; all kinds of citrus flowers; fennel flowers; jasmine flowers; lavender flowers and leaves; very strong-smelling roses; rosemary flowers and branches; scented pelargonium flowers and leaves; tī kōuka flowers.

TIPS

Traditionally, odourless lard is used for pomades, but I've found that it's hard to find lard here that's odourless enough to use.

For a vegan pomade, mango butter and virgin coconut oil are favourite bases.

Some people like to use shea butter or cocoa butter as a base, but these are very hard. If you use either of these, melt it and mix in a little of another butter or oil to soften it a bit before beginning the enfleurage.

As with a tincture, you may need to do 10 or more recharges to get a strong-enough fragrance. Perfumes handcrafted from scratch take time and care.

If you don't have enough flowers to do a change at any time, you can store your pomade in the fridge, without flowers sitting in it, until you have collected some more.

BLENDING WITH POMADES

- Pomades will mix with other pomades and infused oils. They also blend with essential oils, absolutes and carbon dioxide extracts, but note that these fragrances can overpower them. If you first dilute an essential oil in a vegetable oil at 5–10 per cent strength and add it carefully and sparingly, drop by drop, you should be able to control the balance of scents. Mix and check the fragrance after each addition.

- Pure alcohol tinctures can also be mixed carefully and gradually into some pomades.

> **YOUR ENFLEURAGE FRAME**
>
> Traditionally, enfleurage uses wooden-framed glass sheets stacked on top of each other. Real enfleurage frames are just about impossible to come by, although you can make one yourself. Otherwise, a glass oven dish with a lid is a good substitute. Even two plates, saucers or shallow bowls made of a non-reactive material that can be held together will do for small quantities. If your containers are small enough, you may be able to use a sturdy rubber band to secure them together.

Infused oils

To make an infused oil for use in perfumery or cosmetics, use the same method as for making a culinary infused oil (see recipe, page 181), but add very fragrant aromatics. Any odourless vegetable oil will work as the base, or if you want an oil that is beautiful on the skin, good-quality extra-virgin olive oil is perfect and has a gentle scent of its own to add to the mix.

heavily scented foraged treasures
oil

Wash the foraged treasures and pick them over to remove foreign material. Leave them in a dry place for a few hours to wilt and reduce their water content.

Crush the wilted plants slightly, or cut or tear them into pieces. Cram them into a jar or bottle, and pour oil over them.

Be scrupulous about filling the bottle with oil as near to the top as you can, as this will reduce the amount of oxygen sealed inside the container when the lid is on.

Make sure no plant material is sticking above the surface, and poke it down if it is.

Place the infusing oil, tightly covered, in a cool, dark place. Keep an occasional eye on it to make sure no plant matter has bobbed above the surface.

Infuse for 1–3 days, then strain through muslin, very gently pressing the plant material to get as much of the oil out of it as possible without causing it to disintegrate.

If you'd like a stronger infusion, recharge with a new batch of plant material for another 1–3 days. Repeat this as many times as you like, until the infusion is as strongly aromatic as you like.

When you're happy with your infused oil, strain it well — any bits left in the oil may encourage mould.

Decant it into a sterilised bottle and store in the fridge. To help it keep longer, let it stand for a few days, then decant it again, leaving behind any sediment that has settled. How long these keep will depend on the particular shelf life of the oil you use.

POSSIBILITIES

Fragrant broom flowers; fennel leaves, flowers and seeds; unripe kawakawa fruit, either fresh or dried; lavender; mānuka leaves; pine, spruce and fir bark, resin, needles, tips and cones; rose petals; rosemary; scented pelargonium leaves and flowers; wild jasmine.

TIPS

- Jojoba oil and fractionated coconut oil are commonly used in artisan perfumery and cosmetics because they are virtually odourless and have an extremely long shelf life compared to many other oils. Jojoba oil is particularly kind to the skin. Recently, I've also been enjoying avocado oil as a skin-care oil.
- Good olive oils smell divine in their own right, and some have almost floral notes. Perhaps it's my imagination, but I'm sure I can detect the olive family relationship to jasmine in the bouquet of some local olive oils, so they blend well with jasmine and rose flowers.

BLENDING WITH INFUSED OILS

- Infused oils can be mixed with other infused oils and pomades.
- Infused oils also blend with essential oils, absolutes and carbon dioxide extracts, although those fragrances can be overpowering. However, if you first dilute these in a vegetable oil at 5–10 per cent strength and add them carefully and sparingly, drop by drop, you should be able to control the balance of scents. Mix and check the fragrance after each addition.
- Pure alcohol will mix with fractionated coconut oil.

Wild perfume formulas

A rich, satisfying perfume generally contains top, middle and base notes. Much of a perfumer's art lies in the blending, although they also have to know each individual ingredient intimately in order to make effective blends.

You can wear or gift a single fragrant extract that you love, or blend extracts to create something more complex. Start by blending just 2–3 ingredients — just as when you mix lots of paint colours, it's easy for fragrance blends to become muddied.

You'll be able to experiment more easily with scent combinations if you make extracts of single plants and try blending them in different combinations in very small quantities. However, you can also make blending part of the extraction process. This can be simple and fun. Try the recipes below, using store-cupboard staples plus some wild foraged plants. Use them as inspiration for your own formulas.

Perfume blends, like wine, change and mellow over time. You might want to start using some of your blend straight away, but you can also seal some up and store it for a few weeks, months or even years to see how it develops.

Simple balsamic tinctured perfume

This two-stage tincture creates a perfume with a base note (vanilla), a middle note (rose or jasmine) and a top note (peppercorns).

1 vanilla bean pod sliced into several pieces
about 20 black or pink peppercorns or a mix of coloured peppercorns
½ cup vodka
a continual supply of rose petals, jasmine and/or sweet broom flowers

Put the vanilla bean pod and peppercorns into a jar.

Add the vodka, making sure the vanilla bean pod and peppercorns are covered.

Leave to infuse for a week.

Strain out the vanilla bean pod and peppercorns. Put the petals and/or flowers into a jar and pour the vanilla-peppercorn infusion over them.

Strain and recharge the tincture with new flowers every 24 hours until you're happy with it.

Decant into a nice bottle, give it a better name, and label it!

Simple kawakawa perfume

Using the intensely aromatic dried female fruits of kawakawa is one of the best ways to capture the plant's beautiful scents.

½ vanilla bean pod, sliced into several pieces
3 whole cloves
a handful of dried tākawa peppercorns (see recipe, page 124)
½ cup vodka
a few thin slices of fresh ginger

Put the vanilla bean pod, cloves and tākawa peppercorns into a jar.

Pour the vodka over to cover well.

After 3 days, strain out the vanilla, cloves and peppercorns.

Put a few thin slices of fresh ginger into another jar and pour the tincture over the ginger.

Leave to infuse for another 24 hours or so.

Decant into a nice bottle and add a label.

VARIATIONS

- Kawakawa perfume works well with the addition of rose scent. Put some heavily scented rose petals into a clean jar and pour the kawakawa perfume in, making sure the rose petals are covered. Leave for 24 hours and repeat with fresh rose petals several times until you are happy with the result.
- Instead of rose petals, you can add rose water to the kawakawa perfume just before decanting (see mock rose water recipe, page 169).

Jaftelier

This is my homage to California-based Mandy Aftel of Aftelier Perfumes, whose perfume Chocolat begins with an infusion of cocoa and vanilla. She adds several jasmine absolutes, then tops it off with blood orange essential oil.

1 vanilla bean pod, sliced into several pieces
2 teaspoons cacao nibs or good-quality roasted cacao beans
around ½ cup vodka
a continual supply of jasmine flowers
1 orange

Put the vanilla bean pod and cacao nibs or beans into a small jar. Pour the vodka over to cover well.

After 3 days, strain and remove the vanilla and cacao nibs or beans.

Fill the jar with jasmine flowers and pour the vanilla-cacao infusion over them.

Leave to infuse for 24 hours.

Strain and recharge the tincture with new flowers every 24 hours or so until you're happy with it.

Finally, add thin peel from the orange (use a potato peeler) and leave to infuse for a further 24 hours.

Decant into a nice bottle and attach a label.

A WARNING ABOUT CITRUS

From lime and tangerine to grapefruit, citrus scents are a staple of natural perfumery, providing fresh, gorgeous top notes. You can use ripe or unripe fruits. Tincture the peels, infuse them in oil or grate them finely into a pomade, but do be careful. The oils in citrus skins contain phototoxins, which can permanently discolour your skin when exposed to sunlight. Therefore, use citrus zest only in products you're sure will be applied to parts of your body that stay out of the sun.

Alternatively, use a distilled citrus oil, as the distillation process denatures the phototoxins. If you are concerned about phototoxicity, make sure you are buying a distilled citrus oil, not a cold-pressed oil. If you have a still, citrus peel is a rewarding item to distil, as it has a high yield compared to many other plants.

Balsamic pomade

Don't wear this pomade on any part of your skin that is likely to be exposed to the sun (see 'A warning about citrus', above).

- 2 vanilla bean pods
- ¼ cup mango butter or extra-virgin coconut oil
- a continual supply of heavily scented flowers over several days or more
- ¼ teaspoon citrus zest

Cut the vanilla bean pods lengthwise and scrape out the seeds. Stir these thoroughly through the mango butter or coconut oil.

Use the enfleurage technique to infuse the mango butter or extra-virgin coconut oil with the fragrance of your chosen flowers.

When you're happy with the strength of the pomade, stir the citrus zest through the pomade. Keep the pomade in a jar and use as a fragrance or body balm.

POSSIBILITIES

Fragrant broom flowers; citrus flowers; daphne flowers; jasmine flowers; jonquil flowers; tī kōuka flowers.

ENFLEURAGE TROUBLESHOOTING

- If you have too much trouble removing bits of plant matter from your fat, try using the same suspension-in-muslin method recommended for use with daphne (see 'Divine daphne pomade', below).
- If you're in a warm environment and your fat or butter is too sticky or soft to stay where it's put, use your fridge. The process can be a little slower, but you can basically let most of the enfleurage happen in the fridge, taking out the frame only to change the flowers.

DIVINE DAPHNE POMADE

Daphne is a late-winter treat, filling the chilly air with its strong perfume. The flowers aren't suitable for tincturing or infusing in oil because of their toxic sap, but they are among the best for a pomade. Because of their toxicity, keep the flowers suspended in muslin slightly above the fat.

Simply use a small, lidded casserole dish and a square of muslin that's bigger than the dish. Smear the fat (mango butter works well) on the bottom and up the sides of the casserole dish, then place the muslin over the top, with edges draped over the sides of the dish. Place the flowers onto the muslin, and put the lid of the casserole dish on so that it holds the muslin in place. Pull the edges of muslin tight so that the fabric becomes taut inside and holds the flowers above the fat.

Change the flowers every 1–2 days. After about 10 changes the smell should be impressive. But keep going to make it even stronger if you have the flowers, the time and the patience.

Daphne blooms in the winter, when the flowers are often damp from rain. To avoid mould, dry them fully before placing them in the pomade.

Using fixatives

A fixative is just that — it fixes a perfume *in situ* so that its fragrance lasts longer on your skin or hair. Glycerine makes a great fixative for water- or alcohol-based perfumes, giving them a slightly silkier texture, too, and you need only a few drops. Many base-note fragrant extracts are also fixatives for middle and top notes. Below are a few of the most common.

Animal magic

Many perfumes have a primal, earthy touch. Animal secretions — including musk from the musk deer, civet paste from civets and castoreum from beavers — have been highly prized as perfumery ingredients for centuries. Although these intense animal ingredients can smell repulsive undiluted, they add mysterious, sexy allure when watered right down and blended with other fragrances. Many are also unparalleled as fixatives — for example, musk can retain its scent for centuries.

While there is often cruelty involved in harvesting these ingredients, there are a few substances from animals, or containing animal notes, that are perfect for the ethical perfumer, such as ambergris, ambrette seeds and blackcurrant buds.

AMBERGRIS

A secretion produced and excreted by sperm whales, ambergris must surely be the ultimate forager's find — a fist-sized lump is worth thousands of dollars. It can be found on the beaches of Aotearoa, although it's extremely rare.

If you want to get hold of some ambergris without extensive and potentially fruitless beachcombing, there are reputable dealers. It is expensive, but a little goes a long way. You can buy ambergris tinctures, or grind a tiny amount and tincture and age it in alcohol yourself. It is often diluted in alcohol at around 3 per cent strength. Younger ambergris is grey and has oceanic notes. Aged ambergris, which has floated on the waves and been bleached in the sun for decades or even centuries, is almost white and smells sweet.

In small quantities, ambergris is a superb fixative, as well as an 'exultant' — amplifying the other scents in perfumes to which it is added. In larger quantities it has an entrancing smell in its own right that is exotic, yet strangely and compellingly familiar and comforting. I can almost guarantee that the first time you smell it, it won't be what you're expecting.

AMBRETTE SEEDS

You can sometimes buy ambrette seed extract (*Abelmoschus moschatus*) from essential-oil suppliers. It's both harsh and sickly unless you dilute it very, very heavily. Only then does it make an excellent botanical musk substitute. The extract has fixative qualities and adds a seductive, rounded softness to blends.

BLACKCURRANT BUDS

These are leaf buds, not flower buds, and are little flame-shaped bundles of possibility that grow from the branches of blackcurrant bushes. Commercially produced blackcurrant bud absolute is often available and is a valued ingredient in perfumery — its fragrance a marriage of fruitiness and tomcat.

You can also gather the buds from a bush yourself and tincture them in alcohol or infuse them in oil. I'm not sure about their fixative qualities when they're processed this way, but the tomcat scent has a strong and stealthy sillage — it radiates widely and lingers in the air.

Benzoin resin

You can buy powdered benzoin resin from cosmetics or incense suppliers, then dissolve it in pure perfumer's alcohol as a fixative. It's a compelling balsamic base note, and in my opinion is even better when mixed with a little vanilla. You can add it to any of the recipes in this chapter. Use your alcohol-dissolved benzoin in alcohol-based perfumes, or carefully mix a little into a pomade or oil.

Essential oils

There are many readily available essential oils that make strong fixatives. Natural perfumers often work with vetiver, frankincense, myrrh, patchouli and sandalwood.

Indian sandalwood (*Santalum album*), the sandalwood species traditionally used in perfumery, is now endangered. However, there are ethical sources of other *Santalum* species, each of which has its own charms. The recent development of an industry in Australia based around Australian sandalwood (*S. spicatum*) is particularly interesting, especially where the Indigenous custodians of the land are taking the lead.

Essential-oil base notes can be overpowering, so use them very sparingly. Dilute them to 5–10 per cent strength in alcohol or vegetable oil before attempting to add them to your handmade perfume blends. Then use a dropper and add a drop at a time, mixing and testing the fragrance on your skin or a strip of blotting paper after every drop.

Labdanum resin

This sticky, pitch-dark resin has an intoxicating fragrance that is hard to describe. Use it as you'd use benzoin resin, noting that the consistency is different.

Vanilla

This is a time-honoured base note, and the recipes on pages 312–315 show how it can be used in alcohol tinctures and pomades. You can also add bought or homemade pure vanilla essence to any water- or alcohol-based perfume (see the homemade vanilla essence recipe, page 26).

The wide world of ingredients

You'll find many plants growing in your neighbourhood or further afield that don't have main entries in this book but make wonderful perfume ingredients. Below are just a few.

Bay tree

The buds and dried or fresh leaves of the bay tree (*Laurus nobilis*) make a beautiful tincture. Note that the leaves you gather from wild-growing bay will often be much more fragrant than shop-bought ones.

Daphne

Delicious-smelling daphne flowers (*Daphne* genus) produce one of the best homemade pomades (see 'Divine daphne pomade', page 315).

Jonquil

Jonquil flowers (*Narcissus jonquilla*) are marvellous for enfleurage. When they bloom in spring, make the most of it, because they don't last long and you'll want to make sure you can do several recharges before they die away. Note that jonquils are slightly toxic, so you may want to use the same method as for daphne (see 'Divine daphne pomade', page 315).

Lilac

Lilac (*Syringa vulgaris*) is in the Oleaceae family, the same family as olives and jasmines, but it doesn't give its scent up to extraction nearly as readily as jasmine. Nonetheless, if you're persistent you can make a delicately scented pomade or oil using lilac. Select the most fragrant flowers you can find, and recharge your pomade or oil as many times as possible.

Ornamental conifers

Some cypress trees (Cupressaceae family) and other ornamental conifers have marvellous-smelling leaves and cones that tincture well in alcohol.

Herbs

Thyme, coriander and various other herbs are used in perfumery. You can extract the scent from herbs using any of the methods described earlier in this chapter. Coriander lends itself especially well to perfume blends.

Spices

Many kitchen spices are widely used in perfumery, including cloves, cinnamon, ginger and pepper, although use the first two of these very sparingly as they're strong and can also irritate the skin.

Found colours

Extracting dyes and inks from vegetable or mineral materials you find around you can become an obsession. Recently I became excited about making writing inks, but my longest-standing love is dyeing fibres that I spin — usually hemp, wool or alpaca. Occasionally, I also overdye an old garment to try to breathe new life into it. Lots of people share these interests — or love to work with raw fabrics or pre-spun yarns.

Once you start natural dyeing, it's hard not to start questioning where your garments and other fabric products come from. The need for affordable clothing and furnishings has most of us stuck in an industrial catch-22. In industrialised nations like New Zealand, we often rely on clothes that have likely been sewn in sweatshops overseas or are made of fabric produced in sweatshops. And let's call sweatshops what they are: a modern form of slavery where those of us who benefit from them don't have to think about them. They're usually out of sight and out of mind, unless a disaster like the 2013 Dhaka garment factory collapse temporarily reminds us of them.

There is also the entirely entwined environmental damage that the clothing industry inflicts. Synthetic petrochemical fibres like polyester, nylon and acrylic not only rely on the oil industry for their raw materials, but are made with enormously polluting processes. That includes colouring them with synthetic dyes. Then, once they're made, bought, worn and repeatedly washed, they begin to shed synthetic microfibres into the environment, which are poisoning ecosystems and food chains everywhere.

Natural fibres like cotton don't release microfibres, but massive cotton crops are responsible for environmental destruction and degradation. What about organic fair trade cotton? This is a bit better, but how many of us can afford it?

Then there are animal fibres. These may be natural, but how much do you know about how the animals they are from lived and died? What level of animal welfare are you personally comfortable with?

I've created a personal manifesto listing my aims for supporting ethical clothing practices — see the following box. I'm not suggesting this is the only approach, but thinking it through and writing it down has helped me crystallise my thoughts, and motivated me to try to stick to what feels most right to me (even if I don't always succeed). I'd recommend it as an exercise!

AN ETHICAL CLOTHING MANIFESTO

- Buy natural fibres for spinning from known producers, where it's possible to find out the provenance.
- Favour local alpaca when possible, and producers with a strong focus on humane farming.
- Favour hemp when it comes to plant-based fibres, as this seems to cause less environmental damage than many other crops.
- Buy clothes second-hand as often as possible, favouring those made from natural fibres (the microfibre-shedding problem with synthetics gets worse over a garment's lifetime).
- Turn second-hand synthetic garments into items that are useful but don't need to be washed, such as rag rugs and wall hangings.
- When washing synthetics, use a short cycle and a washing bag to minimise and contain microfibre shedding.
- Gather natural dyestuffs sustainably and with reverence.

Dyeing with foraged plants

Just as with natural perfumery, natural dyeing can involve adjusting your tastes so that you revel in the subtler, perhaps kinder beauty that nature offers, compared with louder, flashier offerings from factories. That's not to say that you can't get incredibly bold, bright colours from nature, but they can be rarer.

Foraging for colour is always an adventure. With some plants, what you see is what you get, but many hide colourful secrets. Throw them into a dye bath with a willing fabric or fibre and see what they have to give. For example, fennel flowers share their sunny gold, and harakeke pods give all their darkness and then some, but silver-blue eucalyptus trees hide souls of red and orange.

Never be afraid to experiment. Marigold flowers, buddleia flowers, cleavers roots, fennel leaves, rosemary leaves, comfrey leaves, blackberry leaves, dyer's chamomile, goldenrod flowers, yarrow flowers, coprosma bark, and dock leaves and roots are all good to use, whether you're a beginner or more experienced. Try different plants, and every part of each plant. Try plants in different seasons and with different mordants. Try dyeing different fibres with the same dye. Try soaking dye plants for different lengths of time, or upping the quantity of plant material used . . . the possibilities are endless.

However, some outcomes are predictable. Natural plant dyes will always colour animal fibres; for example, silk, wool, angora, mohair and alpaca. They will also often colour plant fibres; for example, hemp, cotton and bamboo. However, only rarely will they colour synthetic fibres — most synthetic fibres repel plant dyes.

The dyeing process sometimes shrinks fibres. Wool, angora and alpaca are especially susceptible, but there are ways to minimise the risk (see page 330). Silk doesn't shrink, although you do have to be careful not to let the dyeing liquid get too hot or it will weaken the fibre, which may then start to disintegrate.

THRIFTY DYEING

Buy old, dull, unlovable garments from op shops to experiment on — but check the labels first and remember that you won't be able to dye synthetics. You don't have to dye a whole garment either. Unravel knitted or crocheted garments and dye the yarn, then make something else. Or unpick a sewn garment, dye the individual pieces and stitch them into something new.

Using mordants

The word 'mordant' means 'biting' and a mordant is a chemical that 'bites' into your fibre and primes it, allowing it to take on a more colourful dye. Some plant dyes really need a mordant in order to take, while others produce deep, rich, colour-fast results without one. There are also many plant dyes that produce quite different results depending on whether or not you use a mordant and which one you use.

There are various mordants, but some, like chrome, are highly toxic and should be used with great care. Like many home dyers, I don't use chrome at all. However, there are three mordants that are safe to use at home:

- potassium aluminium sulphate mixed with cream of tartar, for animal fibres
- aluminium acetate, for plant fibres
- copper sulphate, for animal fibres.

All three are readily available from fibre arts supplies stores and sometimes also at chemists and farm-supply stores. The two alums are good general mordants, while copper sulphate (which is nearly as safe) adds depth to green and blue colours, although it also gives interesting results with any dye.

DISPOSING OF YOUR MORDANTS

An alum mordant solution can be safely tipped on your garden — just bear in mind that it will lower the pH. To dispose of copper-sulphate mordant safely, leave a hunk of steel (not stainless-steel) wool in the mordant solution and over a few hours or days it will react with the copper sulphate to produce an iron-sulphate solution and copper. The iron sulphate can be tipped on your garden, and the remaining solids disposed of as general waste.

Mordant recipe

This recipe gives instructions for using mordants to prepare fibre for dyeing. The quantities are per 100 g (3½ oz) of dry fibre or fabric.

4 teaspoons potassium aluminium sulphate and 1 teaspoon cream of tartar for animal fibres

OR 4 teaspoons aluminium acetate for plant fibres

OR 1 teaspoon copper sulphate for plant or animal fibres

Mix mordant into a solution with water — enough to cover your fibre or fabric very well and give it room to move.

Place the fibre or fabric into the water, making sure it's all pushed down under the surface. I use a wooden spoon or stick for this.

Bring the mix to a very slow simmer. Let it simmer for around half an hour.

Leave the fibre or fabric in the solution overnight.

Either dye the fibre or fabric as soon as you remove it from the mordant, or dry it on a washing line and store it in the dark until you're ready to dye it. Mordanted fibre will store for months.

Preparing to dye

Collect all the equipment and ingredients you'll need before embarking on your dyeing project. Follow these simple steps to minimise the mess and inconvenience, and to maximise your likelihood of success.

- Decide what you want to dye, then what you want to dye it with.
- Decide whether you'll use a mordant or not.
- If using a mordant, mix it and soak the fibre or garment you want to dye in it, according to the instructions on page 329.
- Gather enough of your chosen wild plant. The general rule is that you need about 2 litres (3½ pints) of plant material (or a bit more, to be sure) per 100 g (3½ oz) of fibre or fabric. Too much is better than too little.
- You can soak your plant material in water overnight or longer to help it release its colourants, although this isn't usually necessary.
- Breaking your plant matter up a little can also be helpful.
- Make sure you have a long wooden spoon and a large pot reserved specifically for dyeing. A stockpot bought from a second-hand shop is a good option. Always keep your dyeing pots and cooking pots separate.

MINIMISING THE RISK OF SHRINKAGE

Fibres shrink if moved around while wet, and with sudden changes of temperature from hot to cold. To avoid these hazards, follow the advice below.

- Stir the fibre in the dye pot as little as possible – preferably not at all. Having a very large pot with plenty of water flowing around the folds of the garment means you won't have to stir it to make sure the whole garment is being dyed evenly.
- Keep a close eye on the pot to make sure it doesn't boil but stays at a gentle simmer or just below simmering point.
- Don't try to speed things up by rapidly cooling the dye pot and its contents. Leave it to cool in its own time.
- Alternatively, use a solar cooker as the temperature stays low and even (see page 266).

The art of dyeing

One of the delights of natural dyeing is the aromatic steam that fills the kitchen as you work. Another is the scent of the fibre when you lift it from the pan — an item coloured with natural plant dyes is softly fragrant. The sweet aromas of harakeke pods, fennel and eucalyptus can linger for ages.

Method

Put your wild plant material and the water it's been soaking in (if it has) into your dye pot. The pot needs to be large enough to hold all the fibre or fabric plus enough dyeing liquid to cover it so that it has plenty of room to move. Add more water if necessary. This doesn't mean the final colour will be less intense, because it's the ratio of fibre or fabric to plant material that counts.

Drop the fibre or garment into the pot. You may want to put it in a net bag if there are lots of plant bits in the water (picking these out of the fabric afterwards can be a pain).

Bring the pot to simmering point very slowly and carefully. If you heat it too fast, the fibre can burn on the bottom of the pot.

Keep the liquid simmering or just below simmering point — but definitely not boiling — for 20 minutes to 1 hour. Keep a careful watch on it. You may want to check the depth of colour in the fibre occasionally, but don't stir the pot.

When you have achieved the shade you want, turn the heat off and leave everything in the pot to cool. One cool, gently remove the garment or fibre from the pot and rinse it in cool or warm water until the water runs clear. If you leave the item in the pot for a day or two, it doesn't matter — dyes are not impatient.

Dye plants

The following table lists a few commonly growing dye plants that I've experimented with and the results I got — although note that yours might be different. The blanks indicate combinations I haven't yet tried. You could also experiment with berry dyes, but beware that they are fugitive dyes, washing out or fading rapidly. They're fun if you don't want a permanent result.

Dye plant	**Alum mordant** (Aluminium acetate for plant fibres; potassium aluminium sulphate plus cream of tartar for animal fibres)	**Copper sulphate mordant**	**No mordant**
apple tree bark	light ginger	rich dark brown	medium brown
avocado pips and/ or skins (with added cloudy ammonia until the pink is right)	dusty pink	darker dusty pink	–
dandelion flowers	golden yellow	–	–
elder leaves	pale olive green	olive green	
fennel flowers	vibrant, almost fluorescent golden yellow	–	greenish gold
harakeke seedpods	almost black	rich dark brown	medium brown
ivy leaves – new (note that old leaves will give browns rather than greens and yellows)	pastel yellow on wool; didn't take well to hemp	light olive green	–
olive leaves and/ or bark	very rich golden yellow	rich olive green	creamy yellow
silver dollar gum leaves (you can achieve yellows by dyeing for a shorter time)	vibrant, deep red-orange	brick red	orange
windfall beard lichen (*Usnea* genus, unknown species)	rich ginger	–	rich ginger
walnut shells	–	–	light, slightly pinkish brown

THIS PAGE Common lichens around urban and suburban areas. At top left is *Usnea*.

HARAKEKE-POD AND WALNUT-SHELL DYES

Harakeke pods and walnut shells take slightly longer than green plants to give up their colour. Pound and crush harakeke pods a little and soak them in water for 3 days or more before using. Apparently, over time they can ferment and get quite stinky, although this has never happened to me. At any rate, don't worry if they smell — they'll still give beautiful colour.

Walnut shells need to be soaked even longer — a week or more. The water will turn black and a bit smelly but, as with the harakeke pods, the shells still produce a lovely dye.

MYCOPIGMENTS

Dyes from fungi and lichens, called mycopigments, can be rich and vivid, and often don't require mordants. While beard lichens lend themselves well to hot-water dyeing (see the table on page 332), there are other fungi and lichens that give exciting results — including pinks and purples — with alkaline fermentation.

A simple method is to soak the fungus or lichen in a 50:50 mix of cloudy ammonia and water for several weeks, giving it a stir as often as you remember. To use the dye, strain out the lichen or fungus, then gently heat your fabric or fibre in the dye bath to simmering point for about 45 minutes. Leave it to cool and soak overnight.

It's important not to rip lichens off plants, as they take a long time to grow and are vital in supporting ecosystems. Instead, use windfall lichens for your dyeing projects. For more information on mycopigments, see the 'Resources' section (page 345).

Making inks

Once you've finished a dyeing project, you can thriftily turn the leftover colour solution into a simple natural ink. Boil it down until it's very concentrated, then add a fixative, such as a few drops of gum tragacanth (although this isn't always necessary). You can use your ink with a paintbrush or in a dip pen. For inspiration, search for natural homemade inks online — there are plenty of exciting blogs and videos out there (see also page 345).

Play as you forage

The world invites us to play. Children know this; the rest of us often forget. In this section are a few ideas. The games Conkers and Poohsticks come from British Isles tradition. Educator Harko Brown has put out a range of resources on traditional tākaro — Māori games and sports (see page 347).

Small adventures

Any walk in nature can involve curiosity, discovery and play — just grab a field guide and go hunting for new plants and trees to identify. You could also choose a nature-based theme for the day and head out with that in mind. See what you observe around that theme; explore what it gets you thinking about. Talk about it, write about it or make art about it. A few starter ideas for themes include breezes, tangles, memories, cloaks, song, clouds, damp and dry, shadows, scents, circles, holes and flight.

Below are a couple of other discovery games.

Find my tree

Take turns to be blindfolded, spun around, and led to a tree or plant. The blindfolded person gets to know their tree or plant by touch and smell, then they're spun around again and led away. The blindfold is taken off, and they have to find their tree or plant.

Go find

This is a simple game where the participants take turns to set each other the task of finding something; for example, the smallest, largest or most asymmetrical pine cone; a kawakawa leaf with three holes in it; a rock with red on it; the most intact skeleton leaf; a pink yarrow flower and a white yarrow flower. You can play the game in endless ways, with or without time limits and competitively or non-competitively. Or put together a list of things to find and turn it into a scavenger hunt.

Other games

Conkers

You can't eat horse chestnuts (see page 147), but you can play conkers with them. This simple game has been popular since at least the nineteenth century, and variations are played around the world.

MATERIALS

Each player needs to gather a selection of horse chestnuts and then choose from these the ones they think will make the best conkers. They should be smooth, firm, uncracked and symmetrical. You can test conkers by putting them in a bowl of water — floaters are no good. Choose conkers that sink to the bottom, then fit them out.

Drill a hole through the middle of each horse chestnut using a nail, a thick needle, an awl or a small screwdriver. You can also use an electric drill — a smooth, clean hole is best to help maintain the conker's strength.

Cut a 25 centimetre (10 inch) length of string and thread it through the conker, tying a knot at one end to hold the conker on. You can also use a shoelace.

BASIC RULES

- Players take turns using their conker to hit someone else's conker. In each round there is a defender and an attacker.
- The defender wraps the string of their conker around their hand and lets the conker hang down, perfectly still, at whatever height the attacking player chooses.
- The attacker wraps the string of their conker around their hand and uses the other hand to draw the conker back and then release and swing it forward on its string to hit the defending conker.
- If the attacker misses, they get two more chances. If they hit, it's the other player's turn to attack.
- Players continue playing until one conker is destroyed — usually when it splits in two and falls to the ground.

BONUS SHOTS

- If the strings get tangled, both players yell, 'Strings!' The one who yells first gets a bonus shot.
- If the attacker's hit makes the defender's conker swing around in a full circle on its string, the attacker gets a bonus shot.

SCORING

- Traditionally, conkers is an ongoing schoolyard game that lasts an entire season, with each conker accumulating points over days, weeks or months. Every time a conker is victorious, it adds one point to its score, but also adds its opponent's score to its own. If it beats a new conker, it therefore wins only one point. But if it beats a conker with, say, a score of three, it wins four points, which are added to any points it has already accumulated.
- A new conker is called a 'none-er', meaning that it has beaten none yet.
- A conker is called a 'one-er' if it has a score of one, a 'two-er' with a score of two and so on.
- Mental tallies are not always reliable — you might want to keep track of scores on paper!

CHEATING

The harder your conker, the more likely it is to win. You can deviously harden your conkers by baking them or soaking them in vinegar. One-year-old conkers are well hardened too. That's why it's considered cheating to use them — new conkers should be found each year.

Poohsticks

This simple game, invented by author A. A. Milne for his character Winnie-the-Pooh and first described in *The House at Pooh Corner* (1928), is a much-loved pastime. The bridge in Ashdown Forest, East Sussex, where Milne and his son Christopher Robin first played Poohsticks, has been renamed Poohsticks Bridge and attracts tourists from all over the world. Meanwhile, Oxfordshire hosts an annual World Poohsticks Championships at Day's Lock on the River Thames. To play the game, all you need is one stick per player and a stream with a bridge over it.

MATERIALS

Each competitor chooses a stick and shows it to the others. All sticks must be recognisable, so you can tell which is whose when they're floating on the water. If they're not recognisable, find a way to mark them.

BASIC RULES

- Competitors stand in a row along the bridge and face upstream. Each competitor holds their stick out over the water. Everyone's hands must be at the same height.
- Someone calls, 'Ready, steady, drop!' On 'drop', everyone drops their stick. Throwing is not allowed.
- Everyone hurries to look over the downstream side of the bridge to see which stick emerges first. The person whose stick emerges first is declared the winner.
- Repeat!

VARIATIONS

- When Winnie-the-Pooh first played the game he used fir cones. Other foraged plant material that floats can be used, including leaves and flowers, as long as the bits are big enough when floating for players to be able to identify them.
- Winnie-the-Pooh also played the game alone the first time. Play solitaire Poohsticks by holding a stick or other item in each hand and dropping them at the same time, pitting one against the other.
- If there is a stream without a bridge, set a starting point and a finishing point. Drop your stick or other item in at the starting line, and see which stick reaches the finishing line first.

Resources

Foraging for food

AOTEAROA BOOKS

Andrew Crowe, *A Field Guide to the Native Edible Plants of New Zealand*, Auckland: Collins, 1981.

This classic has rarely, if ever, been out of print. It covers numerous native plants and fungi, offering historical, medicinal and culinary information, as well as identification details.

Monique Fiso, *Hiakai*, Auckland: Penguin, 2020.

This new classic, detailing uses of native plants as culinary ingredients and containing stunning recipes, is by the phenomenal chef and owner of Wellington's Hiakai restaurant, Monique Fiso.

David Fuller, *Māori Food and Cookery*, Auckland: Reed, 1978.

This hard-to-find book contains a wealth of information about cooking both hunted and gathered ingredients.

Sheila Natusch, *Wild Fare for Wilderness Foragers*, Auckland: Collins, 1979.

Sheila Natusch, a prolific writer about Aotearoa history and natural history, produced this anecdotal guide to wild resources of the bush and seashore.

Murdoch Riley, *Māori Vegetable Cooking: Traditional and Modern Methods*, Paraparaumu: Viking Sevenseas, 1988.

This small but dense book illustrates a rich variety of Māori cuisine.

Charles Royal and Jenny Kaka Scott, *Cooking with Charles Royal*, Wellington: Huia Publishers, 2010.

Pioneering Māori chef Charles Royal shares accessible, contemporary recipes using some of his favourite native ingredients.

Gwen Skinner, with illustrations by Christine Brown, *Simply Living: A Gatherer's Guide to New Zealand's Fields, Forests and Shores*, Auckland: A. H. & A. W. Reed, 1981.

Again, this is out of print, but it can be found second-hand. It contains recipes for food, drink and cosmetics.

INTERNATIONAL BOOKS

Frances Bissell, *The Scented Kitchen: Cooking with Flowers*, London: Serif, 2007.
This treasure will inspire beginners and enthusiasts alike.

Shep Erhart and Leslie Cerier, *Sea Vegetable Celebration: Recipes Using Ocean Vegetables*, Summertown, TN: Book Publishing Company, 2001.
This wonderful little book from the United States contains all sorts of vegetarian recipes using seaweed.

Euell Gibbons, *Stalking the Wild Asparagus*, Chambersburg, PA: Alan C. Hood & Company, 1962.
Euell Gibbons drew on a lifetime of foraging — sometimes from necessity — to write this groundbreaking book. Each chapter is a highly informative and entertaining examination of a wild plant or group of plants, focusing mostly on their uses as food. A large amount of the information is specific to the United States, but New Zealanders will nonetheless find plenty to apply locally.

John Kallas, *Edible Wild Plants: Wild Foods from Dirt to Plate*, Layton, UT: Gibbs Smith, 2010.
In this newer classic, US forager John Kallas focuses on fifteen commonly growing weeds, all of which are found in Aotearoa, and describes the harvesting and uses of the different parts in incredible detail.

Richard Mabey, *Food for Free*, London: Collins, 1972.
Many plants introduced to Aotearoa originated from the United Kingdom, so this British book contains plenty that's of relevance to New Zealanders. It's good for both culinary ideas and plant identification.

ONLINE SOURCES

Friendly Foraging: www.rnz.co.nz/national/programmes/thiswayup/collections/foraging
Radio New Zealand interviews with the author on *This Way Up* about foraging for particular plants (2008–11).

The Rubbish Trip: therubbishtrip.co.nz
Hannah Blumhardt and Liam Prince, 'the no-waste nomads', travel Aotearoa running workshops on living with zero waste, foraging included.

Toi Te Ora Public Health: www.toiteora.govt.nz/botulism
The 'Botulism' page of this website includes good information on prevention.

Wild Capture – Wild Foods and Foraging – NZ: www.facebook.com/forageNZ
A Facebook group run by Aotearoa forager and fisher Peter Langlands, who is a fount of knowledge about foraging, and generous with it.

Plant-identification guides

BOOKS

In addition to the following, any or all of Andrew Crowe's identification guides are a great addition to the forager's library.

Owen Bishop and Audrey Bishop, with photographs by Nic Bishop, *New Zealand Wild Flowers Handbook*, Auckland: Hodder & Stoughton, 1994.

Geoff Brunsden and Liz Brunsden, *Wildflowers of New Zealand*, Auckland: New Holland Publishers NZ Ltd, 2004.
A valuable ID book, as a plant's flowers can be one of the best ways to distinguish it.

John Salmon, *The Native Trees of New Zealand*, Auckland: Reed Methuen Publishers Ltd, 1980.

C. J. Webb, W. R. Sykes and P. J. Garnock-Jones, *Flora of New Zealand, Volume IV: Naturalised Pteridophytes, Gymnosperms, Dicotyledons*, Christchurch: Botany Division, DSIR, 1988.

ONLINE SOURCES

iNaturalist: inaturalist.nz
A community dedicated to cataloguing and identifying Aotearoa nature — for experts and occasional or new enthusiasts alike.

New Zealand Plant Conservation Network | Rōpū Hononga Koiora Taiao ki Aotearoa: www.nzpcn.org.nz
This organisation is focused on protecting Aotearoa's Indigenous flora, and its website is a stunning and valuable repository of information.

Plants For a Future: www.pfaf.org
This is an international database of 7000 useful plants.

Royal New Zealand Institute of Horticulture: www.rnzih.org.nz
This website includes a page on 'Poisonous Plants in New Zealand', available at: www.rnzih.org.nz/pages/poison.html

Solar-cooking resources

BOOKS

Lorraine Anderson and Rick Palkovic, *Cooking with Sunshine: The Complete Guide to Solar Cooking with 150 Easy Sun-cooked Recipes*, Lebanon, IN: De Capo Press, 2006.

A classic for anyone interested in solar cooking.

ONLINE SOURCES

Solar Cookers International: www.solarcookers.org

Includes links to their solar-cooking wiki, which provides information on all aspects of solar cooking.

Natural-healing and well-being resources

BOOKS

Linda Buzzell, *Ecotherapy: Healing with Nature in Mind*, San Francisco, CA: Sierra Club Books, 2009.

A series of essays exploring the new discipline of ecotherapy, which brings together psychology and ecology.

Carole Fisher and Gilian Painter, *Materia Medica of Western Herbs for the Southern Hemisphere*, New Zealand: Janus, 1996.

This standard local reference guide for herbalists lists many species that grow wild in Aotearoa, along with some that are cultivated but have not naturalised.

Elizabeth Francke, *Make Your Own Cosmetics and Fragrances*, Auckland: Heinemann Reed, 1988.

Martin Jordan and Joe Hinds, *Ecotherapy: Theory, Research and Practice*, London and New York, NY: Palgrave, 2016.

An academic textbook for students and practitioners of ecotherapy.

Murdoch Riley, *Māori Healing and Herbal*, Paraparaumu: Viking Sevenseas, 1988.

This classic details the use of many native plants in rongoā.

Jeanne Rose, *Jeanne Rose's Kitchen Cosmetics*, Berkeley, CA: North Atlantic Books, 1993.

AOTEAROA SUPPLIERS OF BODY-CARE INGREDIENTS

Go Native: www.gonative.co.nz
Pure Nature: www.purenature.co.nz

Natural-pigment resources

BOOKS

India Flint, *Eco Colour: Botanical Dyes for Beautiful Textiles*, Fort Collins, CO: Interweave Press, 2010.

A seminal book on contemporary natural dyeing that remains relevant.

Sarah Hudson, *Mana Whenua*, self-published, 2020.

This book springs from the Kauae Raro Collective, whose members work with clays gathered from unceded Māori lands. You can order a copy from https://kauae-raro.myshopify.com.

Jason Logan, *Make Ink*, New York, NY: Abrams, 2018.

New York artist Jason Logan provides inspiration and recipes for urban-foraged inks.

Ann Milner, *Natural Wool Dyes and Recipes*, Dunedin: John McIndoe, 1971.

Try to get hold of a second-hand copy of this treasure, which is full of ideas and information about dyeing with wild plants and lichens.

ONLINE SOURCES

Mushroom and Lichen Dyers United: www.facebook.com/groups/mycopigments

This Facebook group is a good starting point for support and information about mycopigments.

Courses

RONGOĀ COURSES

Te Wānanga o Raukawa: www.wananga.com
Heke rongoā (one-year diploma).

Te Wānanga o Aotearoa: www.twoa.ac.nz
Certificate and diploma in rongoā.

Titoki Education and Learning: www.titokieducation.co.nz
The opportunity to learn with Donna Kerridge and Rob McGowan.

FORAGING AND HERBALISM COURSES

These groups and individuals run courses, and their websites also often provide a wealth of information and resources.

Cottage Hill Herbs: www.cottagehillherbs.co.nz
Donna Lee offers a range of courses about herbs and common weeds, and their uses.

Herb Federation of New Zealand: herbs.org.nz
Offers a very reasonably priced, modular correspondence course in herbs and their uses.

Homegrown Botanica: www.homegrownbotanica.co.nz
Herbalist Felicity Joy offers regular workshops, usually around Kāpiti and Wellington.

Human Bushcraft and Wild Living: www.human.org.nz
Weed walks and hands-on bushcraft and foraging courses for adults and teens.

Julia's Edible Weeds: www.juliasedibleweeds.com
Julia Sich runs information-packed workshops — mostly around Tauranga, but she can travel.

ECOTHERAPY COURSES

Earthbody Institute: www.theearthbodyinstitute.com
A California-based school that offers online ecotherapy courses.

Games and activities

NGĀ TAONGA TĀKARO — TRADITIONAL MĀORI GAMES

Harko Brown and Yves Brown, *Ngā Aro-Tākaro: 100 Māori Games Artefacts*, self-published, 2019.

Details 100 pieces of equipment for Māori games, including how to identify and harvest the materials, and how to make the equipment according to tikanga.

OTHER GAMES

A Deck for Wonder-walking: www.amytwon.com

US-based artist Amy T. Won has produced a beautiful deck of cards to inspire reconnection with nature and creativity.

He mihi
Acknowledgements

Many people have helped make this book, directly and indirectly.

Over the past few years I've had the privilege to learn from amazing teachers of rongoā, tikanga and writing. I'm grateful every day that I've had the opportunity to experience the knowledge and wisdom of Rita Tupe, Maudy Tupe, Mate Tihema, Keelan Ransfield, Anahera Gildea, Krissi Smith, Emily Perkins, Emalani Case and Damien Wilkins. I'm also grateful to the other ākonga with whom I've shared these journeys. You know who you are — I've learned a lot from every one of you, and that learning continues.

To my family, the Knoxes; my children, the Moala-Knoxes; and also to the Moala family and the Malcolm-Garnock-Joneses, who are all part of the fabric of our household life — you are the best. Thank you for everything.

To my friends — you kind, creative, brilliant people — you help me constantly, whether you're providing solidarity, a listening ear, an escape from the daily grind, or just living your life inspiringly. I am so lucky to know you. And to my little rōpū of wāhine o te pene — I can't even imagine a writing life without the safe space we've made for sharing and critiquing work, at the same time as hashing out the big pātai . . . a never-ending process.

Enormous thanks to Jenny Hellen and Leanne McGregor from Allen & Unwin, without whom this book's second edition would not exist. You have both been unfailingly kind, patient and helpful as well as smart, careful and insightful. I am in awe of how much you hold in your heads at once. Thanks also to the fantastic Nic McCloy, who commissioned and midwifed the first edition of this book, and to the marvellous Abba Renshaw, who helped it find its way in the world.

Lottie Hedley! I had so much fun travelling around with you on your photo mission, and your work is stunning. Megan van Staden: thank you for designing this book. It looks so much more beautiful than I imagined it could. To Susi Bailey, I can't thank you enough for the time, care, skill and patience you put into editing. And thank you also for sharing your insights into allergies.

I'm thankful to Kate Stone and Claire Davis for proofreading the book so thoroughly, and for doing it under some pressure. And Robin Briggs, thank you for providing what the book has needed for so long — an index! Lovely to make the old family connection, too.

Phil Garnock-Jones: a massive thank you for your photographs, for your immense botanical expertise, and for your generosity in sharing both.

Everyone acknowledged here has helped me make this book, but every error is my own.

Lastly, to the many people over the years who have shared their foraging stories, ideas and and knowledge with me, I thank you so much, and I hope to keep learning from you in future. Nāu te rourou, nāku te rourou, ka ora ai te iwi.

Additional image credits

Glossary of reo Māori terms

Note that these translations from te reo Māori into English are approximate as the two languages don't map directly onto each other.

aroha love, compassion
hapū kinship group
kairongoā rongoā practitioner
kaitiakitanga guardianship
karakia ritual chant, incantation, prayer
kotahitanga unity, solidarity
mana whenua rights over the land
mātauranga knowledge
ngahere bush, forest
pūkenga lecturer
raranga weaving
rongoā an expansive Māori system of healing
rongoā rākau Māori plant medicine
taiao the natural world
taonga treasure
wairuatanga spirituality
whakapapa genealogy, a framework of relationships that links everything together
whakataukī proverb
whenua land

Index

Page numbers in bold indicate photographs; headings in bold indicate recipe groupings.

N

O

P

The information contained in this book is provided for general purposes only. The reader should consult and cross-reference multiple sources to ensure proper plant identification. If in any doubt, consult a health professional before touching or eating any plant matter.

First published in 2013
This revised edition first published in 2021

Allen & Unwin
Level 2, 10 College Hill, Freemans Bay
Auckland 1011, New Zealand
Phone: (64 9) 377 3800
Email: auckland@allenandunwin.com
Web: www.allenandunwin.co.nz

83 Alexander Street
Crows Nest NSW 2065, Australia
Phone: (61 2) 8425 0100

A catalogue record for this book is available from the National Library of New Zealand.

ISBN 978 1 98854 767 1

Design by Megan van Staden
Set in Newzald
Printed in China by C & C Offset Printing Co., Ltd.

10 9 8 7 6

FSC www.fsc.org
MIX
Paper | Supporting responsible forestry
FSC® C008047